BERUFSKOLLEG 2017
Prüfung zum Erwerb der Fachhochschulreife

Englisch

Baden-Württemberg
2011–2016

MP3-CD

STARK

© 2016 Stark Verlagsgesellschaft mbH & Co. KG
5. ergänzte Auflage
www.stark-verlag.de

Das Werk und alle seine Bestandteile sind urheberrechtlich geschützt. Jede vollständige oder teilweise Vervielfältigung, Verbreitung und Veröffentlichung bedarf der ausdrücklichen Genehmigung des Verlages.

Inhalt

Vorwort
Stichwortverzeichnis

Hinweise und Tipps für die Prüfung der Fachhochschulreife

1	Vorbereitung auf die Prüfung	I
2	Struktur der Prüfung	III
3	Hinweise und Tipps zur schriftlichen Prüfung	V

Übungsaufgaben

Übungsaufgabe 1

Hörverstehen	1
Leseverstehen	3
Textproduktion	4
Lösungsvorschläge	10

Übungsaufgabe 2

Hörverstehen	17
Leseverstehen	19
Textproduktion	20
Lösungsvorschläge	27

Übungsaufgabe 3

Hörverstehen	34
Leseverstehen	36
Textproduktion	37
Lösungsvorschläge	43

Übungsaufgabe 4

Hörverstehen	50
Leseverstehen	52
Textproduktion	53
Lösungsvorschläge	59

Fortsetzung siehe nächste Seite

Original-Prüfungsaufgaben

Prüfung 2011
Hörverstehenstest 2011-1
Lösungsvorschläge 2011-4
Schriftliche Hauptprüfung 2011-11
Lösungsvorschläge 2011-20

Prüfung 2012
Hörverstehenstest 2012-1
Lösungsvorschläge 2012-4
Schriftliche Hauptprüfung 2012-13
Lösungsvorschläge 2012-22

Prüfung 2013
Hörverstehenstest 2013-1
Lösungsvorschläge 2013-4
Schriftliche Hauptprüfung 2013-11
Lösungsvorschläge 2013-20

Prüfung 2014
Hörverstehen 2014-1
Leseverstehen 2014-3
Textproduktion 2014-4
Lösungsvorschläge 2014-11

Prüfung 2015
Hörverstehen 2015-1
Leseverstehen 2015-3
Textproduktion 2015-5
Lösungsvorschläge 2015-11

Prüfung 2016
Hörverstehen 2016-1
Leseverstehen 2016-3
Textproduktion 2016-5
Lösungsvorschläge 2016-11

MP3-CD

Übungsaufgabe 1:	Aufgabe 1 a	Track 1
	Aufgabe 1 b	Track 2
Übungsaufgabe 2:	Aufgabe 1 a	Track 3
	Aufgabe 1 b	Track 4
Übungsaufgabe 3:	Aufgabe 1 a	Track 5
	Aufgabe 1 b	Track 6
Übungsaufgabe 4:	Aufgabe 1 a	Track 7
	Aufgabe 1 b	Track 8
Prüfung 2011:	Aufgabe 1	Track 9
	Aufgabe 2	Track 10
	Aufgabe 3	Track 11
Prüfung 2012:	Aufgabe 1	Track 12
	Aufgabe 2	Track 13
	Aufgabe 3	Track 14
Prüfung 2013:	Aufgabe 1	Track 15
	Aufgabe 2	Track 16
	Aufgabe 3	Track 17
Prüfung 2014:	Aufgabe 1 a	Track 18
	Aufgabe 1 b	Track 19
Prüfung 2015:	Aufgabe 1 a	Track 20
	Aufgabe 1 b	Track 21
Prüfung 2016:	Aufgabe 1 a	Track 22
	Aufgabe 1 b	Track 23

Die Hintergrundgeräusche auf der CD stammen aus folgenden Quellen: *freesound, freesoundeffects* und *pacdv*

Jeweils im Herbst erscheinen die neuen Ausgaben
der Prüfungsaufgaben mit Lösungen.

Autoren:

Übungsaufgaben: Rainer Jacob
Lösungen Prüfungsaufgaben: Hans Georg Lang

Vorwort

Liebe Schülerinnen und Schüler des Berufkollegs,

mithilfe der **Übungsaufgaben im Stil der Prüfung** und der **Original-Prüfungsaufgaben** in diesem Band können Sie sich umfassend auf die **schriftliche Prüfung** zum Erwerb der Fachhochschulreife vorbereiten. Was in den einzelnen Prüfungsteilen von Ihnen erwartet wird, und wie Sie sich auf die Prüfung vorbereiten können, erfahren Sie im Kapitel „Hinweise und Tipps für die Prüfung der Fachhochschulreife", das auch **konkrete Lerntipps** und **sprachliche Hilfen** enthält.

Seit dem Prüfungsjahrgang 2014 gibt es eine **neu strukturierte Prüfung**. So ist z. B. der Hörverstehenstest nun in die schriftliche Hauptprüfung integriert. Anhand der Übungsaufgaben im Stil der neuen Prüfung können Sie sich optimal vorbereiten. Aber auch die Original-Prüfungen 2011 bis 2013 bieten Ihnen Übungsmaterial zu Aufgabenstellungen, die in der aktuellen Prüfung relevant sind.

Zu allen Aufgaben gibt es ausführliche **Lösungen**. Vor allem bei Aufgaben zur Textproduktion sind diese als Musterlösungen zu sehen, die Ihnen als Anregung dienen und möglichst viele inhaltliche Aspekte sowie Formulierungsmöglichkeiten aufzeigen sollen.

Sollten nach Erscheinen dieses Bandes noch wichtige Änderungen in der Prüfung 2017 vom Kultusministerium bekannt gegeben werden, finden Sie aktuelle Informationen dazu im Internet unter: www.stark-verlag.de/pruefung-aktuell.

Ihnen eine gute Vorbereitungszeit und viel Erfolg in der Prüfung!

Ihr Stark Verlag

Stichwortverzeichnis

alcopops 60 ff.
advertising 2014-4 ff.

bank account 15 f.
binge drinking 60 f., 2016-5 ff.

canteen food 59 f.
cartoons
– advertising 2014-5
– (modern) binge drinker 2016-6
– body scan (airport) 2011-15
– cultural diversity 21
– emissions 2011-18
– environment (destruction) 2013-16
– Fair Trade 2015-10
– gender 2016-9
– genetically modified food (GM) 38
– globalisation 5
– mobility 2011-18
– outsourcing (health) 2011-17
– racism 2012-17
– refugees 2015-7
– youth gangs 2013-15
– water shortage 2013-19
– working children 54
– working conditions (developing countries) 2012-18, 2015-10
casual dress at work 2012-1, 2012-4
charity work 11
child
– labour 2016-3 f.
– welfare 3
computers 2011-1, 2011-4
cybercrime 32 f.

developing countries 5, 14 f., 50, 63 f. 2015-2, 2015-8, 2016-3 f.

development aid 28

e-books 2011-12, 2011-20
e-commerce 32
education 48 f.
emissions (CO_2) 2011-27 f., 2015-3 f.
energy 17, 27, 65
energy efficiency 2015-3 f.
environment 2014-2

Facebook parties 2013-16
Fair Trade 2015-8 ff.
food
– labelling 2015-1
– free sugars 2016-2
– waste 15 f., 2012-13, 2012-22
fossil fuels 65
future of publishing 2011-11, 2011-20

gangs 2013-13
genetically modified food (GM) 1, 37
global trade 36
globalisation 4 ff., 14 ff., 36
gun control 2014-1

hotel reservation 18, 28 f.
hunger 15 f.

immigration 30 ff., 2012-16, 2015-5 f.
infrastructure 2015-3 f.
internet
– challenges and opportunities 32 f.
– electronic commerce 32
– internet safety 52 f.
– social networks 52 f., 2016-1

job search 35, 44

land grabbing 2015-2

materialism 3 f.
media 2011-1, 2011-4, 2011-11, 2011-20
mobile phones 2011-1, 2011-4

noise pollution 2013-11

obesity 15 f., 2016-2

pollution (cars) 2011-18, 2011-27 f.

racism 2012-15, 2012-23
renewable energy sources 65
road safety 2012-20 f., 2012-27 f.

sabbatical 2012-3, 2012-9
school exchange 2011-2, 2011-6 f.
slavery 2016-3 f.
Smart City 2015-3 f.
society
– alcoholism 2016-5 ff.
– multiculturalism 20 ff., 30 f.
– poverty 85 f., 2013-2
sport
– sports events 2011-16, 2011-23 f.
– young people and sport 2014-8 ff.
starvation 15 f.
statistics and charts
– advertising 2014-7
– alcohol consumption 2016-6
– child work 53 ff.

– cultural diversity (England and Wales) 58
– cultural diversity (Germany) 20 f.
– gender (jobs) 2016-8 f.
– globalisation 41 f.
– GM food 38 f.
– migration 2015-6
– mobility 2011-19
surveillance in stores 2011-13 f.

travelling 2013-17
travelling with children 19 f.

university 49

wind power 64 f.
world of work
– benefits for employees 2014-3 f.
– women in male jobs 2016-8 ff.
– working abroad 2011-16, 2011-24 f.
– working children 53 ff., 2016-3 f.
– working environment 2012-1, 2012-4 f., 2015-8 ff., 2016-1
– working women 2016-8 ff.

young drivers (accidents) 2012-19 ff., 2012-27 f.
youth (crime) 2012-2, 2012-6 f.
youth (unemployment) 2013-1

Hinweise und Tipps für die Prüfung der Fachhochschulreife

1 Vorbereitung auf die Prüfung

Die Prüfung der Fachhochschulreife im Fach Englisch umfasst drei unterschiedliche Kompetenzbereiche bzw. Fertigkeiten, auf die Sie sich gezielt vorbereiten können:

Hörverstehen

Obwohl das Hörverstehen im Unterricht immer wieder geübt wird, kann man auch in der Freizeit einiges dafür tun, um es zu verbessern. So können Sie sich im Fernsehen bzw. Internet englische Nachrichten (z. B. CNN oder BBC) ansehen oder auf dem Weg zur Schule englische Podcasts zu verschiedenen Themen anhören, die man auf den jeweiligen Webseiten englischsprachiger Sender und Zeitungen findet. Weiterhin kann man Spielfilme auch noch einmal in der Originalversion ansehen. So gewöhnt man sich nach und nach an das Sprechtempo in der Fremdsprache.

Leseverstehen

Um das Leseverstehen zu trainieren, bietet es sich an, immer wieder einmal einen englischen Text zu lesen. So können Sie z. B. eine englische Sprachzeitschrift abonnieren oder im Internet Artikel englischsprachiger Zeitungen abrufen, um sicherzustellen, dass Sie regelmäßig und automatisch englische Texte zu lesen haben. Englische Bücher im Original zu lesen ist schon schwieriger, da hier deutsche Wortangaben oder Umschreibungen fehlen. Es gibt jedoch auch vereinfachte Textausgaben, die Vokabelerklärungen und Hinweise enthalten, oder E-Books mit Wörterbuchfunktion.
Natürlich ist es auch ratsam, im Unterricht mitzuarbeiten, denn die Schulbücher orientieren sich an den Inhalten der Prüfung und vermitteln das Fach- und Themenvokabular, das anschließend in der Abschlussprüfung verwendet wird. Auch sollten Sie Ihren Wortschatz kontinuierlich erweitern und regelmäßig wiederholen. Um dem Gedächtnis eine gewisse Stütze zu geben, sollten Sie bei einem neuen Wort, wenn möglich, immer auch die Wortfamilie und deren Bedeutungen mitlernen und außerdem Wörter mit gleicher *(synonyms)* oder gegenteiliger *(opposites)* Bedeutung notieren. Dadurch entstehen Verknüpfungen im Gehirn, die das einzelne Wort nicht isoliert stehen lassen, sondern in einen Kontext einbetten. Ein einsprachiges Wörterbuch ist

ganz ähnlich aufgebaut. Auf diese Weise wird auch die schnelle und sinnvolle Verwendung des Wörterbuchs eingeübt.

Textproduktion

Bei Aufgaben zur Textproduktion ist es hilfreich, bereits verschiedene *useful phrases* (siehe Beispiele auf S. VII) zur Hand zu haben. Es reicht jedoch nicht, diese einfach auswendig zu lernen, denn den einen oder anderen englischen Aufsatz sollten Sie schon einmal geschrieben haben. Als Hilfestellung dient dabei die Methode *Modelling of Excellence*. Dabei liegt Ihnen ein Musteraufsatz (z. B. in diesem Buch) vor, nach dessen Vorlage Sie einen eigenen Aufsatz zu einem ähnlichen Thema oder Bild erstellen. Diese Methode ist gewinnbringend, wenn man die Standardsätze, die *useful phrases*, verinnerlicht hat und in einem neuen Kontext anwenden kann.

Mögliche Themen

Die Prüfungsaufgaben beziehen sich auf Lehrplaninhalte, die Sie im Laufe Ihres Unterrichts bereits kennengelernt haben. In der Prüfung können Themen aus folgenden Bereichen vorkommen:

Arbeitswelt und Arbeitsmarkt	– Bildung und Ausbildung im 21. Jahrhundert – Studium und Auslandsaufenthalt – Arbeitsplatz, Arbeitnehmer und Arbeitgeber – Transport und Verkehr
Medien und Konsum	– Werbung – Konsumverhalten (z. B. Markenbewusstsein, Trendverhalten, Teleshopping, *electronic shopping*) – Gesundheit und Ernährung (z. B. *obesity* und *anorexia*) – Möglichkeiten und Gefahren moderner Medien
Gesellschaftliche und politische Realität zu Beginn des 21. Jahrhunderts	– Kulturelle Vielfalt – Herausforderungen des modernen Sozialstaates – Aspekte des globalen Arbeitsmarktes – Internationale politische Zusammenarbeit und Krisenherde
Wissenschaftliche und technische Realität zu Beginn des 21. Jahrhunderts	– Ressourcenproblematik – Umwelt – Energie – Gentechnik
Aktuelles Geschehen	– Einwanderung und politisches Asyl – Der Jugendliche in der Gesellschaft (Kriminalität, Arbeitslosigkeit, Drogen) – Die Kluft zwischen Arm und Reich – Entwicklungs- und Industrieländer

2 Struktur der Prüfung

Teil A: Hörverstehen

Das **Hörverstehen** besteht aus zwei Aufgabenteilen. In einer Aufgabe müssen Meinungen und Standpunkte erkannt und vorgegebene Satzanfänge auf Deutsch richtig ergänzt werden. Eine weitere Aufgabe besteht darin, einzelne Aussagen an der richtigen Stelle in ein Raster einzufügen. Es können statt des Rasters aber auch offene Fragen gestellt werden. Auch hier antworten Sie auf Deutsch.
Die Hörverstehensprüfung dauert 30 Minuten und es dürfen keine Hilfsmittel verwendet werden. Die beiden Aufgabenteile werden nacheinander bearbeitet, wobei man sich die Aufgabenstellung vor dem ersten Hören durchlesen kann. Die Einlesezeit wird vom Lehrer bestimmt und beträgt in der Regel eine Minute. Man hört den Text immer zweimal, wobei man zwischen dem ersten und dem zweiten Hören zwei bis drei Minuten Zeit zur Bearbeitung hat. Nach dem zweiten Hören lässt der Lehrer den Prüflingen nochmals 4 bis 5 Minuten zum Fertigstellen der Aufgabe, bevor das Arbeitsblatt abgegeben werden muss.

Teil B: Leseverstehen

Das **Leseverstehen** wird in Form einer Mediationsaufgabe abgeprüft. Hier müssen Sie einem englischen Text wichtige Informationen entnehmen und diese auf Deutsch, z. B. für einen Zeitungsartikel, aufbereiten. Sie dürfen hier ein einsprachiges Wörterbuch benutzen.

Teil C: Textproduktion

In Teil C müssen Sie selbst einen Text auf Englisch verfassen. Sie sollen für Ihren Aufsatz verschiedene Materialien, die Ihnen vorliegen, einbeziehen. Sie müssen dabei zwischen zwei Themen bzw. Materialsets wählen. Auch für die **Textproduktion** dürfen Sie ein einsprachiges Wörterbuch benutzen.

In der folgenden Tabelle finden Sie einen Überblick über die Prüfungsstruktur:

Aufgabe	Prüfungsanforderung	Punkte
Teil A: Hörverstehen	zwei Aufgaben mögliche Aufgabenformate: z. B. Satzergänzung, offene Fragen, Raster mit Lücken	15
Teil B: Leseverstehen	eine Aufgabe (Mediation) einem englischen Sachtext gezielt Informationen entnehmen und in einen eigenen Text integrieren	15

Teil C: Textproduktion Wahlmöglichkeit zwischen **Composition 1** und **Composition 2**	materialgestützter Aufsatz: Verfassen eines Aufsatzes zu einem bestimmten Thema unter Verwendung verschiedener Materialien (Bildvorlage, Statistik, Schaubild, Kurztext, Zitat etc.)	30

Für die Prüfung stehen insgesamt 200 Minuten zur Verfügung:

Teil A: Hörverstehen: 30 Minuten

            20 Minuten Pause

Teil B + C: Leseverstehen und Textproduktion: 170 Minuten

Berechnung der Gesamtnote:

Die Gesamtnote berechnet sich folgendermaßen:

$$\frac{\text{Anmeldenote} + \text{Prüfungsleistung}\,(\times 2)}{3} = \text{Endnote}$$

Das Ergebnis der schriftlichen Prüfung zählt im Hinblick auf die Endnote doppelt, d. h., die Anmeldenote (sie ist immer eine ganze Note, während es in der Prüfung auch halbe Noten gibt), in die die Klassenarbeiten aus dem Schuljahr einbezogen sind, zählt ein Drittel. Hieraus wird die Bedeutung der Prüfung ersichtlich. Aus diesem Grund lohnt es sich besonders, die Prüfungsanforderungen und -aufgaben sowie die Tipps zu ihrer Bearbeitung und die Lösungsvorschläge genau anzusehen.

3 Hinweise und Tipps zur schriftlichen Prüfung

Hörverstehen

Bei den beiden Aufgaben zum Hörverstehen müssen Sie jeweils einen Hörtext (Interview/Gespräch/Telefonat etc.) auswerten und das Verstandene auf Deutsch in einem bestimmten Schema wiedergeben. So müssen Sie z. B. vorgegebene Satzanfänge mit den richtigen Informationen ergänzen und den Satz in korrektem Deutsch zu Ende führen. In der Regel sind es zu jedem Satzanfang zwei Informationen, die gefunden werden müssen. In einer anderen Aufgabe müssen Sie offene Fragen in ganzen Sätzen oder verständlich in Stichpunkten beantworten. Alternativ kann auch verlangt werden, ein Raster mit Lücken zu ergänzen, in das man stichwortartig die gefragten Informationen schreibt. Beide Teile ergeben zusammen 15 Punkte.
Konzentrieren Sie sich in der Prüfung beim erstmaligen Hören auf die Inhalte und notieren Sie nur Stichpunkte, evtl. verpassen Sie sonst während des Schreibens wichtige Informationen. Nutzen Sie die Pause zwischen den Hördurchgängen und danach, um Ihre Antworten ins Reine zu schreiben.

Leseverstehen (Mediation)

Bei der Aufgabe zum Leseverstehen müssen Sie, in Form einer Mediation, auf der Basis eines englischen Textes einen eigenen Text auf Deutsch verfassen, z. B. einen Artikel. Dabei wird gefordert, dass Sie die Inhalte in einem vorgegebenen Kontext in eigenen Worten wiedergeben. Eine Zusammenfassung des Inhalts ohne Berücksichtigung des Kontextes entspricht ebenso wie eine reine Übersetzung nicht der Aufgabenstellung und wird dementsprechend mit null Punkten bewertet. Der Text soll logisch aufgebaut und in vollständigen und verständlichen Sätzen formuliert sein.

Mögliche Vorgehensweise:
Aufgrund der Aufgabenstellung und der geringen Bearbeitungszeit von nur 45 Minuten bis zur endgültigen Version müssen Sie sehr gezielt vorgehen.
– Lesen Sie sich den Text einmal durch, ohne Wörter nachzuschlagen (max. 10 Minuten Einlesezeit).
– Lesen Sie die Aufgabenstellung genau durch und unterstreichen Sie die dazugehörigen Informationen im Text.
– Schreiben Sie sich die im Text gefundenen Informationen sinngemäß auf Deutsch auf einem eigenen Blatt auf. Bis dahin sollten nicht mehr als 15 Minuten vergangen sein.
– Formulieren Sie einen Einleitungssatz.
– Bauen Sie nun die Informationen, die Sie sich notiert haben, je nach Aufgabenstellung in einen eigenen Text ein.

Eine andere Vorgehensweise bestünde darin, sich zunächst die Aufgabenstellung anzusehen, ohne den Text gelesen zu haben. Als Nächstes entwirft man anhand der Aufgabenstellung eine Überschrift, evtl. eine Anrede und einen Einleitungssatz, den man der Aufgabenstellung entnehmen kann. Erst jetzt sieht man sich den Text an und sucht nach allen Informationen, die zur Aufgabenstellung passen und die man dann gemäß der Aufgabenstellung in eigenen Worten formuliert.

Textproduktion

Hier müssen Sie einen längeren **materialgestützten Aufsatz** schreiben. Sie bekommen dabei zwei Themen zur Auswahl, die jeweils fünf verschiedene Materialien mit unterschiedlichen Aspekten zum Thema beinhalten. In den Aufsatz müssen Sie mindestens drei Materialien einbeziehen und diese auch benennen. Für den materialgestützten Aufsatz erhalten Sie insgesamt 30 VP.

Mögliche Vorgehensweise:
- Sehen Sie sich zuerst alle Materialien durch. Unterstreichen Sie die interessanten Informationen und machen Sie sich auf einem gesonderten Blatt Stichpunkte auf Englisch.
- Entscheiden Sie dann, welche Materialien Sie in Ihrem Aufsatz verwenden wollen.
- Schreiben Sie eine Einleitung, bevor Sie den Hauptteil auf der Basis der ausgewählten Materialien verfassen. Ordnen Sie die aus den Materialien gewonnenen Informationen und schreiben Sie einen zusammenhängenden Text in eigenen Worten.
- Fassen Sie danach die wichtigsten Ergebnisse und Überlegungen zusammen und formulieren Sie abschließend noch Ihre eigenen Gedanken.
- Der Textumfang sollte 300 bis 500 Wörter betragen.

Tipps:
- Die Hinführung zum Thema (Einleitung) ist wesentlicher Bestandteil einer guten Darstellung und einer umfassenden Behandlung des Themas. Zusätzlich zu den Inhalten der Materialien kann man in seinen Materialaufsatz aber auch eigenes Wissen zum Thema einbringen.
- Was den Inhalt angeht, sollten Sie folgende Punkte beachten:
  - Gute Verknüpfung von mindestens drei Materialien
  - Klarer Aufbau und logische Strukturierung des Inhalts, d. h. Einleitung, eigene Argumentation mit Angabe der Quellen (Materialien) und Schluss. Vergessen Sie auch nicht, zwischen den einzelnen Abschnitten Überleitungen einzubauen und Ihre Argumentation mit Beispielen zu illustrieren.
  - Verfassen Sie Ihren Aufsatz in eigenen Worten, d. h., zitieren Sie nicht direkt aus den Materialien. Es ist auch wichtig, die Gedanken in verständlichem Englisch zu formulieren, sodass man Ihrer Argumentation folgen kann.
- Um Ihre sprachlichen Fertigkeiten unter Beweis zu stellen, werden angemessene Ausdrücke sowie ein variantenreicher Wortschatz von Ihnen erwartet. Außerdem sollten Sie beim Satzbau komplexere Sätze den einfachen Sätzen vorziehen, d. h. stets auch Nebensätze einbauen, anstatt nur einfache Hauptsätze zu verwenden. Des Weiteren sollten Sie verschiedene sprachliche Konstruktionen benutzen (z. B.

Aktiv/Passiv, verschiedene Zeiten, Partizipialkonstruktionen, Relativsätze, Bedingungssätze). Natürlich sollten Sie auch auf die Rechtschreibung achten.

Folgende **Wendungen** können beim Verfassen Ihres Aufsatzes hilfreich sein:

Einleitung/Hinführung zum Thema:
– *Let me begin/start by pointing out that ...*
– *To begin with/First of all I would like to mention that ...*
– *It is highly discussed at the moment ...*
– *Nowadays many people are worried about (the fact that) ...*

Formulierungen zur Pro-/Kontra-Argumentation:
– *The main motive/aspect for/against this is that ...*
– *Another argument for/against ... is that ...*
– *The next positive/negative aspect to consider is that ...*
– *A further problem to be mentioned is that ...*
– *The real reason for this is that ...*
– *Another aspect in favour of/against ... is that ...*
– *Despite all these arguments in favour of/against ...*

Formulierungen zur linearen Fragestellung (Problemlösung):
– *There are many things people can do to ...*
– *The first thing people can do for/against ... is ...*
– *Another idea to do something for ... would be to ...*
– *The next suggestion I have is that we should ...*
– *Another possibility to ... would be to ...*
– *A consequence of this would be (that) ...*
– *And we shouldn't forget to ...*

Schlussformulierungen:
– *Weighing the pros and cons I come to the conclusion that ...*
– *In my opinion ...*
– *As I made the same/a different experience in my life ... I think that ...*
– *I know many people who ...*
– *To sum up the arguments given, it can be concluded/said that ...*
– *On the whole/All in all we can say that ...*
– *My point of view concerning this topic is that ...*

Oft sind auch **Diagramme** Teil des Materialiensets. Auf der folgenden Seite sind die häufigsten Arten aufgeführt sowie mögliche Formulierungen für deren Interpretation und Bewertung.

a) Kreis-/Kuchendiagramm

Das **Kreis- oder Kuchendiagramm** *(pie chart)* wird normalerweise gewählt, um den Anteil von unterschiedlichen Gruppen an einem Ganzen darzustellen.

b) Balken-/Säulendiagramm

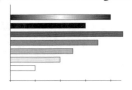

Das **Balken- oder Säulendiagramm** *(bar chart)* verwendet man, um Mengenverhältnisse und Prozentanteile zu beschreiben.

c) Kurvendiagramm

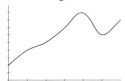

Das **Kurven- oder Liniendiagramm** *(line graph)* zeigt Veränderungen und Entwicklungen in einem bestimmten Zeitraum und evtl. auch Tendenzen für die Zukunft.

Interpretation und Bewertung:
– *The most significant trend is that ...*
– *This suggests that there is a relation between ... and ...*
– *The biggest change is ...*
– *These facts lead to the assumption that ...*
– *We can draw the conclusion that ...*

Auch **Bildvorlagen** (Comic, Karikatur etc.) sind meist Teil des Materialiensets. Sie müssen das Bild dabei nicht im Detail beschreiben, sondern seine Aussage erkennen und in Ihren Aufsatz sinnvoll integrieren. Folgende Formulierungen können Ihnen dabei helfen:
– *The picture shows ...*
– *The picture shows/illustrates a typical scene/situation ...*
– *On the left/right you can see ...*
– *The picture makes fun of/mocks ...*
– *The picture conveys the message that ...*
– *The artist wants to point out that ...*

Fachhochschulreife Englisch (Berufskolleg Baden-Württemberg)
Übungsaufgabe 1

Teil A: Hörverstehen

Aufgabe 1a – Satzergänzungen *(8 VP)*

Radio Avon hat Passanten auf der Straße zum Thema „Genetisch veränderte Nahrungsmittel" befragt.

- Hören Sie aufmerksam zu und beenden Sie auf Deutsch die unten stehenden Sätze. Pro Antwort werden zwei verschiedene Informationen (je 1 VP) aus dem Hörtext erwartet.
- Sie hören den Ausschnitt aus der Sendung zweimal. Während des Hörens dürfen Sie sich Notizen machen.

(1) James	Er sieht keine Risiken, weil …
	(2 VP)
(2) Ernestine	Sie ist besorgt, weil sie nicht weiß, …
	(2 VP)
(3) Robert	Er sieht in der neuen Technik vor allem Vorteile, nämlich …
	(2 VP)
(4) June	Sie ärgert sich über die Menschen in der westlichen Welt, da …
	(2 VP)

Aufgabe 1 b – Raster mit Lücken *(7 VP)*

Sie hören einen Podcast über eine Veranstaltung.
- Hören Sie aufmerksam zu und vervollständigen Sie auf Deutsch das unten stehende Raster mit Informationen aus dem Podcast. In den mit X gekennzeichneten Kästchen sind keine Einträge erforderlich.
- Sie hören den Bericht zweimal. Während des Hörens dürfen Sie sich Notizen machen.

Name	Ort/Land 0,5 VP	Adressaten- gruppe 0,5 VP	Projekt 1 VP
(1) Micaela	X		
(2) Jessica			
(3) Jacqueline	X		
(4) Wilfredo			

Teil B: Leseverstehen

Aufgabe 2 – Mediation (15 VP)

Sie sind Redakteur einer Zeitschrift für Jugendliche und wollen ein Interview mit einem deutschen Politiker zum Thema „Kinder und Konsum" führen.
- Fassen Sie die Informationen der folgenden Internetseite auf Deutsch als Vorbereitung für das Interview zusammen.
- Formulieren Sie ganze deutsche Sätze.

Trapped in materialism

New research by Ipsos MORI for UNICEF UK has shown that children in the UK feel trapped in a "materialistic culture" and don't spend enough time with their families.

Following on from UNICEF's pioneering report in 2007, which ranked the UK bottom in child well-being compared to other industrialised nations, the research released today gives an in-depth comparison of over 250 children's experiences across three developed countries: the UK, Sweden and Spain.

Children in all three countries told researchers that their happiness is dependent on having time with a stable family and plenty of things to do, especially outdoors, rather than on owning technology or branded clothes.

Despite this, one of the most striking findings is that parents in the UK said they felt tremendous pressure from society to buy goods for their children; this pressure was felt most acutely in low-income homes.

The research also shows that parents in the UK are committed to their children but they lose out on time together as a family due in part to long working hours. They often try to make up for this by buying their children gadgets and clothes.

Consumer culture in the UK contrasts starkly with Sweden and Spain, where family time is prioritised, children and families are under less pressure to own material goods and children have greater access to activities out of the home.

"Right now politicians are grappling with the aftermath of the riots and what they say about our society, culture and families," said David Bull, the UNICEF UK Executive Director. "The research findings provide important insights, and it is vital that those in power listen to what children and their families are saying about life in the UK."

In response to the research UNICEF UK is calling on the UK Government to:
- encourage businesses to pay a living wage, so parents don't have to take on several jobs to make a living, which affects the amount of time they can spend with their children
- insist local authorities assess the impact of public spending cuts on children so that funding is protected for play facilities and free leisure activities
- follow Sweden's example and stop advertisements being shown before, during or after programmes aimed at under-12s.

Reg Bailey, Chief Executive of The Mother's Union, who led an independent review of the commercialisation and sexualisation of children earlier this year, said: "If the Government is serious about creating a more family-friendly society – and it has repeatedly set out to do so – then this report is to be welcomed for its thought provoking challenges." *(428 words)*

© UNICEF, www.unicef.org.uk/Latest/News/Research-shows-UK-children-caught-in-materialistic-trap/

Teil C: Textproduktion

Aufgabe 3 – Materialgestützter Aufsatz   *(30 VP: 10 VP Inh./20 VP Spr.)*

Choose between composition 1 or composition 2.

Write a composition about the chosen topic.
- Use the information of at least three of the given materials.
- Name which ones you are using.
- You can add your own ideas.
- Do not write three separate compositions but one covering all the materials chosen.

Composition 1

Write a composition about the topic "Globalisation – winners and losers in our global village".

Material 1

Globalisation means that everybody and everything in our digital age is connected. Every country, every organisation, every individual has become part of a worldwide network. The most noticeable feature of globalisation is the removal of trade barriers between nations which offers a lot of advantages. Firms can produce more cheaply in countries where labour costs are low. As there is also more competition between manufacturers, consumers in industrialised countries can buy goods at lower prices. Critics say that lower production costs are achieved at the expense of workers in developing countries. However, it should not be overlooked that due to globalisation jobs are created in those countries where production is cheap. This has an overall positive effect because it brings down unemployment rates and improves living standards for people there who can now earn a decent wage to keep their families. Furthermore, as recent developments in the Arabian world have shown, globalisation of ideas and the free exchange of information can also have political consequences. Human rights supporters can spread information and call for solidarity.

Material 2

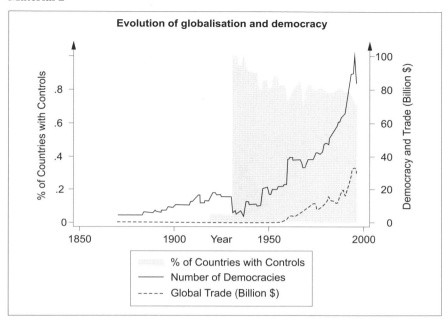

© Eichengreen, Barry/Leblang, David: BIS Working Papers No 219. Democracy and globalisation. Herausgegeben von der Bank for International Settlements. Basel 2006, S. 47

Material 3

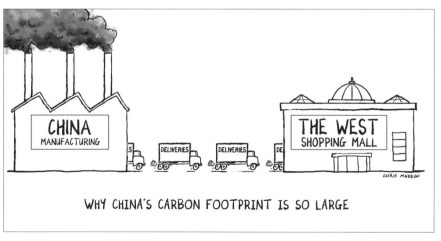

© Chris Madden/cartoonstock.com

Material 4

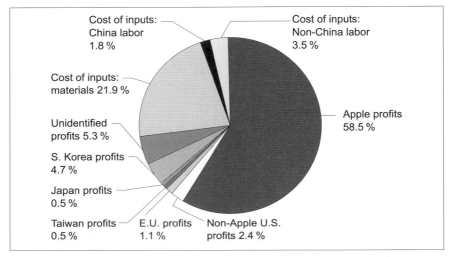

© Kenneth L. Kraemer/Greg Linden/Jason Dedrick: *Capturing Value in Global Networks: Apple's iPad and iPhone.* University of California, Irvine, University of California, Berkeley and Syracuse University, July 2011

Material 5
„Wir bleiben Gewinner der Globalisierung"

Handelspartner außerhalb Europas werden für Deutschlands Exporteure immer wichtiger. Im vierten Quartal 2011 nahmen die Ausfuhren in Länder außerhalb der EU im Vergleich zum Vorjahreszeitraum deutlich um 10,3 Prozent auf 113,4 Milliarden
5 Euro zu. Das geht aus einer veröffentlichten Aufstellung des Statistischen Bundesamtes hervor. „Die Zahlen unterstreichen, was wir seit Jahren sehen: Wir gewinnen zunehmend an Unabhängigkeit von unseren Kernmärkten in der EU", sagte der Geschäftsführer des Bundesverbandes Großhandel, Außenhandel, Dienstleistungen (BGA), André Schwarz, der Nachrichtenagentur dpa in Frankfurt. „Diese Entwick-
10 lung hat im vierten Quartal an Dynamik gewonnen." Gemessen am Gesamtwert der exportierten Waren, der sich laut Bundesamt in den Monaten Oktober bis Dezember auf 269 Milliarden Euro summierte, ist Europa nach wie vor der wichtigste Absatzmarkt für Waren „Made in Germany". Die Exporte in EU-Staaten machten mit 155,5 Milliarden Euro knapp 58 Prozent aus.

© dpa; Handelsblatt

Composition 2

Write a composition about the topic "Feeding the world – between hunger and obesity".

Material 1

Text 1

Drought has left 13 million people on the brink of a full-scale humanitarian crisis in West Africa, a leading British charity has said.

Oxfam said tens of thousands of people in the Sahel region of west and central Africa could die in the coming months if the international community did not distribute much needed aid immediately.

The charity said western governments and aid agencies risked making the mistakes of last year in the Horn of Africa, where the famine may have been far less severe had there been a swifter response to the crisis as it developed.

In parts of Chad, Mali and Niger, the malnutrition rates have exceeded 15 %, with more than one million children at risk of starvation.

© Titel: *Oxfam says drought leaves 13m on brink of crisis in Africa*. Wales Online, 9 March 2012

Text 2

As much as half of all the food produced in the world – two billion tonnes worth – ends up being thrown away, a new report has claimed.

The waste is caused by poor infrastructure and storage facilities, over-strict sell-by dates, "get-one-free" offers, and consumer fussiness, according to the Institution of Mechanical Engineers.

Each year countries around the world produce some four billion tonnes of food. But between 30 % and 50 % of this total, amounting to 1.2 to 2 billion tonnes, never gets eaten, says the report Global Food; Waste Not, Want Not.

In the UK, up to 30 % of vegetable crops are not harvested because their physical appearance fails to meet the exacting demands of consumers. Half the food purchased in Europe and the United States is thrown away after it is bought, the report adds.

© Titel: *Half of all food "thrown away"*. Evening Standard, 10 Jan. 2013

Material 2

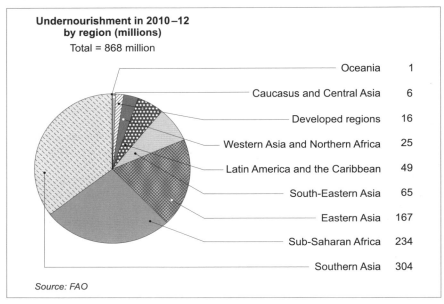

© Source: Food and Agriculture Organization of the United Nations, Graph Undernourishment in 2010–2012, by region (millions), http://www.fao.org/hunger/en/

Material 3

© Mike Baldwin/cartoonstock.com

"You've got the blood pressure of a teenager – who lives on junk food, TV and the computer."

Material 4

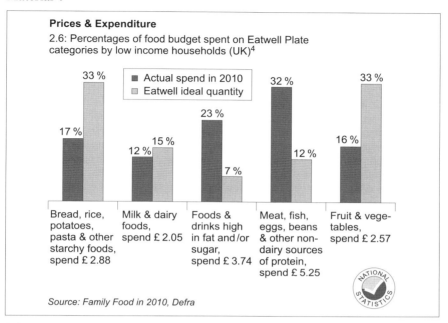

Prices & Expenditure
2.6: Percentages of food budget spent on Eatwell Plate categories by low income households (UK)[4]

Source: Family Food in 2010, Defra

© Department for Environment, Food and Rural Affairs: Family Food 2010. A National Statistics Publication. London: 2011

Material 5

Futtermittel- und Agrosprit-Produktion vernichten Nahrungsmittelanbau

Mit dem verschwenderischen Einsatz von Nahrungsmitteln für Agrosprit und steigendem Fleischkonsum steigt die Konkurrenz um die Landnutzung zwischen Nahrungs- und Futtermitteln sowie Sprit. Die Nahrungsmittelkrise im Jahr 2008 hat dazu
5 geführt, dass Investoren umfangreich Land pachten oder kaufen. Seit dem Jahr 2000 wurden 773 solcher Geschäfte bekannt und getätigt. Sie umfassen insgesamt 33 Millionen ha Fläche. Knapp die Hälfte dieser Landgeschäfte betrafen Afrika. Viele Landgeschäfte werden im Geheimen abgeschlossen und bleiben unbekannt. Agrarkonzerne sichern sich zunehmend wichtige Wasser- und Landrechte. Sie bauen z. B. Getrei-
10 de für Biosprit oder Futtermittel für den Export an. Oftmals bieten Regierungen Flächen feil, welche als unverkauft und ungenutzt gelten. Doch in den wenigsten Fällen liegt das Land tatsächlich brach; meist wird es von mittellosen Familien zum Anbau von Nahrungsmitteln verwendet. Diesen Kleinbauern und -bäuerinnen fehlt dann der Zugang zu Land und Wasser, um sich und ihre Familien zu versorgen. Ihr Grund-
15 recht auf Nahrung wird verletzt. © Oxfam Deutschland e.V.

Lösungsvorschläge

Teil A: Hörverstehen

Aufgabe 1a – Satzergänzungen

Transcript:

1. **James:** I think, it's ridiculous. Some people seem to get really scared when they hear the words "genetically modified". As if their lives were in danger. I'm not sure if they really know what GM means. They simply follow that fashionable trend of our time "going green, going back to nature". As if this were possible in our world today! I don't understand all this fuss. I say, don't panic, keep cool. I'm sure the food manufacturers know how to avoid possible side-effects and have taken all precautions. In addition, the government has made laws which protect us against health hazards.

2. **Ernestine:** I'm worried about food safety. As a consumer you don't really know what's in the foodstuff they sell you in supermarkets or in restaurants. You just have to believe that it doesn't affect your health. That's why it always comes as a shock to me when news of food scandals hits the headlines. Remember BSE, foot and mouth disease, salmonella, and the bird flu in Asia? Scares you, really. We have the saying "You are what you eat". But what about if you can't be sure what you eat? I believe that a healthy diet is important and I'm against any tampering with our food. And GM food is dangerous. That's why I don't want it on the shelves.

3. **Robert:** People are against GM food because they don't trust the new technology. In my opinion, people's fears are exaggerated and in reality GM food works and is a good idea. In the United States, large proportions of maize and soya have been genetically modified for years without any problem. Therefore we should welcome the advantages of the new technology. Food production can be increased, so that the starving people in the Third World can be fed properly. But not only that, it can also increase the quality of our food.

4. **June:** I've heard about GM food, but to be honest, I don't really know what it means. What's more, I'm not really bothered or interested. There are much bigger problems in my opinion, and food is not one of them. It really annoys me that people here worry so much about what they eat. They should be happy and contented that they get enough, that they don't starve. We're too well off in our western world. What's worse, we throw away too much food. This is the real problem, and not whether you have got some funny ingredients in your foodstuff.

Beachten Sie, dass immer zwei Argumente pro Sprecher verlangt sind. Nicht immer werden diese gleich zu Anfang genannt. Sie können sich bereits beim Hören einzelne Stichworte auf Englisch notieren und die Antworten dann auf Deutsch ausformulieren.

(1) James	Er sieht keine Risiken, weil … • **die Hersteller alle Nebenwirkungen vermeiden können** • **und die Regierung Gesetze zum Schutz der Gesundheit erlassen hat.**
(2) Ernestine	Sie ist besorgt, weil sie nicht weiß, … • **was unsere Nahrungsmittel enthalten,** • **und weil es bereits zahlreiche Lebensmittelskandale gab.**
(3) Robert	Er sieht in der neuen Technik vor allem Vorteile, nämlich … • **die Erhöhung der Nahrungsmittelproduktion (gerade für die hungernden Menschen in den Entwicklungsländern)** • **und die Verbesserung der Nahrungsmittelqualität.**
(4) June	Sie ärgert sich über die Menschen in der westlichen Welt, da … • **sie sich zu große Sorgen um ihre Nahrungsmittel machen** • **und zu viel wegwerfen.**

Aufgabe 1 b – Raster mit Lücken

Transcript:

Last night more than 500 people watched the nomination ceremony of the charity organization "Do Something" in Los Angeles. Every year the organisation presents young people and their social work in a special event in which the audience is asked to decide on the best project of the year. The winner of the top prize receives a grant of $ 100,000. Here are some of the nominees:

23-year-old Micaela Connery grew up with her cousin Kelsey, who is disabled. From early on and through her own experience, she became familiar with the problems of children with disabilities. They are often excluded from activities, such as sports, excursions or games. Micaela wanted to change this. She founded a theatre company, called Unified Theater, in which young people with and without disabilities work together to stage plays. Over 1,000 people have participated in the productions.

Jessica Posner, who is 23, founded a school for girls in Kibera, which is a part of Nairobi, the capital of Kenya. Kibera is one of the largest slums in Africa. It's the place where the poorest of the poor fight for survival. In this jungle of poverty girls especially are at risk of being raped and forced into prostitution. Only 8 per cent of them ever get an education. Jessica Posner started the first free school for girls in Kibera, which gave children new hope for a better future.

Jacqueline Murekatete was born in Rwanda, in Africa. In 1994, when Jacqueline was nine, she lost her parents, brothers and sisters and most of her relatives during the civil war between the Tutsi and Hutu in Rwanda. Young Jacqueline was lucky to escape alive because she was taken to live with her uncle in America. The memory of the war, which had made her an orphan, never left her. In 2007, she founded Jacqueline's Human Rights Corner. She travelled widely and told her own story in high schools, universities, churches, workshops, and conferences to educate people in all countries about human rights.

23-year-old Wilfredo worked for one year in Haiti, one of the poorest countries in the world. He realised that people who live in the country, in particular, had no proper health care. Because of the bad hygienic conditions thousands die of illnesses such as tuberculosis, typhoid, diarrhoea or malaria. In order to improve medical care for rural communities Wilfredo Perez created a Public Health and Education Program where he trained young Haitians to be public health workers.

After the presentation of the nominees the audience took a vote, the result of which is to be announced next Thursday.

Vier für die Auszeichnung nominierte Kandidaten werden vorgestellt. Achten Sie darauf, wo die Kandidaten tätig sind (Ort oder Land), um wen sie sich kümmern (Adressatengruppe) und wofür sie ausgezeichnet wurden (Projekt).

Name	Ort/Land 0,5 VP	Adressatengruppe 0,5 VP	Projekt 1 VP
(1) Micaela	x	junge Menschen mit Behinderungen	Theatertruppe für behinderte und nicht behinderte Kinder (Unified Theater)
(2) Jessica	Kibera (Nairobi)	Mädchen aus armen Familien	kostenlose Schule (first free school for girls)
(3) Jacqueline	x	Menschen überall auf der Welt	über Menschenrechte sprechen (Human Rights Corner)
(4) Wilfredo	Haiti	Menschen auf dem Land	Gesundheitsfürsorge (Public Health and Education Program)

Teil B: Leseverstehen

Aufgabe 2 – Mediation

Der Artikel berichtet über die Ergebnisse von UNICEF-Studien, die belegen, dass Kinder im Vereinigten Königreich weniger glücklich sind als z. B. in Schweden und Spanien. Er zeigt die Gründe dafür auf und informiert über geforderte Konsequenzen. Hier sind die wichtigsten Punkte (auf Englisch) aus dem Artikel aufgeführt, die Sie dann für Ihre Zusammenfassung verwenden können:

(Ergebnisse zweier UNICEF-Studien)
- *UNICEF report (2007) about child well-being ranked the UK bottom*
- *new UNICEF report: children's happiness is dependent on having time with a stable family*
- *owning technology or branded clothes less important*

(Gründe für weniger Zufriedenheit im Vereinigten Königreich)
- *parents lose out on time together as a family*
- *they try to make up for this by buying their children gadgets and clothes*
- *in Sweden and Spain children and families are under less pressure*

(Konsequenzen/Forderungen)
- *UNICEF UK is calling on the UK Government to encourage businesses to pay higher wages, to provide funds for play facilities and free leisure activities and to stop advertisements in programmes aimed at under-12s*

Im Materialismus gefangen

In einer Studie von 2007, die die Zufriedenheit von Kindern in Industrieländern untersuchte, belegte das Vereinigte Königreich den letzten Platz. Nun wurde eine weitere Studie veröffentlicht, in der Erfahrungsberichte von Kindern im Vereinigten Königreich, in Schweden und Spanien ausgewertet wurden. Für Kinder aus allen drei Ländern bestand Glück darin, Zeit in einer stabilen Familie zu verbringen und die Möglichkeit zu haben, die Freizeit aktiv zu gestalten, v. a. mit Aktivitäten im Freien. Weniger wichtig war der Besitz von Elektronik und Markenkleidung.

Die Eltern britischer Kinder, besonders diejenigen mit geringerem Einkommen, sehen sich einem gesellschaftlichen Druck ausgesetzt, ihren Kindern Konsumgüter zu kaufen. Oft geschieht dies aus schlechtem Gewissen, da für die Kinder wegen der hohen Arbeitsbelastung meist nur wenig Zeit bleibt. In Schweden und Spanien ist dieser Druck geringer.

UNICEF UK fordert daher von der Regierung, sich bei Firmen für eine Bezahlung einzusetzen, von der Familien leben können, damit Eltern nicht mehrere Jobs annehmen müssen. Auch soll die Finanzierung der öffentlichen Ausgaben für Kinder (z. B. kostenlose Spiel- und Freizeitmöglichkeiten) gesichert sein. Außerdem sollte, wie in Schweden, Werbung in Sendungen für Kinder unter 12 Jahren verboten werden.

(188 words)

Teil C: Textproduktion

Aufgabe 3 – Materialgestützter Aufsatz

Composition 1

Es empfiehlt sich, in der Einleitung kurz zu erklären, was mit Globalisierung gemeint ist. Im Hauptteil gehen Sie dann auf die Gewinner und Verlierer der globalisierten Welt ein. Sie können Ihren Aufsatz folgendermaßen strukturieren:

(Einleitung)
- *definition of globalisation: people around the world are closely connected (global village)*

(Hauptteil)
winners of globalisation:
- *internationally operating companies can produce more cheaply in low-labour-cost countries (Far East, India, China)*
- *consumers in the West profit from cheaper prices*
- *workers in low-labour-cost countries have jobs and can support their families*

losers of globalisation:
- *workers in Asia, for example, if exposed to unfair and unhealthy working conditions*
- *workers in industrialised countries (workplaces are exported)*
- *the environment: more toxic gas emissions*

(Schluss)
- *positive effects politically: globalisation can help spread democratic structures*

Unter Verwendung aller Materialien:

Globalisation – winners and losers in our global village

We are living in the age of globalisation, which means people all around the world are closely connected – thanks to progress in computer and Internet technology. The world has become a smaller place, it has shrunk so much that some experts even talk of us living in a global village. In addition, advances in transport – by air or sea – mean that even distant corners of the globe can be reached in a relatively short time.

The winners of globalisation are internationally operating companies. *(Material 5)* They can have their goods manufactured in countries where workers earn less than in industrialised nations. *(Material 1)* Among the low-labour-cost nations are, above all, countries in the Far East. India and China, for example, which have a vast and more and more qualified workforce. A look at the production costs of an iPhone, for example, shows that labour costs there are very low and that Apple's profit is huge. *(Material 4)* All in all, it pays for companies to have products manufactured overseas. Consumers also profit from the globalized market. When products can be offered at a lower price, competition increases. This, in turn, makes articles cheaper for buyers in the industrialised countries.

Critics of globalisation say that the West profits, but people in developing countries suffer. In the first place, production costs in Asian factories are lower because workers in India or China earn much less than workers in developed countries. In addition, poor working conditions, long working hours and discrimination in Asian factories often make the headlines. So you might say we save money at the cost of Chinese or Indian workers. This is true to a certain extent, but – thanks to globalisation – more people in Asia now have jobs which enable them to support their families and increase their standard of living. *(Material 1)*

However, an increased production in low-labour cost countries also has its drawbacks for workers in industrialised countries. Jobs are lost when production is exported to India or China. Workers in factories in the West are made redundant if they cannot be retrained.

Another problem is the increasing pollution of the environment. In developing countries the production often takes place in factories which emit high amounts of carbon gases into the atmosphere and thus efforts in the industrialised nations to fight global warming are neutralized. *(Material 3)*

In spite of the negative aspects of globalisation, which have to be tackled, more and more people profit from globalisation, not only economically but also in the political field. Democratic movements in totalitarian states have greater chances of bringing about changes in the political system of their homelands when they can muster support from the world community via Internet. The revolutions in Arabian countries ("Arab Spring") in 2011 are ample proof of this positive side of globalisation. *(Materialien 1 und 2)*

(477 words)

Composition 2

Sehen Sie sich die Materialien genau an und halten Sie stichwortartig das jeweilige Thema und evtl. eine Hauptaussage fest. Durchgehendes Thema der vorgelegten Materialien ist die Diskrepanz zwischen dem Hunger in vielen Entwicklungsländern und dem Nahrungsüberschuss sowie Fehlentwicklungen aufgrund falscher Ernährung in den reichen Industriestaaten. Aus den Materialien wird ersichtlich, wo Menschen hungern und warum das so ist. Entsprechend sollten Sie Ihre Antwort strukturieren.

Unter Verwendung der Materialien 1,2,4 und 5:

Feeding the world – between hunger and obesity

(Einleitung)

Hunger and starvation are still a huge problem in many parts of the world. Every one of us knows the pictures of starving people, very often small children dying in the arms of their mothers.

(Hauptteil)

Organisations such as Oxfam or the Food and Agriculture Organization of the United Nations publish reports to make the public aware that famine rages for example in Africa's Sahel zone, in parts of Chad, Mali and Niger. *(Material 1, Text 1)* Those who manage to survive from day to day suffer from malnutrition. The vast majority of undernourished people live in Asia and Africa, whereas in developed regions only a small fraction of the population is affected. *(Material 2)*

In view of these deplorable facts, it seems rather scandalous that half of all the food produced in the world gets thrown away. In rich countries, there is more food available than people can eat and food frequently lands in the dustbin. Even whole crops are wasted because farmers do not harvest lettuce, for example, or other vegetables if the produce doesn't look perfect and they fear that it won't be sold in supermarkets *(Material 1, Text 2)* as consumers are known to prefer fresh and appealing looking products.

One of the main reasons for the unequal distribution of food in the world today is the climate in Africa and Asia, where floods and droughts regularly destroy harvests. Apart from these natural disasters there is another factor which is responsible for the scarcity of food. International companies buy up farm land in Africa, for example, in order to grow grain for cattle feed or to produce energy. *(Material 5)* The cultivation of so-called biofuel crops takes fertile land away from local farmers, which leads to food shortage and makes food too expensive for poorer people to buy.

In large parts of Asia and Africa people suffer because they do not get enough food, whereas in rich countries people become ill because they eat too much or the wrong kind of food. Particularly families with a low income mostly don't attach a lot of importance to a healthy diet. They spend much more money on food which is not good for them, above all fatty foods and sugary drinks, than on good nutrition. *(Material 4)*

(Schluss)

All in all, farmers grow enough to feed the world – the problem is the unequal distribution of agricultural produce. Food should be distributed more equally so that everyone gets enough to eat. People in rich countries should stop wasting food and try to be more aware of their diet. In order to achieve this aim we have to educate children about nutritional facts and teach them to appreciate healthy food.

(450 words)

Fachhochschulreife Englisch (Berufskolleg Baden-Württemberg)
Übungsaufgabe 2

Teil A: Hörverstehen

Aufgabe 1a – Offene Fragen *(5 VP)*

In der Radiosendung „World of Work" geht es heute um das Thema „Energie- und Ressourcensparen im Büro". Die Reporterin Sandra Nash hat einige Büroangestellte zu diesem Thema interviewt.

▶ Hören Sie aufmerksam zu und beantworten Sie die Verständnisfragen in ganzen Sätzen auf Deutsch. Es genügt je eine Information.
▶ Sie hören die Aufnahmen zweimal. Während des Hörens dürfen Sie sich Notizen machen.

1. Warum hat Jackie Smiths Chef die teuren Energiesparlampen angeschafft? *(1 VP)*

2. Wie soll der Stromverbrauch in Steve Millers Büro gesenkt werden? *(1 VP)*

3. Auf welche Weise soll in Sarah Matthews' Firma die Energieverschwendung durch die Klimaanlage vermieden werden? *(1 VP)*

4. Worüber beklagten sich in John Bowmans Büro einige Mitarbeiter/Mitarbeiterinnen? *(1 VP)*

5. Wie versucht Sally Jones in ihrer Firma Papier zu sparen? *(1 VP)*

Aufgabe 1 b – Satzergänzungen *(10 VP)*

Sie hören fünf Anrufe, die auf dem Anrufbeantworter des Hotels Savoy Central in Bath eingehen.

▶ Hören Sie aufmerksam zu und beenden Sie auf Deutsch die unten stehenden Sätze mit Informationen über die Anliegen der Anrufer. Es werden jeweils zwei Informationen erwartet.

▶ Sie hören die Kurztexte zweimal. Während des Hörens dürfen Sie sich Notizen machen.

1. Mr Edwards weist darauf hin, dass ... *(2 VP)*

   _____

   _____

2. Mrs Clark möchte, dass das Hotel ... *(2 VP)*

   _____

   _____

3. Mrs Goodwin storniert ihre Reservierung, weil ... *(2 VP)*

   _____

   und sie möchte ...

   _____

4. Mr Munroe beschwert sich, weil ... *(2 VP)*

   _____

5. Mr Crawfords Sekretärin möchte von der Hotelleitung zwei Angebote, nämlich ... *(2 VP)*

   _____

   _____

Teil B: Leseverstehen

Aufgabe 2 – Mediation (15 VP)

Sie arbeiten in einer Agentur, die Reisen für spezielle Kundengruppen entwickelt und verkauft. Bisher waren das hauptsächlich Studienreisen und Seniorenreisen. Ihr Chef plant, das Angebot auszuweiten und Reisen für Eltern mit Kleinkindern anzubieten. Im Internet sind Sie auf den Erfahrungsbericht einer Mutter gestoßen.

▶ Verfassen Sie für Ihren Chef und die Mitarbeiter der Agentur auf Deutsch einen Leitfaden für die Beratung von Eltern, die mit ihren Kleinkindern verreisen wollen. Nehmen Sie den Erfahrungsbericht der Mutter als Grundlage.
▶ Formulieren Sie ganze deutsche Sätze.

Travelling with young children

Taking your children abroad can be exciting, challenging and hard work. Cathy Owen talks to one mum who has set up a business with £ 4 m of sales – helping parents find the best child-friendly holidays. After 12 years in the travel industry exploring the world for work, Sian Williams thought she would be a dab-hand at taking her five-
5 month-old baby on holiday to Cuba.

But the reality of taking a young child abroad brought home just how much her life had changed.

"The flight was fine because it is actually easier to travel with a baby when they are very young. But when we got to Cuba I found that the formula I had brought with
10 us had burst all over the bag. I managed to save some and thought it would be easy enough to buy some later on in the holiday. What I hadn't banked on was that no one in Cuba seemed to understand what formula was. I went everywhere, asked people on the street, went to every supermarket and no one had a clue what I was talking about. The holiday was a real eye-opener and I learned a lot from it."

15 After her experiences with Erin, now six, Sian decided to try to write about more family-friendly places to go on holiday. Friends and colleagues in the tourism industry and the travel media came forward with recommendations and before Sian knew it, she had a list of baby-friendly accommodation ... Different people like different places and it can all depend on your style of parenting and how confident you are
20 travelling.

"I would recommend that parents check out places where there are a lot of facilities on site, like a swimming pool or say a farm that does feeding rounds in the morning you can take part in. It means that you are keeping the children occupied and it takes the pressure off parents having to think of things to do. Also, check out if you
25 can get meals delivered to where you are staying. You don't want to be cooking like you do at home, but it can be difficult getting a babysitter, so a lot of places deliver food to your home. It just makes it a bit more special. If the parents are relaxed, then the children are more likely to be relaxed too and everyone has a good time. You can find a lot of places abroad run by ex-pats with young children, so they know what

you want and where you can get what you need. It is all very well having somewhere that has high chairs and cots; you need to find out if they are actually enthusiastic about having families and not just the equipment. Are they the kind of people who know that it takes far more than a travel cot and a highchair to make a family-friendly holiday? Like most parents, I thought holidays and mini-breaks would never be the same again with a baby or toddler in tow. Thankfully I was wrong." *(505 words)*

© *Cathy Owen; Media Wales Ltd. WalesOnline™*

Teil C: Textproduktion

Aufgabe 3 – Materialgestützter Aufsatz   *(30 VP: 10 VP Inh./20 VP Spr.)*

Choose between composition 1 or composition 2.

Write a composition about the chosen topic.
- Use the information of at least three of the given materials.
- Name which ones you are using.
- You can add your own ideas.
- Do not write three separate compositions but one covering all the materials chosen.

Composition 1

Write a composition about the topic "Living in a multicultural society".

Material 1

The 1960s witnessed the beginning of worldwide migration. Increasingly, people find themselves in surroundings where not only their clothes, food and drink set them apart from local inhabitants, but also their language, their ways of thinking and their beliefs. In Europe, as previously in the USA and Canada, the growing diversity of cultures and religions leads to tensions and conflicts.

These conflicts often take place in the schools, in many cases over questions of clothing, religious signs and symbols. The "Islamic scarf" and the crucifix come to mind. Should schoolgirls or teachers be allowed to wear veils in public schools? Does an Islamic girl have the right to be excused from co-educational gym classes because her religion – at least according to her reading of the Koran – forbids her from wearing gym clothes in the presence of the opposite sex?

© *Jutta Limbach (Übersetzer: John Lambert); signandsight.com*

Material 2

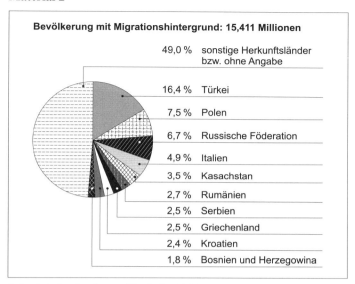

Bevölkerung mit Migrationshintergrund: 15,411 Millionen

%	Herkunftsland
49,0 %	sonstige Herkunftsländer bzw. ohne Angabe
16,4 %	Türkei
7,5 %	Polen
6,7 %	Russische Föderation
4,9 %	Italien
3,5 %	Kasachstan
2,7 %	Rumänien
2,5 %	Serbien
2,5 %	Griechenland
2,4 %	Kroatien
1,8 %	Bosnien und Herzegowina

© *Statistisches Bundesamt, Wiesbaden 2008*

Material 3

"Not to worry. Diversity can only enrich our culture."

© *Joe di Chiarro/cartoonstock.com*

Material 4

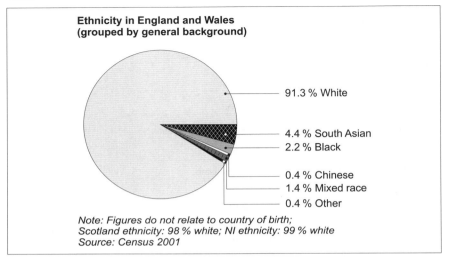

Material 5

Über die Kriminalitätsbelastung von Aussiedlern wurde in der ersten Hälfte der 90er-Jahre längere Zeit auf der Grundlage von Aufsehen erregenden Presseberichten und persönlichen Eindrücken spekuliert. Subjektive Meinungen und in den Medien mehrfach präsentierte negative Einzelbeispiele prägten maßgeblich das Bild des gewalt
5 bereiten, alkoholisierten Aussiedlers, der als „Sozialschmarotzer" nicht zu Arbeit und Ausbildung zu motivieren ist und sich äußerst passiv ins soziale Netz der Bundesrepublik Deutschland fallen lässt.

In der zweiten Hälfte dieses Jahrzehnts wurden die ersten einschlägigen Erhebungen zu diesem Thema veröffentlicht, fundierte empirische Belege lagen erstmals im
10 Jahr 2000 vor. So konnten Strobl/Kühnel in der Kriminalität von Aussiedlern und Deutschen keinen statistisch signifikanten Unterschied feststellen … Der Alkoholkonsum der einheimischen Deutschen sei etwas höher als der Alkoholkonsum der Aussiedler.

© *Johannes Luff; Polizei Bayern*

Composition 2

Write a composition about the topic "Challenges and opportunities of the World Wide Web".

Material 1

Can the high street survive the convenience of online purchasing?

I bought a new book the other day. I walked into a high-street bookseller's, looked at the hardback I had been fancying – and then promptly walked back out again after deciding it was too costly.

That evening I logged onto the internet, bought the same book from an online retailer, and had it delivered to my door for a lower price than if I had carried it home myself.

In doing so, I not only saved myself a couple of quid, but became part of an increasing trend in UK retail.

On the high street the conditions are harsh. Big names like Habitat and Focus are shutting up shop while a slew of others issue profits warnings on an unprecedented scale.

The number of retail firms which appointed administrators rose to 43 in the three months to June from 40 in the same period last year.

But while the cold winds are blowing through our town centres and retail parks, the world of online retail looks increasingly like the land of eternal sunshine.

Even famous names such as Woolworths, now absent from the high street, can enjoy a sort of retail afterlife on the worldwide web. And while Habitat may be closing all but a few London stores, we in the provinces will still be able to take advantage of its online offering.

When it comes to the growth in internet retail the figures speak for themselves. According to the latest IMRG Capgemini e-Retail sales index, British shoppers spent 19 % more on the internet in the first half of 2011 than in the same period a year earlier.

The overall figure added up to a hefty £ 31.5bn and in June alone the average shopper apparently spent £ 86 online.

© *Rhodri Evans, Wales Online, Jul 29 2011*

Material 2

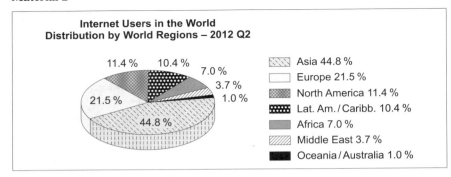

© 2000–2013, Miniwatts Marketing Group. All rights reserved

Material 3

© Mark Lynch/cartoonstock.com

Material 4

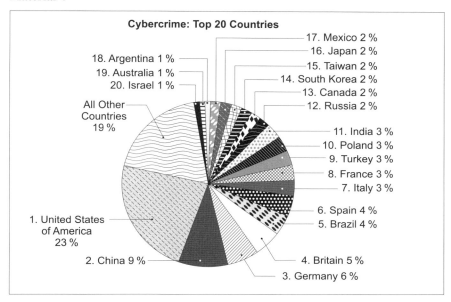

© *Business Week, Symantec*

Material 5

Was weiß Google alles über Sie?
Wenn Sie herausfinden wollen, was Google über Sie weiß und gespeichert hat, können Sie dazu verschiedene Google-Seiten nutzen.
　Die Seite Webprotokoll zeigt alle Suchanfragen eines Users an, egal ob nach Webseiten, Videos oder Bildern. Er kann prüfen, wann er nach welchen Stichworten gesucht hat – und Ergebnisse aus der Liste löschen. Das geht nur, wenn man das Webprotokoll aktiviert hat – wenn nicht, speichert Google auch nichts.
　Der Konzern verspricht, mit Hilfe des Protokolls die Ergebnisse besser personalisieren zu können. Doch Vorsicht: Genau damit ermöglicht man es Google, die Suchanfragen zu speichern. Dann wird das Suchverhalten in einem Cookie gesichert, das auf dem Computer hinterlegt wird. Um es zu deaktivieren, ruft man das Webprotokoll auf und klickt auf „Gesamtes Webprotokoll entfernen".
　Wer ein Google-Konto besitzt, sollte einen Blick in das Google-Dashboard werfen. Auf der Seite zeigt der Anbieter, was er über den Nutzer weiß: Welche Dienste nutzt er und was tut er? Dort steht zum Beispiel, welche Apps man zuletzt bei Android installiert hat (und wie viele), welche Android-Geräte jemand verwendet, was er zuletzt bei Google+ geschrieben hat, wie viele Kontakte er besitzt, wen er am häufigsten kontaktiert hat und wie viele Mails in seinem Google-Postfach liegen.

Übrigens versucht Google bei jedem Nutzer, das Geschlecht und eine Altersgruppe zuzuordnen. Dazu beobachtet die Firma, auf welchen Seiten sich jemand aufhält, und ordnet dem Nutzer Kategorien und Interessen zu. Ob der Anbieter richtig liegt, kann man ebenfalls nachprüfen.

© *Claudia Frickel, in: Focus Online vom 23. 10. 2012*

Lösungsvorschläge

Teil A: Hörverstehen

Aufgabe 1a – Offene Fragen

Transcript:

1. **Jackie Smith:** My boss is rather keen on saving energy. He says this is not only good for the planet, it's also profitable for the company. He has invested in energy saving light bulbs which are quite expensive. Our boss says they will save us a lot of money in the long run because the modern light bulbs use four times less energy and last 15 times longer than regular ones.

2. **Steve Miller:** I work in a small advertising agency. My boss used to say, "We are only a small firm and our energy consumption doesn't make any difference to the world's energy shortage", so we needn't worry. However, his wife does not agree with him. She now sees to it that we reduce our electricity consumption. For example, she makes sure that we turn off all electrical equipment at the end of the day completely. She has also convinced her husband to buy modern computer monitors which turn themselves off when they are not in use.

3. **Sarah Matthews:** The company I work for is very environmentally-minded. All our computers, printers and photocopiers are energy-saving appliances. In this context, air conditioning is also important. The management has seen to it that the air conditioning does not waste energy. This is why the system will shut down when the windows are open. In addition, heat generating equipment, such as photocopiers, is placed away from the air conditioning unit.

4. **John Bowman:** My boss says, heating the work place is extremely expensive, that's why everything is being done to save heating costs. When our office was renovated the building was properly insulated and the heating system was modernised. Thermostats regulate the room temperature and keep it the same level all the time. I, for my part, don't like the office being too hot. However, a few colleagues of mine have already complained that rooms are often a bit chilly, especially in the early mornings or when they have to work late.

5. **Sally Jones:** As a manager of a multinational company I'm very concerned about the amount of waste we produce every year. In my view, we waste too much paper. Therefore, I have thought about a few recommendations to our staff. First of all, I think we should re-use paper. I mean, there are cases when we can use the other side of each sheet of paper when printing. In addition, I think we should change from paper-based to electronic correspondence. That means we can send documents and letters to customers via email instead of by post.

✏ Einzelne Sprecher geben mehrere Begründungen für das Energiesparen. Sie brauchen dann aber jeweils nur eine Begründung (in einem ganzen Satz) wiederzugeben.

1. Energiesparlampen sparen Geld, weil sie weniger Energie verbrauchen und viel länger halten. (... *save us a lot of money ... use four times less energy and last 15 times longer ...*)

2. Nach Büroschluss müssen alle Geräte ganz ausgeschaltet werden. (... *turn off all electrical equipment at the end of the day completely.*) /
Es wurden moderne Computer angeschafft, die sich von selbst ausschalten, wenn sie gerade nicht genutzt werden. (... *modern computer monitors which turn themselves off when they are not in use.*)

3. Die Klimaanlage schaltet sich aus, wenn die Fenster geöffnet werden. (... *the system will shut down when the windows are open.*) /
Wärme ausstrahlende Geräte wurden aus der Nähe der Klimaanlage entfernt.
(... *heat generating equipment ... is placed away from the air conditioning unit.*)

4. Sie beklagten sich, weil die Arbeitsräume zu kalt sind, besonders früh am Morgen oder spätabends. (... *rooms are often a bit chilly, especially in the early mornings or when they have to work late.*)

5. Sie schlägt vor, in bestimmten Fällen auch die Rückseite des Papiers zu benutzen/ auf papierlose Übermittlung von Dokumenten umzustellen.
(... *re-use paper.*)/(... *change from paper-based to electronic correspondence.*)

Aufgabe 1 b – Satzergänzungen

Transcript:

1. **Mr Edwards:** I wish to confirm that the meeting with our business partners from the Kuwait Group will take place next Monday at 10 o'clock in the Charlotte Room as planned. The only difference is that there will be another three guests in our party. So could you please make sure the necessary arrangements as to our lunch and later the seating in the conference room are updated, in particular the Internet service. I think, we'll need another three laptops and another overhead projector. Refreshments should be served at 4:30, as arranged with your headwaiter.

2. **Mrs Clark:** I'm calling you on behalf of my son. He's five and we stayed at your lovely hotel for a week. Everything was fine, until at the very last moment, a catastrophe happened. Well, at least that's what our little Simon thinks. We lost his favourite soft toy. It's called Snoopy, you know, that clever dog from the Peanuts series. Simon takes it to bed every night. He just can't go to sleep without Snoopy. When we were leaving yesterday, we probably left Snoopy somewhere in the bed beneath the bed covers. Could you please check if it was found when the room was cleaned? That would be very nice. By the way, we stayed in

room 345. Oh, but of course, you know which room we stayed in and you also have our address which you could forward Snoopy to.

3. **Mrs Goodwin:** Unfortunately, my husband broke his left arm yesterday. We were looking forward so very much to our stay in your hotel, but because of my husband's accident we have to cancel our reservation. The name is Mr and Mrs Goodwin. We wanted to stay for a week from Monday 12th. Of course we are still keen on going on our holiday and will do so in about three months' time. Therefore I would ask you to reserve a suite for my husband and I the first week in July, if that is possible. Could you check it please, and call me back on 376 3856 087.

4. **Mr Munroe:** I'm very sorry, but I have to get this off my chest. We, that is my wife and I, were very disappointed with our last stay at your hotel. In the first place, what really annoyed us, was the room, and especially the bathroom, was not cleaned properly. We complained about this negligence to the house manager and he promised to see into the matter. Well, the problem was solved, but then we found out that the room service was not available after 10 pm. That should not happen at a hotel of your class and standing.

5. **Ms Jennings:** This is Sheila Jennings speaking. I'm the secretary of Mr Crawford, CEO of Glaxone Incorporated in Exbourne. Our firm is planning an incentive event for 14 of our clients in the city of Bath and would like to use your hotel as a base for three days. Could you please submit an offer for the reservation of 14 rooms, including breakfast, from 3rd to 6th September. We understand that a concert will take place on 4th September in the Convention Centre, and would like to reserve 25 tickets. As we are thinking about entering into further business connections with you we expect a favourable offer. My email address is sheila.jennings@glaxone.co.uk.

Es sind immer zwei Informationen je Anrufer gefordert. Versuchen Sie, schon beim ersten Hören mindestens eine Information pro Sprecher in Stichworten festzuhalten, und ergänzen Sie nach dem zweiten Hören die einzelnen Sätze.

1. Mr Edwards weist darauf hin, dass **drei weitere Gäste erwartet und drei zusätzliche Laptops und ein Overheadprojektor benötigt werden**.
   (... another three guests ... another three laptops and another overhead projector.)

2. Mrs Clark möchte, dass das Hotel **ihr das Kuscheltier ihres Sohnes nachschickt, falls es gefunden wurde**. *(... check if it was found ... forward Snoopy.)*

3. Mrs Goodwin storniert ihre Reservierung, weil **ihr Mann sich den Arm gebrochen hat**, und sie möchte **in der ersten Juliwoche eine Suite buchen**.
   (... husband broke his left arm ... reserve a suite ... the first week in July ...)

4. Mr Munroe beschwert sich, weil **das Zimmer und das Bad nicht sauber waren und weil nach 22 Uhr kein Zimmerservice mehr zur Verfügung stand.** *(... room, and ... bathroom ... not cleaned properly ... room service not available after 10 pm.)*
5. Mr Crawfords Sekretärin möchte von der Hotelleitung zwei Angebote, nämlich **für die Reservierung von 14 Zimmern und die Bestellung von 25 Konzerttickets.** *(... reservation of 14 rooms ... to reserve 25 tickets.)*

Teil B: Leseverstehen

Aufgabe 2 – Mediation

Entsprechend der Aufgabenstellung ist die Zusammenfassung für den Chef und die Mitarbeiter der Agentur, also für den internen Gebrauch, gedacht. Die hier angeführten Gesichtspunkte sollten die Mitarbeiter beachten, wenn sie Eltern beraten, die mit kleinen Kindern verreisen wollen.

Beachten Sie bei der Beratung von Eltern, die mit kleinen Kindern verreisen wollen, Folgendes:
– Beruhigen Sie die Eltern. Reisen mit kleinen Kindern, insbesondere mit Babys, sind im Allgemeinen kein Problem. Das gilt auch für Flugreisen.
– Weisen Sie Eltern, die eine Fernreise (z. B. nach Kuba) wählen, darauf hin, genug Babynahrung mitzunehmen.
– Schlagen Sie einen Urlaubsort vor, der für Kinder Beschäftigungsmöglichkeiten bietet (z. B. Unterkunft mit Swimmingpool oder ein Bauernhof).
– Für Eltern, die nicht selbst kochen möchten, eignet sich ein Urlaubsquartier, das einen Essenslieferservice anbietet.
– Es kann vieles vereinfachen, eine Ferienunterkunft zu wählen, die von im Ausland lebenden Landsleuten betrieben wird, die sich vor Ort auskennen.
– Achten Sie auf die Kinderfreundlichkeit des Ferienortes. Kinderfreundlichkeit ist dabei nicht allein eine Frage der Ausstattung.

Insgesamt gilt: Wenn die Kleinen zufrieden sind, dann sind es die Eltern auch und können den Urlaub genießen.

Teil C: Textproduktion

Aufgabe 3 – Materialgestützter Aufsatz

Composition 1

In Ihrem Aufsatz sollen Sie sich mit dem Zusammenleben von Menschen verschiedener Herkunft in einer Gesellschaft auseinandersetzen. Sehen Sie sich zuerst alle Materialien an und entscheiden Sie dann, welche Sie in Ihren Aufsatz integrieren wollen.

Beispiel für die Strukturierung des Aufsatzes:

(Einleitung)
emergence of multicultural societies:
– USA: model of a multicultural society
– in Europe: immigration on a larger scale after WW II
(Hauptteil)
positive aspects of a multicultural society:
– immigrants bring new ideas
– add to the diversity of a country
– promote mutual understanding
– are a boost to its economy
challenges of a multicultural society:
– "clash" over cultural/religious symbols
– prejudice against newcomers
– failed integration
(Schluss)
– efforts on both sides necessary for a successful multicultural society
– sensible immigration quotas

Unter Verwendung aller Materialien:

Living in a multicultural society

The United States is arguably the best example of a multicultural society. The 19th century saw large numbers of people, mainly from Europe, immigrating to the New World. In Europe, migration on a larger scale set in after World War II when the booming European economies needed workers. Britain was the first country to receive immigrants from her former colonies in the Caribbean and Asia, who made the United Kingdom the multi-ethnic society it is today. *(Material 4)* Germany, for example, is also on the way to becoming a more diverse society. More than 15 million people of various cultural and ethnic backgrounds live in the country today. Most of them came from Turkey or Southern and Eastern European countries. *(Material 2)*

A country can gain a lot from the peaceful existence of people from different cultures. Hard-working immigrants with new ideas and plans can add to the diversity of a country, and the interchange of cultures can lead to better understanding. The United States, in the words of President John F. Kennedy "a nation of immigrants", profited from the industriousness and abilities of the newcomers who contributed greatly to the country's economic rise. However, the bitter irony is that the indigenous inhabitants are the losers in the multicultural society of the New World. Instead of profiting from the diversity of the melting pot of nations, the Native Americans were pushed aside to the brim of extinction by the waves of newcomers. *(Material 3)*

Today, multiculturalism is increasingly being discussed, as the growing diversity of cultures and religions has also led to tensions and conflicts. *(Material 1)* In Germany, the authorities opposed the wish of Muslim women teachers who wanted to wear a headscarf in class, which has a religious significance in Islam, but is seen by many in the Western world as a symbol of women's suppression.

It is also prejudice against newcomers which makes mutual understanding and integration difficult. Young resettlers from Kazakhstan, for example, are often seen as lazy drunkards committing crimes and exploiting the country's social system. However, statistics and police reports show that these assumptions are completely unfounded. *(Material 5)*

In Britain, the riots in the summer of 2011 showed that failed integration into mainstream British society and the lack of prospects for the future can lead to the unrest of young people, many of whom – but not all – had an immigrant background. The disturbances make it clear that integration and fair treatment is the key to a peaceful multicultural society.

To achieve this, efforts need to be made on both sides. On the one hand, newcomers must be willing to integrate and on the other hand, society has to give immigrants a fair chance to succeed. To finally deal with the fact that Germany is now a country of immigration, introducing sensible immigration quotas and welcoming the positive effects of a multicultural society would be a step in the right direction. *(492 words)*

Composition 2

Sehen Sie die vorgelegten Materialien genau durch und halten Sie in Stichworten fest, worum es im Einzelnen geht. Sie werden feststellen, dass vor allem die Gefahren, die mit dem Internet und den modernen Medien verbunden sind, im Vordergrund stehen. Diese sollten Sie in Ihrem Aufsatz entsprechend der Themenstellung („challenges") ausführlich darlegen, daneben aber auch einige positive Aspekte („opportunities") des World Wide Web erläutern. Es empfiehlt sich, nach einer kurzen Einleitung zunächst auf die Gefahren und dann auf einige Vorteile des Internets einzugehen. Selbstverständlich ist auch eine andere Reihenfolge möglich.

Unter Verwendung aller Materialien:

Challenges and opportunities of the World Wide Web

(Einleitung)

The use of new communications technology such as mobile phones or the Internet has greatly increased in recent years. People all over the world have Internet access. Most users live in Asia – in countries with large populations such as India and China

– accounting for almost half of the world's users. *(Material 2)* The expansion of the World Wide Web has been accompanied by positive and negative effects.

(Hauptteil)
Many retailers use the Internet as a platform for selling their merchandise. E-commerce is the keyword, and for many firms the Internet has become a very profitable distribution channel. However, retailers who have shops in the city suffer as a result, and the number of those who have had to close their doors has recently risen, because they cannot compete with the cheap prices offered by online sellers. *(Material 1)*
Another deplorable negative effect of new media technologies is the lack of personal communication. Nobody writes letters any more, and people now seem to talk less face-to-face, but use tweets and blogs instead. *(Material 3)*
Furthermore, criminals use the potential of the Internet for unlawful activities, which the police have termed cyber crimes. The number of such crimes is surprisingly high in the United States. Almost a quarter of all cyber crimes are committed there, although the US accounts for only 12 per cent of the world's Internet users. In Asia, where most users live, cyber crimes are not as frequent (India 3 per cent, China 9 per cent). *(Material 2 und 4)*
Another point which worries many people is the security of personal data on the Web. Every time a user logs onto a site or tries to find information via the search engine Google, for example, personal data are collected and stored. Experienced users will regularly look up the special pages which tell them what Google knows about them. *(Material 5)* On the whole, however, it appears to be rather difficult to delete information once it has been published on the Web. Everybody needs to be aware that "the Web never forgets" and should be careful not to give away too many personal details or post very private personal photos.
In spite of all these challenges, the Web also offers unparalleled benefits to firms and individuals alike. Using the Web, firms can do business worldwide and attract more customers than they can in high-street shops. Buyers find online shopping more convenient and often cheaper. *(Material 1)* In addition, Internet retailers usually offer a wider selection. Jobseekers can inform themselves about employment opportunities. People can keep in touch via e-mail or Skype with families and friends who live in distant countries. Adventurers who travel the world can inform their friends at home about their whereabouts, students who study abroad can tell their parents how they are getting on. The phrase "Information at your fingertips", coined by Bill Gates in the 1990s, has become a reality. Anyone can look up practically any subject that is of interest at any time on the Internet.

(Schluss)
Considering the pros and cons, it seems fair to say that, despite all the disadvantages and hidden dangers on the web, the Internet is of enormous advantage for most businesses and individuals as long as they know how to use it wisely. *(545 words)*

Fachhochschulreife Englisch (Berufskolleg Baden-Württemberg)
Übungsaufgabe 3

Teil A: Hörverstehen

Aufgabe 1a – Satzergänzungen *(5 VP)*

Zwei Aussteller unterhalten sich auf einer Computermesse.
▶ Hören Sie aufmerksam zu und vervollständigen Sie auf Deutsch die unten stehenden Aussagen. Pro Aussage wird eine Information erwartet.
▶ Sie hören das Gespräch zweimal. Während des Hörens dürfen Sie sich Notizen machen.

1. In wirtschaftlich schwierigen Zeiten wollen Firmen ihre Geräte länger behalten, da ... *(1 VP)*

2. Es gab einen ungeheuren Ansturm auf das neue Tablet, weil ... *(1 VP)*

3. Viele Besucher wollen die Produkte des Ausstellers haben, aber ... *(1 VP)*

4. Viele Schnäppchenjäger kommen am Ende der Messe, weil ... *(1 VP)*

5. Daten und Fotos sind auf einem externen Server wahrscheinlich sicherer als ... *(1 VP)*

Aufgabe 1b – Raster mit Lücken *(10 VP)*

Sie hören fünf Kurzberichte von Schulabgängern, die über ihre Pläne nach Abschluss ihrer Schulausbildung sprechen.

- ▶ Hören Sie aufmerksam zu und vervollständigen Sie auf Deutsch das unten stehende Raster mit Informationen aus den Berichten.
- ▶ Sie hören die Kurzberichte zweimal. Während des Hörens dürfen Sie sich Notizen machen.

Sprecher(in)	Wunschtätigkeit 1 VP	Gründe 1 VP	Wunschort 0,5 VP
(1) Leo			
(2) David			
(3) Zoe			
(4) Meryl			

Teil B: Leseverstehen

Aufgabe 2 – Mediation *(15 VP)*

Die Schülerzeitung plant eine Sonderausgabe über das Thema „Globalisierung". In einem Artikel soll es um das „Symbol des weltweiten Handels", den Container, gehen.
- In Ihrer Funktion als Redakteur schreiben Sie diesen Beitrag anhand der entsprechenden Informationen im folgenden Artikel.
- Formulieren Sie ganze deutsche Sätze.

The Symbol of Global Trade

In 2008 the British Broadcasting Corporation (BBC) started a project to illustrate how closely countries have become connected through trade. Everybody was talking about our global economy and the BBC wanted to show what this meant in real life by sending a shipping container around the world. In the course of 421 days the BBC
5 Box, as it was called, travelled more than 50,000 miles. The Box used different means of transport on its worldwide journey: 47,000 miles aboard different container ships, 3,000 miles by train and 1,300 miles by roads. Its cargo included 15,000 bottles of whisky (which was shipped to China), 4,000 bathroom scales and more than 95,000 tins of cat food. During the project visitors of the BBC website could always
10 follow the route the Box was taking by GPS. After the end of the project the container was transported to Africa where it was refitted as a permanent soup kitchen for poor people.
    The shipping container has become the symbol of global trade. Many people think it was invented in China – not true. The first shipping container was invented
15 and patented in 1956 by an American named Malcolm McLean. McLean was not an ocean shipper, but was a trucker and by 1956 he owned the largest trucking fleet in the South and the fifth largest trucking company in all the United States. He saved his money and bought his first truck in 1934. During those years all cargo was loaded and unloaded in odd sized wooden crates. The process was very slow and certainly
20 not standardized. After observing this slow and inefficient process for 20 years, he finally decided to step back and develop some standardized way of loading cargo from trucks to ships and warehouses. Malcolm then purchased Pan Atlantic Tanker Company, which owned a bunch of fairly rusted tankers. He re-named the new shipping company Sea-Land Shipping. With this shipping company he could finally
25 experiment with better ways to load and un-load trucks and ships. After many experiments, his final design is what we know now as the Shipping Container. ... super strong, uniform design, theft resistant, stackable, easy to load, unload, truck, rail, ship, and certainly store. (...) The final boost to standardize McLean's concept was the US Navy and by the early 70's (containers) were globally accepted. So in fact, al-
30 though McLean had the first concept and working system in 1956, it was the US military who finally did what was necessary to make the ISO shipping container accepted by every shipping line and every country of the world. Because it was so much faster and organized to load-unload, the cost of loading freight was reduced by more

than 90 %. Thus, the cost of products you sell or buy were reduced greatly because of
the invention and standardization of the ISO shipping container. In 1956, loose cargo
cost $ 5.86 per ton to load. Using an ISO shipping container, the cost was reduced to
only 16 cents per ton. The shipping container invention of Malcolm McLean has certainly changed the world and thus, it has changed the lives of every human on the planet.

(523 words)

ab Z. 13: ISBU Association, Inc. Copyright 2012. http://www.isbu-association.org

Teil C: Textproduktion

Aufgabe 3 – Materialgestützter Aufsatz *(30 VP: 10 VP Inh./20 VP Spr.)*

Choose between composition 1 or composition 2.

Write a composition about the chosen topic.
- Use the information of at least three of the given materials.
- Name which ones you are using.
- You can add your own ideas.
- Do not write three separate compositions but one covering all the materials chosen.

Composition 1

Discuss the topic "Genetically modified food (GM food)".

Material 1

Consumers are worried about the potential dangers of genetically engineered foodstuffs. Several corporations have applied for permission to the government to increase the production of genetically engineered food, such as meat or fish for human consumption. Opponents say that no scientist can foresee the possible side effects of genetically modified food and strongly advise the authorities to refuse the applications. The critics say, as we do not know for sure if eating GM foods can affect people's health we mustn't allow ourselves to be used as guinea pigs. We are not only responsible for our own well-being, but also for the health of unborn children. If pregnant women consume GM food we do not know what damage they might be causing their unborn babies.

Material 2

© Steve Greenberg/cartoonstock.com

Material 3

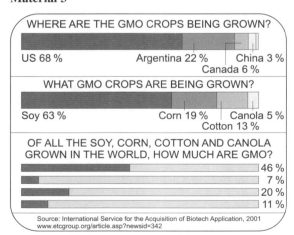

© 2001 ISAAA, International Service for the Acquisition of Agri-Biotech Applications

Material 4

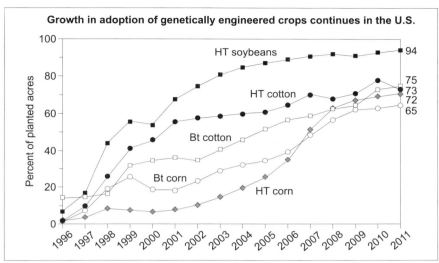

HT = crops which are resistant to certain herbicides *(Pflanzenschutzmittel)*
Bt = crops which are resistant to insects

© *Daten nach: Jorge Fernandez-Cornejo/William D. McBride: Adoption of Bioengineered Crops. Agricultural Economic Report No. (AER810) 67 pp, May 2002 USDA*

Material 5

BASF hat heute angekündigt, dass sie ihre Aktivitäten im Bereich der Pflanzenbiotechnologie auf die Hauptmärkte in Nord- und Südamerika konzentriert. Im Zuge dieser Veränderungen wird das Unternehmen das Produktportfolio und die Standortstrategie der Gruppengesellschaft BASF Plant Science neu ausrichten. Die Unternehmenszentrale der BASF Plant Science wird von Limburgerhof/Deutschland nach Raleigh/North Carolina/USA verlegt. Die Aktivitäten im Bereich Forschung und Entwicklung werden im Wesentlichen an den Standorten Raleigh, Gent/Belgien und Berlin/Deutschland gebündelt. Die Entwicklung und Kommerzialisierung aller Produkte, die ausschließlich auf den europäischen Markt ausgerichtet sind, werden gestoppt. Die bereits eingeleiteten Zulassungsprozesse werden weitergeführt.

„Wir sind davon überzeugt, dass die Pflanzenbiotechnologie eine der Schlüsseltechnologien des 21. Jahrhunderts ist. Andererseits fehlt in weiten Teilen Europas immer noch die entsprechende Akzeptanz bei der Mehrheit der Verbraucher, Landwirte und Politiker", sagte Dr. Stefan Marcinowski, Mitglied des Vorstandes der BASF und zuständig für Pflanzenbiotechnologie.

© *Pressestelle BASF*

Composition 2

Discuss the topic "The importance of education in our globalized economy".

Material 1

CBI criticises schools over "inadequate" literacy and numeracy

Survey of over 500 firms shows many employers dissatisfied with school leavers' numeracy and use of English

Almost half of all employers have paid for remedial training for school and college leavers who lack a basic grasp of English and maths, according to the CBI. Companies also find school leavers lacking in the broader attributes required for work, with 69 % saying school leavers have inadequate business awareness, and more than 50 % finding shortcomings in their ability to manage themselves. The survey of more than 500 firms shows that 42 % are dissatisfied with school leavers' use of English, and more than a third are concerned about numeracy. Twelve per cent of employers provided remedial literacy training for graduates. The government is expected to announce this week that teenagers failing to get good GCSEs in English and maths should be required to pursue these subjects after 16. At present, 4 % of such teenagers go on to achieve this by the age of 19. The CBI survey findings echo the view of the Wolf report on vocational education, published in March, which said English and maths were "the most generally useful and valuable vocational skills on offer", and that less than half of English teenagers had good passes in these core GCSEs by 16.

© *Jeevan Vasagar, in: The Guardian, Monday 9 May 2011*

Annotation:
CBI: Confederation of British Industry – head organization of British employers in the UK

Material 2

	Public sector 'secondary' schools in the UK				
	Number of schools	Pupils (thousands)	Full-time teachers (thousands)	Pupils per school	Pupil:teacher ratio
1905	630	113	…	179	…
1914	1,083	207	12	192	17.2
1925	1,602	510	25	318	20.3
1935	1,704	627	31	368	20.3
1945	…	…	…	…	…
1955	6,093	2,191	112	360	19.6
1965	6,817	3,217	176	472	18.3
1975	5,680	4,190	248	738	16.9
1985	5,262	4,244	268	806	15.9
1995	4,479	3,656	228	816	16.0
2005	4,230	4,002	247	946	16.2
2010	4,149	3,907	…	942	15.4
2011	4,121	3,889	247	944	15.3
2012	4,072	3,856	…	947	15.3

© Paul Bolton; sn04252-1.pdf; House of Commons Library, Education: Historical statistics; Standard Note: SN/SG/4252; Last updated: 27 November 2012; www.parliament.uk

Material 3

© Steve Delmonte/cartoonstock.com

"I called you in to talk to you about your son not being able to sit still."

Material 4

The numbers of men and women applying for and entering university

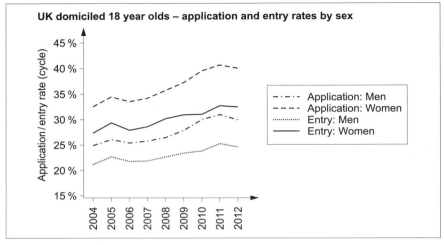

© UCAS "End of cycle report 2012", www.ucas.com

Material 5

Mädchen sind in der Schule deutlich besser als Jungen

Der Göttinger Neurobiologe und Lernforscher kann nicht erkennen, dass Jungen in der Schule das finden können, was sie für eine gute Entwicklung brauchen. Sie seien im Durchschnitt extrovertierter und suchten noch stärker als Mädchen nach Anerken-
5 nung und Bedeutung. „Doch Hausaufgaben in der Schule sind keine Aufgaben, an denen Jungen wachsen können." Solche Aufgaben seien in der Schule aber schwer zu finden.
 „Bedeutungsvoll wird Gelerntes für die Jungen eher außerhalb der Schule, im realen Leben", sagt Hüther und fordert, dass sich Schulen mehr öffnen, damit die Schü-
10 ler in die Natur und in die Praxis gehen könnten. Mädchen orientierten sich hingegen weniger stark als Jungen am Außen. „Sie können eher nur um der Noten willen lernen, haben Spaß an Beziehung und sich selbst", erklärt Hüther.

© Lisa Becker: Mädchen lernen besser, Jungen steigen auf. In: FAZ vom 3. 5. 2012

Lösungsvorschläge

Teil A: Hörverstehen

Aufgabe 1a – Satzergänzungen

Transcript:

RALPH: Must have a sit-down. My feet are killing me.
ROBERT: Yeah, I need a break too.
RALPH: How have things been going at your stand?
ROBERT: Extremely busy, you could say, especially during the trade-only days. We've had a lot of IT experts come to our shows and seminars. Many of them long-time customers.
RALPH: What are they interested in this year?
ROBERT: We are doing very well with the services we provide. I have the feeling there is more and more demand for aftersales service and support. Of course, we also demonstrate our latest equipment, but from my point of view there seems to be more money in servicing these days.
RALPH: Interesting. I can imagine that during difficult economic times firms want to hang on to their equipment as long as possible because they had to invest enormous funds in the first place.
ROBERT: Yes. And what about you? How are things going?
RALPH: Yesterday morning, when the fair was opened to the public all hell broke loose. Everybody's mad on our new super-thin notebook and the latest tablet.
ROBERT: I can understand that. And it was to be expected, because you'd been making quite a lot of noise about the tablet months before it was due to be released.
RALPH: That's true. But you must admit, it is a beauty.
ROBERT: I agree, it looks fantastic. I suppose you have sold a lot already?
RALPH: Well, actually not. Lots of people like our stuff, but they don't want to pay for it. At least not the price we are asking. So they keep looking and looking, playing around with it, trying it out, asking for information, although they have read all computer magazine articles about it – and then they wander off again.
ROBERT: I can just imagine.
RALPH: And then there's the bargain hunters. They know all the Internet prices and what our competitors offer, and they just cannot stop haggling.
ROBERT: I know the type. You get many of them near the end of the fair, when they believe we're all tired, want to go home and get rid of our stuff at half price rather than packing it up again. It's always been like that.
RALPH: True. Has security been an important issue with your IT experts?
ROBERT: Of course it has. It's becoming more and more significant, especially when you think about the cloud services. That's why we offer individually designed se-

curity solutions, recovery plans in case of a data disaster. I suppose your bargain hunters are concerned about cloud security too, aren't they?

RALPH: They are, indeed. But I keep telling them that storing their files and photos on a server in California or some other place is probably safer than having it all at home on your hard disk, which might crash after four or five years.

ROBERT: I agree with you.

Achten Sie bei der Satzergänzung darauf, dass Sie den Satz grammatikalisch korrekt vervollständigen.

1. In wirtschaftlich schwierigen Zeiten wollen Firmen ihre Geräte länger behalten, da **sie für die Geräte sehr viel investieren mussten**. *(... because they had to invest enormous funds ...)*

2. Es gab einen ungeheuren Ansturm auf das neue Tablet, weil **schon Monate vor der Einführung viel Werbung dafür gemacht worden war**. *(... quite a lot of noise about the tablet months before it was due to be released.)*

3. Viele Besucher wollen die Produkte des Ausstellers haben, aber **nicht zu dem Preis, den dieser verlangt**. *(... they don't want to pay for it. At least not the price we are asking.)*

4. Viele Schnäppchenjäger kommen am Ende der Messe, weil **sie glauben, dass die Aussteller müde sind und ihre Sachen zum halben Preis loswerden wollen**. *(... we're all tired, want to go home and get rid of our stuff at half price ...)*

5. Daten und Fotos sind auf einem externen Server wahrscheinlich sicherer als **auf der Festplatte zu Hause**. *(... safer than having it all at home on your hard disk ...)*

Aufgabe 1b – Raster mit Lücken

Transcript:

1. **Leo:** I don't feel like taking up work straight after my final exams. I've spent so many years studying at school, I can't stand it anymore. I want to do something different, something practical, with my own hands, I don't know. What I do know, however, is I'm not ready for a nine-to-five job. I don't want to turn up at some office in the morning and stay locked in there for the rest of the day. I need air to breathe – best of all somewhere in Asia. Japan would be cool. I'd love that.

2. **David:** I want to be a manager and study international business management. I have been told that it is not easy to get a place at a good business school, therefore I want to learn another foreign language and get some work experience first. My idea is to look for a work placement with an international company in South America. Spanish is needed in a lot of countries – apart from English, of course. I

don't mind if I don't earn much money; it should be enough, though, to cover my basic living costs. I'm sure that work experience and a foreign language will improve my chances on the job market later.

3. **Zoe:** It's money, I'm after! But no, seriously, though. I am fed up with still being dependent on my parents. I don't want to ask for pocket money any longer. It's not that I want to be rich, I just want to be a little bit more independent. That's the reason why I want to spend a gap year working in a job which is worthwhile moneywise. I'm aware it might be a job which not everybody wants, but I don't mind getting my hands dirty or working long hours. I'm prepared to work anywhere in the world.

4. **Meryl:** Many people say "Money makes the world go round!", but I'm not one of them. Before taking up a job or perhaps going into some sort of further education I want to do something really useful. What I mean is, I want to do something which can help to save our planet. I've read a lot about how people are destroying the environment, almost all over the world. Now, after graduation, is the time for me to do something practical, in real life. Therefore I would like to join a project for the conservation of the Amazon rain forest. I'm sure that I will also benefit as a person from living and working in a totally different environment from the one I've been used to up to now.

Für die Ergänzungen in den Spalten „Wunschtätigkeit" und „Gründe" gibt es einen Punkt, für den „Wunschort" einen halben Punkt. Es genügen jeweils kurze, stichwortartige Angaben.

Sprecher(in)	Wunschtätigkeit 1 VP	Gründe 1 VP	Wunschort 0,5 VP
Leo	etwas Praktisches	hat genug vom Lernen	Asien / Japan
David	Praktikum in einer (internationalen) Firma	will Spanisch lernen / berufliche Erfahrung sammeln (je 0,5)	Südamerika
Zoe	irgendeinen gut bezahlten Job ausüben	will eigenes Geld verdienen	egal, wo
Meryl	Mitarbeit in einem Umweltprojekt (Regenwälder)	möchte etwas für den Umweltschutz tun	Amazonas-Regenwald

Teil B: Leseverstehen

Aufgabe 2 – Mediation

Das Kernstück der Globalisierung ist der weltweite Handel. Ein wesentlicher Faktor für die Entwicklung und Beschleunigung des weltweiten Warenverkehrs war die Erfindung eines genormten Containers. Der Text informiert zunächst über ein Projekt der BBC, die zur Veranschaulichung des internationalen Handels einen Container rund um den Globus schickte. Der zweite Teil des Artikels berichtet über die Erfindung des genormten Containers und dessen Vorteile für den Warentransport. Hier sind einige Punkte aufgeführt, die Sie in Ihren Artikel integrieren können. Achten Sie darauf, den vorliegenden Text nicht zu übersetzen, sondern die Informationen in eigenen Worten zu formulieren.

Projekt der BBC:
- *ein Schiffscontainer wird auf seinem Weg um die Welt mithilfe von GPS begleitet*
- *zeigt, wie sehr die Welt durch den internationalen Handel zusammengewachsen ist.*

Erfindung des ISO-Containers:
- *Erfindung des ersten Schiffscontainers durch den amerikanischen Transportunternehmer Malcolm McLean (1956)*
- *vor McLeans Erfindung: Ladung in Holzkisten befördert*
- *US-Marine verhilft dem Container zum Durchbruch*

Folgen:
- *Frachtkosten um mehr als 90 % reduziert*
- *Schiffscontainer hat die Welt verändert*

Der Schiffscontainer revolutioniert den weltweiten Warenverkehr

Im Jahr 2008 startete die englische BBC ein Projekt, mit dem sie zeigen wollte, wie eng die Welt im Zeitalter der Globalisierung durch den Handel zusammengewachsen ist. Zu diesem Zweck schickte sie einen Container, den sie *The Box* nannte, mit einer Fracht aus unterschiedlichen Artikeln (vom Whisky bis zum Katzenfutter) per Schiff, Eisenbahn und auf der Straße rund um die Welt. Per GPS konnten Besucher der BBC-Internetseite den 47 000 Meilen weiten Weg, den *The Box* in 421 Tagen zurücklegte, verfolgen.

Der Frachtcontainer ist mittlerweile ein Symbol für den globalen Handel. Erfunden wurde er 1956 von einem amerikanischen Transportunternehmer namens Malcolm McLean. 1934 hatte McLean seinen ersten Lastwagen gekauft und 1956 besaß er die fünftgrößte Lastwagenflotte in den USA. Zu der Zeit wurden Waren noch in Holzkisten unterschiedlicher Größe verladen. McLean stellte Versuche an, das langsame Be- und Entladen der Waren zu beschleunigen, und entwickelte schließlich den Frachtcontainer, der fest, von genormter Größe, diebstahlsicher, stapelbar und schnell zu verladen war. Für den Durchbruch von McLeans Entwicklung sorgte die US-Marine, die McLeans Konzept übernahm und damit den ISO-Container (Internationale Organisation für Normung) Anfang der 70er-Jahre zum weltweiten Standard machte.

Weil die Verschiffung mit dem Container viel schneller zu bewerkstelligen war, sanken die Frachtkosten dramatisch. 1956 kostete eine Tonne fast 6 Dollar, mit dem ISO-Container später nur noch 16 Cent. Durch die Verbilligung des Transports veränderte der genormte Container die Welt und wurde zum Symbol des globalen Handels.

Teil C: Textproduktion

Aufgabe 3 – Materialgestützter Aufsatz

Composition 1

Statistiken belegen, dass Gentechnik und gentechnisch veränderte Pflanzen, v. a. in den USA, eine wichtige Rolle spielen und von der Bevölkerung offensichtlich weithin akzeptiert werden. In Europa, insbesondere in Deutschland, überwiegen jedoch die kritischen Stimmen. Der Widerstand ist hier so stark, dass der Chemiekonzern BASF die Forschung in diesem Bereich in die USA verlagerte. Diese und weitere Informationen finden Sie in den Materialien, die Sie als Grundlage für Ihren Aufsatz nehmen können. Wählen Sie mindestens drei Materialien aus und geben Sie diese auch als Quelle an. So können Sie Ihren Aufsatz strukturieren:

(Einleitung)
GM big business in the USA:
– almost 70 per cent of GM crops grown in the United States
– the largest is the soybean (more than 40 per cent of the worldwide production)
– increased cultivation of GM crops (resistant to herbicides and insects)

(Hauptteil)
for and against GM food:
for:
– GM plants and crops help fight poverty and hunger in poor countries
– financial losses for farmers can be avoided
against:
– risks to environment and human health
– technology not fully developed and manageable

(Schluss)
stricter regulations in Europe than in America; BASF transferred laboratory to USA

Unter Verwendung aller Materialien:

Genetically modified food

The country where most GM crops are grown is the United States. Almost 70 per cent of GM crops worldwide are grown there, with the soybean accounting for more than 60 per cent of GM crops. *(Material 3)* The statistics also show that during the last decade American farmers have massively increased the cultivation of plants which have been genetically modified (soybeans, cotton, and corn). These plants yield greater harvests, because they either survive the application of herbicides undamaged or are resistant to insects. *(Material 4)*

Generally speaking, GM food advocates argue that genetically engineered plants and crops are the key to fighting poverty and hunger in poor countries. With the help of biotechnology, scientists can create plants which help avoid financial losses for farmers and, at the same time, guarantee an adequate food supply for people all over the world. For example, a genetically modified type of potato or rice can be grown in areas where this is not possible at the moment or the crop can be transported over longer distances.

In spite of these advantages, opposition to genetically engineered plants and crops is still very strong, especially in Europe. Many people believe that the risks to the environment and human health are too high. *(Material 1)* There are widespread fears that we are conducting an experiment on ourselves. Like the sorcerer's apprentice, we seem to use a technology without being fully aware of the consequences of our actions. *(Material 2)*

It is not surprising then that because of the overall public rejection of GM food, many European governments have introduced strict regulations as to the introduction of genes into food plants. In Germany, not only the production of genetically engineered food is difficult and almost impossible, but also scientific research in this area. As a result, the German chemical giant BASF transferred its GM research department to the USA. *(Material 5)* *(313 words)*

Composition 2

Eine gute Allgemeinbildung ist heute eine wichtige Grundlage für eine Erfolg versprechende Berufsausbildung. Die vorliegenden Materialien zeigen zunächst, dass britische Arbeitgeber mit den Leistungen von Schulabgängern, insbesondere in den Fächern Englisch und Mathematik, die für jede Ausbildung eine große Bedeutung haben, nicht zufrieden sind. Und dies, obwohl die Voraussetzungen für eine gute Ausbildung heute laut Statistik besser denn je sein müssten. In Bezug auf das Leistungsniveau können Sie den Materialien entnehmen, dass Mädchen in der Schule durchschnittlich bessere Leistungen erbringen und sich auch öfter um einen Studienplatz bewerben als Jungen.

Die Musterlösung ist umfangreicher, da auf alle Materialien Bezug genommen wird.
Sie können auch eigene Informationen einbinden. Ihren Aufsatz können Sie folgendermaßen gliedern:

(Einleitung)
changes affecting firms and job seekers in our globalized economy:
 – fiercer competition
 – fewer jobs in production
 – good general school education necessary
(Hauptteil)
 – employers in the United Kingdom complain that school leavers lack basic skills

- – bad results are surprising because education opportunities have improved tremendously
- – statistics show that more girls apply for university than boys
- – girls are often better students at school
- – explanation for gender gap: girls more comfortable with academic work at school

(Schluss)
- – globalized economy is a challenge for young job seekers
- – they must make use of the opportunities to get a good education

Unter Verwendung aller Materialien:

The importance of education in our globalized economy

In our globalized economy, competition has become much fiercer for firms and job seekers. Consequently, it is necessary for young job seekers to have a good general education.

Employers in the United Kingdom complain that school leavers lack basic skills. In particular, they show insufficient knowledge of English and maths, the two skills which are absolutely essential in any workplace. In addition, teenagers who enter the job market often do not know very much about the world of work today, and they are not always able to organise their work well. It is difficult for them to do the work properly and finish it on time. To make up for these deficiencies, many employers have to provide special courses designated to make young people fit for the job. *(Material 1)*

It seems surprising that so many young people leave school today without proper qualifications, as the chances of getting a good education have improved tremendously over the last one hundred years. Since 1905, the number of secondary schools in the United Kingdom has increased from about 600 to more than 4,000, and today nearly 4 million pupils attend secondary schools. *(Material 2)*

Good school-leaving certificates do not only improve applicants' chances on the job market, they also open up the possibility of going into higher education at a college or university. There is statistical evidence that in recent years more girls have applied for a place at university than boys. *(Material 4)* This could be due to the fact that girls are often better pupils at school. This gender gap is difficult to explain, but neurologists assume that girls are more comfortable with the academic work done at school. Experts say that boys often have more active and outgoing personalities and seek peer recognition which they cannot find at school. *(Material 5)* As a result, boys often lack interest in their school work and do not pay attention in class.

It is often the boys, as well, who suffer from ADD (attention deficit disorder). The fact that some children cannot sit still and concentrate may be due to their overexposure to the media, reinforced by playing video games and zapping through television channels or Internet sites. The problem could also be rooted in their genes and/or upbringing in cases where parents display a similar behaviour. *(Material 3)*

On the one hand, job seekers now find it more difficult than in the past to find a proper job. On the other hand, they have better opportunities than ever to get the kind of education which will improve their chances of employment. *(439 words)*

Fachhochschulreife Englisch (Berufskolleg Baden-Württemberg)
Übungsaufgabe 4

Teil A: Hörverstehen

Aufgabe 1a – Satzergänzungen *(5 VP)*

Zwei Kollegen, Martin Wise und Vicky Sullivan, unterhalten sich über das Essen in der Kantine.
- Hören Sie aufmerksam zu und vervollständigen Sie auf Deutsch die unten stehenden Aussagen.
- Sie hören die Aussagen zweimal. Während des Hörens dürfen Sie sich Notizen machen.

1	Vicky und Martin sind sich darüber einig, dass das Kantinenessen schlechter geworden ist, seitdem ...

(1 VP)

2	Die Kampagne des Promikochs Jamie Oliver machte Vicky klar, dass ...

(1 VP)

3	Martin schmeckt das Kantinenessen im Allgemeinen, weil ...

(1 VP)

4	Beide stimmen überein, dass der Preis fürs Essen ...

(1 VP)

5	Aufgrund ihrer Nahrungsmittelunverträglichkeit isst Harriet nicht in der Kantine, sondern ...

(1 VP)

Aufgabe 1 b – Offene Fragen *(10 VP)*

Der englische Journalist Jason Endean ruft seine deutsche Kollegin Petra Neufeld an und spricht mit ihr über das Thema „Alkoholmissbrauch bei jungen Leuten".

▶ Hören Sie aufmerksam zu und beantworten Sie die Fragen in ganzen Sätzen oder verständlichen Stichworten auf Deutsch.
▶ Sie hören das Gespräch zweimal. Während des Hörens dürfen Sie sich Notizen machen.

1. Worüber hat die deutsche Journalistin ihren englischen Kollegen vor einiger Zeit informiert? *(2 VP)*

2. Welche Wirkung hatte die Maßnahme in Deutschland? *(2 VP)*

3. Warum erkundigt sich der englische Journalist über einen Vorgang in Deutschland? *(2 VP)*

4. Wer unterstützt die Pläne der britischen Regierung? *(2 VP)*

5. Warum soll Alkohol vor allem in den Supermärkten teurer werden? *(2 VP)*

Teil B: Leseverstehen

Aufgabe 2 – Mediation *(15 VP)*

Sie bieten in der Volkshochschule eine Veranstaltung „Internet für Einsteiger" an und möchten zu Beginn des Kurses auf einige Grundregeln bei der Nutzung des Internets aufmerksam machen.
- ▶ Erstellen Sie eine Liste, in der Sie die wichtigsten Verhaltensregeln, die im folgenden Artikel genannt sind, zusammenfassen.
- ▶ Formulieren Sie ganze deutsche Sätze.

Dangers of the Internet

The Internet is an amazing source for entertainment, education, and communication. In democratic societies people place great importance on the free and unrestricted flow of information on the net. Every time politicians or police officials ask for more control a huge wave of protest sweeps away any of those plans. However, anyone
5 who goes online should be aware that the enormous potential of the net is also used for fraud and criminal activities.

The most basic safety rule, which everybody and not just young people should observe, is never to disclose private information about themselves and their families. This includes, of course, keeping account logins and passwords safe and never share
10 any of these even with friends. If strangers get hold of this information, it can be used to log into sites, buy and download material at the expense of the accountholder who will only learn later that his credentials have been used illegally. The net offers numerous opportunities to communicate quickly and instantaneously via e-mail or chat. It should go without saying that you must not give personal information about your-
15 self and others to people who you meet only online. There is no way of checking the real identity of the person you are chatting to, or exchanging e-mails with. Another important point about e-mailing is that viruses are frequently distributed as e-mail attachments. If you receive a mail from a source you do not know, it is always advisable not to open it, but delete it straight away in order to avoid infection.

20 It is also essential for users to be extra careful when they post personal reports and photos on social network sites such as Facebook or Myspace. Especially parents, educators and politicians are worried about the safety of children and teenagers using social networking accounts. "The web never forgets", the saying goes, meaning all data and information ever published on the Internet is stored somewhere, even if
25 users deleted it from their accounts. Users of social network sites should be warned not to post personal photos or videos that they would not want their parents or teachers to see. Private and personal information may easily endanger future employment possibilities. It is now quite common for some personnel managers to search social network sites to check on candidates for a job vacancy. They will not hire someone
30 whose pictures they have seen on the net, which show them in a compromising position, for example, extremely happy and slightly drunk at a party. Keep in mind that

the information you post online may not only be read by your friends, but also by a wider audience if you don't adjust your privacy settings.

Shopping on the Internet has increased tremendously over the last years. Most shops on the web do their best to protect buyers from fraud, for example, by publishing the comments of buyers on their websites. Reading customers' comments may be helpful, but it is no guarantee. In any case, study the terms and conditions of the seller before you buy anything. When it comes to paying online, many people are concerned about the security of their credit card numbers. A safe method is to buy from a shop which offers payment through PayPal or is a member of the Trusted Shop group. In these cases the buyer's money is transferred safely over the Internet, and payment is refunded if the ordered items do not arrive. *(568 words)*

Teil C: Textproduktion

Aufgabe 3 – Materialgestützter Aufsatz   *(30 VP: 10 VP Inh./20 VP Spr.)*

Choose between composition 1 or composition 2.

Write a composition about the chosen topic.
- Use the information of at least three of the given materials.
- Name which ones you are using.
- You can add your own ideas.
- Do not write three separate compositions but one covering all the materials chosen.

Composition 1

Write a composition about the topic "Working children".

Material 1

Child domestic workers are also extremely vulnerable to slavery. Due to their young age and separation from their family they are inherently easier to coerce and control. Some are trafficked, while others are in bonded labour, forced to work to pay off a loan their parents have taken.

In most countries the minimum age for employment is 15 years old. Yet child domestic workers are often younger with some starting work as young as six years old. Whilst domestic work is conventionally regarded as formative for girls, in reality many suffer from violence at the hands of their employers. Their conditions of work are frequently hazardous involving the use of chemicals such as bleach, and hot and dangerous instruments such as irons, often without training or protective clothing. Many are denied their right to go to school and lack the opportunity to make friends.

© *antislavery.org*

Material 2

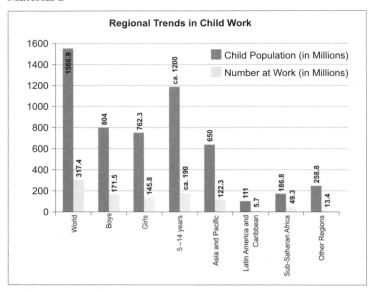

Quelle: http://www.globalmarch.org/campaigns/keepyourpromises/images/graph2.gif

Material 3

"With so little free time, you have to learn to multi-task your TV watching, ipod listening, and texting with your homework."

© Dave Carpenter/cartoonstock.com

Material 4

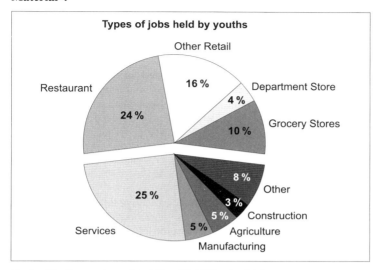

Quelle: http://www.cdc.gov/niosh/docs/97-143/backgr.html

Material 5

Einsatz für Kinderrechte

Schüler aus Hessen wollen mit Unicef etwas gegen die Ausbeutung ihrer Altersgenossen tun.

Wie viel kann ein Kind ertragen? In großen Buchstaben steht diese Frage auf den
5 Plakaten einer Hilfsorganisation mit einem kleinen Jungen, der Steine schleppt. Dieses Plakat hängt an vielen Orten in den Städten der Rhein-Main-Region. Kinder, die solche Plakate oder Bilder im Fernsehen sehen, fragen, warum ihre Altersgenossen in anderen Ländern so leiden müssen. Weil ihre Familien arm sind, ist die schlichte Antwort. Denn das ist meist der Hauptgrund, warum schon Kinder als Soldaten in den Krieg geschickt
10 werden oder für ein bisschen Essen am Tag harte Arbeit leisten müssen. Das finden viele Kinder ungerecht und wollen etwas dagegen tun – als Botschafter für Unicef. Die Hilfsorganisation der Vereinten Nationen fordert jedes Jahr dazu auf, sich für die Rechte von Kindern einzusetzen. In diesem Jahr haben sich 145 Gruppen beworben, 28 davon sind in die Endauswahl gekommen, sieben davon aus Hessen.
15 Aus Hanau und Frankfurt stammen die 15 Kinder und Jugendlichen, die unter dem Titel „Wir machen uns stark" ein Projekt gegen Kinderarbeit organisiert haben. Mit Streichhölzern wollen sie auf die Ausbeutung von Kindern aufmerksam machen. An einem Stand auf dem Wochenmarkt forderten sie Erwachsene auf, die Schachteln mit Streichhölzern zu füllen. So wurde gezeigt, wie mühsam diese Arbeit ist, die in
20 einigen Ländern von Kindern gemacht wird.

© *Frankfurter Allgemeine Zeitung, 18.05.2011, Nr. 115, S. 40*

Composition 2

Write a composition about the topic "Wind power – energy source of the future?"

Material 1

£75bn for UK's biggest offshore wind programme signals new era for renewables
Crown Estate has revealed successful bidders for nine windfarm sites expected to create tens of thousands of new jobs and help the UK meet clean energy and carbon emission targets. According to Greenpeace, Britain already leads the world in the deployment of offshore wind and has more projects installed, in planning or in construction than any other country. Almost 700 MW of offshore turbines are already installed across nine projects, with around another 1.2 GW under construction and a further 3.5 GW in planning stages. By comparison, a large coal-fired power station generates about 1 GW of electricity.

In advance of today's announcement, Greenpeace executive director John Sauven said: "Throughout its history Britain has shown the determination and ingenuity to tackle the great industrial challenges of each era. In the 21st century these qualities are being called on once again, to enable the transition from fossil fuels to clean, renewable sources of energy. Our country is home to some of the best engineers, mechanics and construction professionals in the world. Their expertise will be crucial if we are to harness the massive potential that new technologies like offshore wind have to offer."

© Jha Alok, in: The Guardian

Material 2

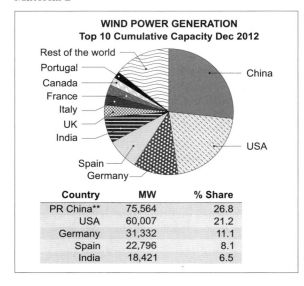

© Global Wind Energy Council (Hrsg.): Global Wind Statistics 2012. Brüssel, 11. 2. 2013, p. 3

Material 3

Jobs in renewable energy

Industry	Estimated jobs worldwide	Selected national estimates
Biofuels	> 1,500,000	Brazil 730,000 for sugarcane and ethanol production
Wind power	~ 630,000	China 150,000 / Germany 100,000 / United States 85,000 / Spain 40,000 / Italy 28,000 / Denmark 24,000 / Brazil 14,000 / India 10,000
Solar hot water	~ 300,000	China 250,000 / Spain 7,000
Solar PV	~ 350,000	China 120,000 / Germany 120,000 / Japan 26,000 / United States 17,000 / Spain 14,000
Biomass power	−	Germany 120,000 / United States 66,000 / Spain 5,000
Hydropower	−	Europe 20,000 / United States 8,000 / Spain 7,000
Geothermal	−	Germany 13,000 / United States 9,000
Biogas	−	Germany 20,000
Solar thermal power	~ 15,000	Spain 1,000 / United States 1,000
Total estimated	**> 3,500,000**	

© REN21.2011.Renewables 2011 Global Status Report. Paris: REN21 Secretariat, p. 47

Material 4

© Chris Madden/cartoonstock.com

Material 5

Nützen Windräder der Unterwasserwelt?
Rund um Windparks fahren keine Schiffe. Pfeiler bilden künstliche Riffe. Offshore-Anlagen können wahre Biotope sein. Doch langfristige Effekte sind noch unerforscht. Wenn fernab vom Festland ein neuer Windpark gebaut wird, ist das für Mee-
5 resbewohner eine Belastung. Die Bohrer sind laut, wirbeln Staub auf und zwingen Fische, Muscheln und andere Tiere zum Umzug. Sobald der Baulärm jedoch verzogen ist, ziehen die ersten Mieter wieder ein. "Die Besiedlung beginnt, wenn sich der Staub gesetzt hat", erklärt Mark Lenz vom Helmholtz-Zentrum für Ozeanforschung in Kiel. Von Frühjahr bis Herbst können sich innerhalb weniger Tage einzellige Al-
10 gen ansiedeln. Dann folgen Seepocken, Muscheln und andere wirbellose Tiere. Bei günstigen Bedingungen herrscht schon innerhalb von einem Jahr am Fuße der Windparks blühendes Leben.

© *Birk Grüling, in: Zeit Online vom 19. 3. 2013*

Lösungsvorschläge

Teil A: Hörverstehen

Aufgabe 1a – Satzergänzungen

Transcript:

MARTIN: Hi Vicky, I see you're not having much, just a little salad. Slimming again?
VICKY: No, no, but there's not much else on offer today that I fancy.
MARTIN: What about the pies, they're quite good.
VICKY: I'm not so keen on pies. Remind me of school dinners, 'cause the pies we got when I was at school tasted horrible. In fact, I never liked any of our school dinners. They were always greasy or over-cooked, especially the vegetables. I hated the cabbage most, I just couldn't eat it.
MARTIN: Oh, I remember that. It was just the same at my school.
VICKY: Mind you, now that I'm working things haven't changed much. Canteen food doesn't have much taste, if you ask me.
MARTIN: I don't know ...
VICKY: I do realise it's not easy to cook for such a large number of people, but still, most of the dishes look rather dry and boring.
MARTIN: I think it depends on the money they are allowed to spend.
VICKY: Of course, and that's why things have got worse since the management cut down the subsidies for the canteen.
MARTIN: Yes, there's just not enough money around.
VICKY: If you watch TV chef Jamie Oliver and his campaign about school dinners it doesn't take you long to realise that the food in our canteen is totally unhealthy.
MARTIN: In which way?
VICKY: Too much stodge, heavy, sticky food, too many pizzas, chips and fatty foods, and not enough fresh salad and vegetables. You can tell that a lot of the stuff comes from tins. Not very good for you.
MARTIN: Well, I must say, on the whole I'm quite happy with the meals you get here. Mind you, I'm not very choosy, I can eat almost anything. Meat, fish, pasta, you name it, I eat it.
VICKY: Perhaps you're the exception.
MARTIN: I think the bad reputation of canteen food has a lot to do with people's expectations. A canteen is not a five-star restaurant. It's just meant to feed you so that you get through your working day all right. What's more, people shouldn't forget that we pay a very reasonable price for a fair-sized meal.
VICKY: That's right. Absolutely.
MARTIN: By the way, I've never seen your friend Harriet down here.
VICKY: She doesn't use our canteen; she suffers from food intolerance.
MARTIN: She can't eat meat, you mean?

VICKY: No, no, she's not a vegetarian. She reacts to some of the chemicals which manufacturers use in the preparation of foods, like glutamate and certain preservatives and artificial colours.
MARTIN: How strange.
VICKY: Harriet says she gets headaches and tummy upsets or her skin feels itchy and irritable. That's why she has to be very careful with what she eats. So she brings her own sandwiches from home.
MARTIN: I see. I'm glad I'm not allergic to anything, really.
VICKY: Anyway, I think we'll have to make a move, 'cause otherwise we'll be in trouble.

Sehen Sie sich die Satzanfänge vor dem Hören genau an, damit Sie wissen, auf welche Informationen Sie achten müssen. Beachten Sie beim Vervollständigen der Sätze den Satzbau der Vorgabe und passen Sie Ihre Lösung grammatikalisch korrekt an.

1	Vicky und Martin sind sich darüber einig, dass das Kantinenessen schlechter geworden ist, seitdem **die finanziellen Zuschüsse gekürzt wurden**. (*... since the management cut down subsidies ...*)
2	Die Kampagne des Promikochs Jamie Oliver machte Vicky klar, dass **das Essen in ihrer Firmenkantine völlig ungesund ist**. (*... the food in our canteen is totally unhealthy.*)
3	Martin schmeckt das Kantinenessen im Allgemeinen, weil **er nicht sehr wählerisch ist und alles verträgt**. (*... I'm not very choosy, I can eat almost anything.*)
4	Beide stimmen überein, dass der Preis fürs Essen **ziemlich günstig ist**. (*... we pay a very reasonable price for a fair-sized meal.*)
5	Aufgrund ihrer Nahrungsmittelunverträglichkeit isst Harriet nicht in der Kantine, sondern **bringt sich Sandwiches von zu Hause mit**. (*... brings her own sandwiches from home.*)

Aufgabe 1b – Offene Fragen

Transcript:
JASON ENDEAN: Hi, Petra, it's me Jason Endean from London.
PETRA NEUFELD: Hi Jason! Nice to hear from you.
JASON ENDEAN: You might wonder why I'm phoning you so early, but I'm in the middle of writing an article for our weekend edition and I just remembered what you told me when we last met in Berlin.
PETRA NEUFELD: Oh yeah, what was it all about?
JASON ENDEAN: You told me that the German government has introduced an extra tax on alcopops, right?
PETRA NEUFELD: That's right. In 2004 the extra tax was introduced because these sweet alcoholic drinks had become so popular with young people, even kids, that

something drastic had to be done because all the information campaigns about the dangers of alcohol abuse and binge drinking had not been successful.

JASON ENDEAN: Yes, I remember that. And what was the result?

PETRA NEUFELD: Well, the government officials were rather pleased with themselves because sales of these colourful little bottles with rum and vodka dropped. The government claims the tax hurt the pockets of the kids and put the drinks out of reach for many, and so they gave up buying them.

JASON ENDEAN: So, you think it was a good decision to make alcopops more expensive?

PETRA NEUFELD: Yes, definitely, because, as I've said, all warnings about the harmful consequences of drinking alcohol at an early age had gone unheard.

JASON ENDEAN: Thank you, Petra. Perhaps you're wondering why I'm asking you about alcopops in Germany?

PETRA NEUFELD: I do indeed, Jason.

JASON ENDEAN: I'm writing an article about plans of our government to do almost the same as yours, which is to make alcohol more expensive. Generally, that is, not just with alcopops, because in Britain we do have a serious alcohol problem.

PETRA NEUFELD: I've read about young men *and* women drinking themselves silly at weekends.

JASON ENDEAN: Yes, binge drinking is a real pest. Therefore, to "turn the tide" against binge drinking, the government is determined to set a minimum alcohol price, which is 40 p per unit of alcohol.

PETRA NEUFELD: How do people react to this plan?

JASON ENDEAN: Most people welcome the government's decision; some would even prefer the minimum price to be 50 p. Health experts, in particular, are all for the new strategy, because every year there are over 20,000 alcohol-related deaths, and alcohol abuse costs the NHS almost 3 billion pounds.

PETRA NEUFELD: I suppose the police are happy too.

JASON ENDEAN: Of course they are. The government claims the 40 p minimum could mean 50,000 fewer crimes a year. Anyway, the patience of the police and emergency services in their dealing with drunken, antisocial or vicious behaviour in public has been stretched to the limit.

PETRA NEUFELD: I see. What about the pubs? Will the higher alcohol price lead to more pubs closing?

JASON ENDEAN: The government believes the new price level will not affect the pubs, it will make alcohol more expensive in the supermarkets. And this is where a lot of people buy their drinks before they go to the pub. We call that preloading.

PETRA NEUFELD: That's the same in Germany. Young people buy cheap orange juice and vodka to get in the right mood. Although in Germany today young people tend to drink less, alcohol abuse and binge drinking, in particular, is still a big problem.

JASON ENDEAN: Let's hope that higher prices will help to tackle this serious social issue – which is not just limited to young people. But we also have to tackle the root of the problem and change the drinking culture.

PETRA NEUFELD: You're right.

✏ *Machen Sie sich auch hier wieder während des Hörens Notizen. Pro Antwort gibt es*
✏ *zwei Punkte. In der Lösung sind die jeweils relevanten Stellen unterstrichen.*

1. Sie hat ihn darüber informiert, dass die <u>deutsche Regierung</u> eine <u>Sondersteuer auf Alcopops eingeführt</u> hat. *(You told me that the German government has introduced an extra tax on alcopops ...)*

2. Der <u>Konsum sank, weil Alcopops</u> für viele Jugendliche <u>zu teuer</u> wurden. *(... sales of these colourful little bottles with rum and vodka dropped ... the tax ... put the drinks out of reach for many ...)*

3. Weil er einen <u>Artikel über einen ähnlichen Plan der englischen Regierung schreibt</u>, nämlich <u>Alkohol zu verteuern</u>. *(I'm writing an article about plans of our government to do almost the same as yours, which is to make alcohol more expensive.)*

4. Die <u>Mehrheit der Bevölkerung</u> und besonders auch <u>Gesundheitsexperten und die Polizei</u> unterstützen die Pläne der Regierung. *(Most people welcome the government's decision ... Health experts, in particular, are all for the new strategy ... the police are happy too ... Of course they are.)*

5. Viele Leute <u>kaufen sich im Supermarkt alkoholische Getränke</u> zum „Vorglühen", <u>bevor sie in einen Pub gehen</u>. *(... this is where a lot of people buy their drinks before they go to the pub. We call that preloading.)*

Teil B: Leseverstehen

Aufgabe 2 – Mediation

✏ *Suchen Sie aus dem Text die Punkte heraus, die für die Kursteilnehmer am wichtigsten sind. Um die Übersichtlichkeit zu wahren, sollten Sie sich auf ca. fünf Grundregeln beschränken.*

Sicher ins Internet

Das Internet kann auf vielfältige Art und Weise genutzt werden, es wird aber auch für kriminelle Aktivitäten missbraucht. Deshalb ist Vorsicht geboten. Hier sind einige Grundregeln, die Sie bei der Nutzung beachten sollten.

– Geben Sie keine persönlichen Informationen, Log-in-Daten oder Passwörter preis. Teilen Sie diese auch nicht mit Freunden.

– Vorsicht auch beim E-Mail-Schreiben und Chatten mit Leuten, die Sie nicht persönlich kennen. In beiden Fällen haben Sie keine Möglichkeit, die wahre Identität Ihres Gegenübers zu prüfen.

– Löschen Sie E-Mail-Anhänge von unbekannten Sendern, weil diese beim Öffnen möglicherweise Viren verbreiten.

– Stellen Sie keine Berichte oder Fotos (z. B. von Partys) ins Netz, die Sie und andere in privaten Situationen zeigen. Dies kann möglicherweise Ihre beruflichen

Chancen beeinträchtigen, da es vorkommen kann, dass Firmen bei Bewerbungsverfahren im Internet gezielt nach Informationen über den Bewerber suchen.
– Wenn Sie im Internet einkaufen, lesen Sie die Geschäftsbedingungen des Verkäufers genau durch. Bezahlen Sie Waren über sichere Dienste wie z. B. PayPal.
Wenn Sie diese Grundregeln beachten, steht einem sorgenfreien Surfen im Internet nichts im Wege.

Teil C: Textproduktion

Aufgabe 3 – Materialgestützter Aufsatz

Composition 1

Kinderarbeit ist ein weltweites Problem, von dessen verheerenden Auswirkungen besonders Kinder in den Entwicklungsländern betroffen sind. In den meisten Untersuchungen geht es um Kinder unter 15 Jahren. UNICEF, die Kinderhilfsorganisation der Vereinten Nationen, führt seit Jahren einen Kampf gegen die Ausbeutung von Minderjährigen als Arbeitskräfte. In vielen armen Ländern sind jedoch die Verhältnisse immer noch so, dass zahlreiche Familien nur über die Runden kommen, wenn ihre Kinder arbeiten. Gehen Sie alle Ihnen vorliegenden Materialien durch und entscheiden Sie, welche Sie in Ihren Aufsatz integrieren wollen.
Beispiel für die Strukturierung des Aufsatzes:

(Einleitung)
Child labour is a worldwide problem:
– about 317 million children are working
– percentage especially high in developing countries
– children working in factories producing for Western multinational firms

(Hauptteil)
– often exposed to unhealthy working conditions
– supplement family income
– pay off parent's debts
– consequences: no childhood, no school education, no future
– contrast: children in the West are privileged and protected by the law

(Schluss)
– UNICEF makes public aware of the problem
– private helpers get involved

Unter Verwendung aller Materialien:
Working children

Child labour is a worldwide problem, as statistics clearly prove. About 317 million children – which is almost one-fifth of all children living in the world today – are working. The percentage of children who have to work is especially high in Africa and Asia. *(Material 2)* Although there are laws in most countries which do not allow the employment of children under the age of 15, these regulations are often ignored, so that some children are only six years of age when they start working. *(Material 1)* Well-known Western multinational firms came under heavy criticism when it was revealed that children in Pakistan and India weaved carpets or sewed footballs together for those companies.

Not only do the children have to work, they are also exposed to working conditions which seriously damage their health. *(Material 1)* In factories they breathe in toxic chemicals or work with dangerous tools such as hot irons. One TV documentary showed young children in India working hard in a quarry carrying heavy stones on their shoulders and breathing in dust for hours.

Many children in developing countries are forced to work because their parents are unemployed or do not earn enough to keep the family. Consequently, children have to work to supplement the family income. The money which children earn is also often used to pay off their parents' loans.

Working children suffer serious consequences for the rest of their lives. To begin with, they have no fair chance of a real childhood, playing together with other children. In addition, they cannot go to school, and without any education they face a grim future with hardly any chance of escaping from a life of misery and poverty.

In contrast, children in industrialised countries live in a completely different and privileged situation. As the cartoon suggests in an exaggerated way, they seem to be mainly occupied with managing their free time with all the electronic gadgets they have to play and TV shows to watch. *(Material 3)* Above all, in Western countries children are protected by the law. They are not allowed to work (although there are certain exceptions). When they are teenagers they can get a job, mostly working in the service industry, in shops or restaurants. *(Material 4)*

What can be done to improve the situation of working children in developing countries? Charity organisations such as UNICEF are trying to make the public aware of the problem of child labour, because many people do not know much about the issue or do not care. In the German State of Hesse, for example, pupils are joining these efforts to fight the exploitation of young people of their age in developing countries, who are forced to work or, even worse, have to fight as child soldiers. *(Material 5)*

(461 words)

Composition 2

Die vorgelegten Materialien beleuchten einige Aspekte, die mit der alternativen Energiequelle „Wind" verbunden sind. Bei genauerer Durchsicht werden Sie feststellen, dass Vor- und Nachteile zur Sprache kommen. Entsprechend sollten Sie Ihre Lösung aufbauen. Für Windkraft sprechen vor allem Umweltgesichtspunkte sowie die Schaffung neuer Arbeitsplätze durch die Bereitstellung der für die Nutzung benötigten Technik. Andererseits gibt es auch Widerstand aus ästhetischen und anderen Gründen, insbesondere von Bürgern, in deren Nachbarschaft Windräder aufgestellt werden sollen. Die Musterlösung ist etwas umfangreicher als erforderlich, da alle fünf Materialien in die Lösung miteinbezogen wurden.

Unter Verwendung aller Materialien:

Wind power – energy source of the future?

(Einleitung)
Among the most pressing problems the world is facing today are the issues of climate change and the increasing demand for energy, both of which are closely connected. We need more and more electricity for computers, machines, robots, and electrical appliances in offices, shops, factories, and private homes. The demand is largely covered by the burning of fossil fuels such as coal and oil; this, however, contributes to global warming. In order to solve the dilemma, environmentalists demand the replacement of fossil fuels with cleaner and renewable sources.

(Hauptteil)
One alternative source which plays an increasingly important role is wind power. It is clean and available in abundance in many parts of the world. In addition, the technology used for generating wind power has made great progress. British engineers are especially advanced in the planning and construction of wind farms and have made Britain the leading nation in the deployment of offshore wind farms. *(Material 1)*
Many countries all over the world have increased their efforts to use wind as an energy source. China, the most populous nation in the world and one with a fast growing economy, heads the list of the world's wind-power generating nations. In 2012, China's share amounted to almost 27 per cent, with the USA (21 per cent) and Germany (11 per cent) close behind. *(Material 2)*
Wind power is not only a clean and renewable energy source, it also generates jobs. In 2010, more than 3.5 million people were employed in renewable energy industries worldwide. About one sixth (630,000) had a job in the wind-power industry *(Material 3)*, which not only manufactures turbines and platforms, but also installs, operates, and maintains wind farms.
In theory, nearly everybody agrees that wind is a clean alternative, but difficulties arise when yet another wind farm is planned. Then people tend to take a "not in my backyard"-stance. Many opponents argue that wind farms are an eyesore and destroy the beauty of the countryside. Ironically, the criticism often comes from people who are responsible for polluting the environment, for example motorists whose cars emit harmful exhaust fumes. *(Material 4)*
Perhaps the disagreement can partly be solved by building more wind farms out at

sea, far away from any built-up areas. Scientists have found that offshore wind farms can even be beneficial for marine life. Not long after the structure for the turbines has been firmly anchored in the seabed, algae begin to grow and mussels start to occupy the underwater columns. *(Material 5)*

(Schluss)
It is obvious, however, that offshore wind farms alone cannot bring about the urgently needed transition from fossil fuels to clean, renewable sources of energy. Compromises have to be made, and a few disturbances caused by wind turbines on land should be accepted as the lesser of two evils. *(466 words)*

Fachhochschulreife Englisch (Berufskolleg Baden-Württemberg)
Hörverstehenstest 2011

Aufgabe 1: Satzergänzung *(8 VP)*

Sonya Ryder vom englischen Radiosender *Channel4U* befragte in Facebook vier Jugendliche zum Thema „Gebrauch digitaler Medien" und gibt deren Kommentare in ihrer Sendung wieder.
▶ Hören Sie aufmerksam zu und vervollständigen Sie auf Deutsch die unten stehenden Sätze. Pro Antwort werden zwei verschiedene Informationen (je 1 VP) aus dem Hörtext erwartet.
▶ Sie hören den Ausschnitt aus der Sendung zweimal. Während des Hörens dürfen Sie sich Notizen machen.

(1) Sam	Er sieht Computer als große Errungenschaft an, da …
(2) Carol	Sie benutzt lieber ihre Digitalkamera als herkömmliche Kameras mit Film, weil …
(3) John	Er kritisiert E-Mails, weil …
(4) Kim	Für sie können Handys ein wirkliches Ärgernis sein, wenn …

Aufgabe 2: Raster mit Lücken (7 VP)

Sie hören Kurzberichte von vier australischen Austauschschülerinnen und -schülern, die über ihre Erfahrungen im jeweiligen Gastland sprechen.
- ▶ Hören Sie aufmerksam zu und vervollständigen Sie auf Deutsch das unten stehende Raster mit Informationen aus den Kurzberichten. Nicht zu allen Punkten in der Tabelle wird von jedem oder jeder etwas gesagt. Sie finden dann ein X im Kasten.
- ▶ Sie hören die Kurzberichte zweimal. Während des Hörens dürfen Sie sich Notizen machen.

Name	Aufenthaltsland	Gesamte Aufenthaltsdauer	Was hat der Aufenthalt persönlich gebracht? (1 Nennung genügt)	Welche Probleme gab es bzw. gibt es? (1 Nennung genügt)
(1) Michael				
(2) Kylie		X		
(3) Fiona				
(4) Keith	X			

Aufgabe 3: Mediation *(10 VP)*

Sie und Ihre Freundin Andrea planen ein Auslandssemester in Manchester (UK) und suchen eine Wohnung nahe der Universität. Andrea liest eine Wohnungsanzeige und ruft den Vermieter an. Sie hören das Telefonat mit.

▶ Sie wollen eine Entscheidung vorbereiten und notieren auf Deutsch die Gründe, die für oder gegen die angebotene Wohnung sprechen.
▶ Sie hören das folgende Telefonat zweimal. Während des Hörens dürfen Sie sich Notizen machen.

Gründe für die Wohnung:

Gründe gegen die Wohnung:

Lösungsvorschläge

Aufgabe 1: Satzergänzung

Transcript:

1. **Sam**
   It's hard to believe that no one had computers a few years ago. I really wonder how people lived without them. There must have been an awful lot of paperwork to do. I can't imagine having to write everything by hand. I also wonder how things used to work without the help of computers because today we need computers for everything: in hospitals, at airports, in banks ... nothing works without computers nowadays. I'm sure I'd be ten times busier than now if I didn't have a computer. I love my computer. It makes everything in my life so convenient. Sure, it freezes and crashes sometimes and of course, I lose data now and again, but that doesn't happen that often. Most of the time my computer is like my best friend.

2. **Carol**
   Digital cameras are so useful. I love my digital camera. I take it with me wherever I go. My friends think I'm mad, but I've got thousands of really good photos. Digital cameras are so much better than the old cameras with film. My digital camera fits in my pocket and takes great photos. The best thing about digital cameras is that they are so easy to use. It's child's play. The good thing is that today's digital cameras make the same high-quality photos that you'd only get using really expensive cameras.

3. **John**
   E-mail certainly keeps me busy. I never used to write as many letters as I do now. In the good old days before computers, we wrote real letters, with paper and envelopes. I wrote one or two letters a week. But now, with e-mail, my in-box is never empty. There's always someone mailing me. I would love to have just one day where I'm free of e-mails. The sad thing is, very few of the mails I get are interesting. I get loads of spam – junk mail trying to sell me things I don't want. It's too much sometimes.

4. **Kim**
   How important to you is your mobile phone? Do you really need it? In the 1980s there were no mobile phones. People still managed to phone their family and friends and do business. I wonder whether mobile phones are a good or a bad thing. Of course, they're very convenient, but they can also be disturbing. There's nothing worse than sitting in a café talking to someone and then they ignore you for ten minutes to answer their mobile phone. I have even seen couples on a date where one person has chatted on the phone for over 30 minutes.

In dieser Aufgabe geht es darum, vorgegebene Satzanfänge mit den wesentlichen Informationen aus den jeweiligen Kommentaren zu vervollständigen. Lesen Sie sich die Satzanfänge genau durch und notieren Sie während des Hörens gezielt die relevanten Informationen in Stichpunkten. Manchmal gibt es auch mehr Informationen, als Sie schließlich für die Bearbeitung der Aufgabe brauchen. Beim zweiten Hören können Sie die Informationen noch einmal überprüfen bzw. ergänzen. Nutzen Sie zum Vervollständigen der Sätze vor allem die Pausen zwischen dem ersten und zweiten Vorspielen sowie nach dem zweiten Vorspielen des Textes.

Sie erhalten für diese Aufgabe insgesamt 8 Punkte, was bedeutet, dass Sie pro Kommentar zwei Informationen erfassen müssen. Für jede richtige Information erhalten Sie einen Verrechnungspunkt.

(1) Sam	Er sieht Computer als große Errungenschaft an, da … • man sie heute überall braucht (in Krankenhäusern, am Flughafen, in Banken, etc.) / heutzutage nichts mehr ohne Computer funktioniert • und sie praktisch sind und das Leben angenehmer machen. / und er ohne Computer viel mehr Arbeit hätte. / und früher ziemlich viel Papier verwendet wurde und man alles von Hand schreiben musste.
(2) Carol	Sie benutzt lieber ihre Digitalkamera als herkömmliche Kameras mit Film, weil … • sie klein und handlich ist / sie leicht zu bedienen ist und man sie überallhin mitnehmen kann • sie qualitativ sehr gute Fotos macht, wie sie sonst nur mit einer teuren herkömmlichen Kamera möglich wären
(3) John	Er kritisiert E-Mails, weil … • sie ihn auf Trab halten, da er so viele bekommt. / es manchmal zu viele sind. / sein Postfach immer voll ist und es keinen Tag gibt, an dem er keine Mails bekommt • nur wenige E-Mails interessant sind. / er eine große Menge Spam- und Junkmails bekommt.
(4) Kim	Für sie können Handys ein wirkliches Ärgernis sein, wenn … • man sich z. B. im Café mit jemandem unterhält, • der/die andere dann einen Anruf auf dem Handy annimmt und ein minutenlanges Gespräch führt.

Aufgabe 2: Raster mit Lücken

Transcript:

1. **Michael**
   I have been in Italy for almost 9 months now, and with three more months to go I can say it has been such an adventure! I won't deny that the first few weeks were difficult, as I came over here with no knowledge of the Italian language and understanding people was difficult enough – not to mention trying to speak! However, as time has gone by this difficulty has got easier day by day. Throughout my exchange I have learnt more about myself and the world around me than I ever could have in a classroom, and, I have no regrets whatsoever regarding my decision to go on an exchange. I would recommend time abroad to absolutely everybody because you gain precious memories, friendships and knowledge which last a lifetime. The only negative thing I can say is that I enjoyed myself so much that I forgot to keep in touch with my family and friends back home!

2. **Kylie**
   Having learnt German at school for a few years, I expected that communication in Austria wouldn't be a problem, and that I would be fluent within a month or so. How naive I was. Learning and speaking a foreign language at school in Australia is very different to being able to integrate yourself into the foreign country itself. That was when I realized I had to drop all expectations and just take each day as it comes. I have been away for a while now, and will be returning home soon. The last months have been a fantastic experience, the kind that helps you develop as a person and this is what you will always remember.

3. **Fiona**
   I can't believe I've been here two months now, and I'm really looking forward to the rest of my one-year stay! Things are going really well here. I've performed in a choir concert and gone and listened to a talk given by a survivor of the Holocaust. I also joined a journalism club. My host family is great, they're very down to earth and my host siblings are a lot of fun. I've made some good friends at school, too; the kids there are all very friendly. I'm actually going to Anaheim on a choir trip; we are leaving tomorrow morning. I get to spend a day at Disneyland and go to Santa Monica pier, along with a couple of other places. In other words, I'm really busy all the time, and, to be honest, sometimes I feel it's all a bit too much for me. But the best thing is that I passed my driving test yesterday! Here in California, the minimum age for driving a car is sixteen.

4. **Keith**
   It's almost three months that I've been here and everything has been absolutely wonderful! School is great – the kids are really nice. They love my accent! All the kids and the teachers are very friendly and welcoming. I have started curling after school and go once a week. Curling is a sport played on ice, which is actually much more difficult than it looks, but it's lots of fun and is a very good social sport, so it's a great way to make friends. I love it. It's also a lot of fun going

to a school where you don't have to wear a uniform! The first days here were a combination of being fantastically exciting and just plain terrifying. For example, I didn't know what time I should get up in the morning, what my family had planned for the day and how often I was allowed to watch TV, so I became really homesick. I think I could say that that was one of the hardest times of my life but now, having to return home next week, those few terrifying weeks all seem worth it.

Bei dieser Aufgabe sollen Sie das unten vorgegebene Raster mit Informationen, d. h. Einzelaussagen aus den vier Kurzberichten australischer Austauschschüler/-innen vervollständigen. Machen Sie sich während des Hörens Notizen. Sie erhalten für diese Aufgabe insgesamt 7 Punkte. Für jede richtige Nennung erhalten Sie einen halben Punkt. In der Musterlösung haben wir verschiedene Alternativen für eine Antwort angegeben, Sie müssen jedoch nur eine Information nennen.
Versuchen Sie, die jeweils passende Information im Hörtext zu erkennen und notieren Sie diese in Stichpunkten. Zeit zum Nachdenken besteht während der Kurzberichte nicht, da Sie sonst weitere Informationen verpassen. Nutzen Sie wiederum die Pausen zwischen dem ersten und zweiten Anhören der Kurzberichte sowie nach dem zweiten Anhören zum Schreiben, um nichts zu versäumen.

Name	Aufenthaltsland	Gesamte Aufenthaltsdauer	Was hat der Aufenthalt persönlich gebracht? (1 Nennung genügt)	Welche Probleme gab es bzw. gibt es? (1 Nennung genügt)
(1) Michael	Italien	12 Monate	mehr über sich selbst gelernt / kostbare Erinnerungen, neue Freundschaften, neues Wissen	mangelnde Sprachkenntnisse am Anfang / Schwierigkeiten, fremde Sprache zu verstehen und zu sprechen / vergessen, Kontakt zu Familie und Freunden zu Hause zu halten
(2) Kylie	Österreich	x	hat sich als Person weiterentwickelt	zu Beginn Integrationsschwierigkeiten / am Anfang zu hohe Erwartungen

(3) Fiona	USA (Kalifornien)	12 Monate	Führerschein gemacht/ gute Freunde in der Schule gefunden/ nette Gastfamilie	Stress durch zu viele Aktivitäten / sie ist ständig beschäftigt
(4) Keith	x	3 Monate	hat Curling gelernt / hat neue Freunde über das Curling gewonnen / hat Schule ohne Schuluniformen erlebt	am Anfang großes Heimweh (durch schlechte Kommunikation in der Gastfamilie)

Aufgabe 3: Mediation

Transcript:

FLAT OWNER: Hello.
ANDREA: Hi I'm calling about the ad for the flat that you posted on the web today. I'm Andrea Schmidt and I am calling from Germany.
FLAT OWNER: Good. I'm pleased you found it.
ANDREA: I'm a bit desperate because I need something right away.
FLAT OWNER: Right. What would you like to know?
ANDREA: First of all, how big is the flat?
FLAT OWNER: It's a two-bedroom flat with a living room, dining-room and kitchen, and a bathroom. There's also room for a washing machine and a dryer.
ANDREA: Okay, and how old is the building?
FLAT OWNER: Well, let's just say it has a lot of history. To be honest, my great-grandfather built it during the 1920s.
ANDREA: Oh, that's interesting! Is the flat furnished at all?
FLAT OWNER: Well, the flat is partially furnished with a fridge, stove, and has a brand new dishwasher in the kitchen.
ANDREA: A new dishwasher? That sounds good! And how much is the rent?
FLAT OWNER: I'm asking £ 630 a month.
ANDREA: Oh dear! That's rather expensive for me.
FLAT OWNER: Well, you could always split the cost with a roommate.
ANDREA: That's an idea! And are utilities included?
FLAT OWNER: Well, the rent includes gas and electricity, but not the phone bill.
ANDREA: And can I rent on a monthly basis, or do I have to sign a contract for a longer period of time?
FLAT OWNER: We require a 12-month commitment for the flat, and if you cancel the agreement anytime during that period, you lose your deposit.
ANDREA: Right and how much is the deposit?
FLAT OWNER: It's £ 3,000.
ANDREA: Really? That is a huge sum you are asking for. Do I get my deposit back

when I move out? That's assuming that I move in.
FLAT OWNER: Generally speaking, we return the deposit, but if you damage the place, then don't expect to get anything back.
ANDREA: Okay. Er ... how close is the flat to the university campus?
FLAT OWNER: It's a 10-minute walk to the university, and you can catch a number of buses right outside the flat.
ANDREA: Oh, so the property is on a busy road. Is the flat noisy?
FLAT OWNER: Well, you have to take the good with the bad: it's a little noisy with the road outside and the airport behind the house, but the place is really convenient because there's a supermarket and a shopping centre right across the street. Just keep the windows closed and a pair of ear plugs handy, and you'll be fine.
ANDREA: I hope you're joking because we really need some peace and quiet to be able to study. Anyway, one last question. Is there any parking space for tenants?
FLAT OWNER: Yes. The flat has two covered parking spaces.
ANDREA: Okay, good. Oh, I nearly forgot to ask: Where exactly is the flat located?
FLAT OWNER: It's one block to the west of the waste water treatment plant. The plant is easy to find, just follow the smell!
ANDREA: Ooh, that doesn't sound too inviting. Well, I'm going to have to think about it, but thanks very much for all the information. Bye.
FLAT OWNER: Thanks for calling. Bye.

Sie hören das Telefonat zwischen Andrea und dem Vermieter zweimal. Machen Sie sich während des Hörens wieder Notizen. Sie erhalten insgesamt 10 Punkte für diese Aufgabe. Das heißt, dass Sie zehn Argumente benötigen, um die volle Punktzahl zu erreichen. In der Musterlösung sind mehr Punkte angegeben, als Sie benötigen. Notieren Sie sich während des Hörens stichpunktartig die Gründe für und gegen die Wohnung. Die Stichpunkte können Sie jeweils kennzeichnen, z. B. durch ein Plus oder ein Minus. Nutzen Sie wiederum vor allem die Pausen zwischen dem ersten und zweiten Hören, sowie am Ende des zweiten Hörens zum Verfassen der Lösung, um von dem Telefonat nichts zu versäumen.

Gründe für die Wohnung
- große Wohnung (4-Zimmer-Wohnung)
- Wohnung teilmöbliert (mit Küchengeräten)
- Mitbewohner erlaubt, daher Aufteilung der Mietkosten möglich
- Nebenkosten (Strom und Gas) im Mietpreis enthalten
- Bushaltestelle direkt vor dem Haus / Entfernung zur Universität nur 10 Minuten zu Fuß
- Supermarkt und Einkaufszentrum in der Nähe
- zwei überdachte Stellplätze fürs Auto

Gründe gegen die Wohnung
- Haus ist alt (aus den 20er-Jahren des letzten Jahrhunderts)
- teure Miete (630 Pfund im Monat inkl. Strom und Gas)

- Kaution ist hoch (3 000 Pfund) und wird bei Beschädigungen nicht rückerstattet
- zwölf Monate Mindestmietzeit; bei Kündigung innerhalb dieses Zeitraums: Verlust der Kaution
- Wohnung ist sehr laut durch Straße vor dem Haus und den Flughafen hinter dem Haus
- starker Geruch durch nahe gelegene Kläranlage

Fachhochschulreife Englisch (Berufskolleg Baden-Württemberg)
Schriftliche Hauptprüfung 2011

Aufgabe 1 – Mediation (10 VP)

Aufgabenstellung

Nach dem Besuch der SMV Ihrer Schule bei der Buchmesse entschließen sich die Redakteure der Schülerzeitung, in der nächsten Ausgabe einen Artikel zu den neuesten Entwicklungen auf dem Buchmarkt und deren Auswirkungen zu veröffentlichen.
- In Ihrer Funktion als Redakteur schreiben Sie diesen Beitrag anhand der entsprechenden Informationen im folgenden Artikel.
- Formulieren Sie ganze deutsche Sätze.

The future of publishing

Like many other parts of the media industry, publishing is being radically reshaped.

More than half of book sales in America take place not in bookshops but at big retailers such as Wal-Mart, which compete to throw bestsellers onto the market at ever higher discounts. Online retailers, too, are already among the biggest distributors of books. In 2009 Amazon sold 19 % of printed books in America. By 2015, according to estimates, it will sell 28 %. And now e-books threaten to reduce sales of the old-fashioned kind.

Publishers think e-books could account for 25 % of the industry's sales in America within three to five years. They may well be right if the iPad and other tablet computers take off, the prices of e-readers keep falling and more consumers start reading books on smart-phones. The number of programmes, or apps, for books on Apple's iPhone recently surpassed that for games, previously the largest category.

Amazon, which currently dominates sales of digital books, has kept prices of many e-book titles and bestsellers at $ 9.99 as they face stiff competition from Sony and Apple. Other firms, including the mighty Google, are likely to enter the race soon, which will only increase the competitive pressure. Publishers worry that this has made consumers expect lower prices for all kinds of books. Unless things change, some in the industry predict that they will suffer a similar fate to that of music companies, whose fortunes faded when Apple turned the industry upside down by selling individual songs cheaply online.

This is particularly alarming for publishers because digital profits are almost as small as print ones. True, e-books do not need to be printed and shipped to retailers. But these costs typically represent only a tenth of a printed book's retail price. Meanwhile, publishers are facing new costs in the form of investment in systems to store and distribute digital texts, as well as to protect them from piracy.

Publishers are investing in the internet in other ways, too. A few are starting to build their own online groups of readers. For instance *Tor.com*, a publisher-run website for science fiction and fantasy enthusiasts, highlights content relevant to its members. Another publisher that has developed an online group focused on poetry found that sales of its books rose by more than 50 % in the six weeks after poems from them had been featured on the site.

Publishers are also pumping plenty of money into "enriched e-books", which combine the printed word with audio, video, and other media to create content that justifies a premium price. Indeed, many publishing executives like to argue that the digital revolution could lead to a golden age of reading in which many more people will be exposed to digital texts. They hope that the shift away from printed books will be slow, giving them more time to adapt to the brave new digital world.

Text based on: *The future of publishing. E-publish or perish. (March 31, 2010)*   *(477 words)*
© *The Economist*

Aufgabe 2 – Leseverstehen: Beurteilen von Aussagen zum Text *(10 VP)*

Stores take close look at habits of customers

The curvy mannequin caught the interest of a couple of teenage boys. Little did they know that as they touched its tight maroon shirt in the clothing store that day, video cameras were rolling.

At an office supply store, a mother decided to get an item from a high shelf by balancing her small child on her shoulder, unaware that she, too, was being recorded.

These scenes may seem like random shopping behaviour, but they are meaningful to stores that are trying to engineer a better experience for the customer, and ultimately, higher sales figures for themselves.

With these types of clips, retailers say, they can help them find solutions to problems in their stores, by installing seating and activity areas for children, for instance, or by lowering shelves so that merchandise is within somewhat of an easier reach.

Privacy supporters, however, are troubled by the number of video cameras, motion detectors and other sensors monitoring the shopping aisles across the country.

Many stores and the consultants they hire are using the appliances not to catch shoplifters but to analyze and to manipulate the behaviour of consumers. And while taping shoppers is legal, critics say that it is unethical to observe people as if they were lab rats. They say they are concerned that the practices will lead to an even greater invasion of privacy, particularly facial recognition technology, which is already in the early stages of development.

Companies that employ this technology say it is used strictly to determine characteristics like age and gender, which they say help them discover how different people respond to various products. But privacy supporters fear that as the technology becomes even more advanced, it will eventually cross the line and be used to identify individual consumers and gather more detailed information on them.

Some degree of privacy, many experts say, is necessary, simply as a matter of respect. "When someone's watching me, I'm going to act differently than when I think I'm alone," a shopper said. "Did I pick my nose? What was I doing? What did they see?"

Some stores use existing security systems for such monitoring and others have installed entirely new systems. They use video cameras in ceilings and sensors near fitting rooms to learn how many customers pass through the doors and where they tend to go most often.

The companies that install and analyze video for retailers say that they are sensitive to privacy issues but that the concerns are mostly overblown. They say they are not using the technology to identify consumers but rather to give them an easier, more convenient and enjoyable shopping experience.

Some retailers are not willing to discuss their use of surveillance technology. And exactly how many cameras are tracking shoppers is not known, partly because cameras are installed and uninstalled during various studies.

⁴⁰ But industry professionals said interest in analyzing shoppers was growing. Video analysis companies said nearly every major chain was or had been a client, including some of the giants like Wal-Mart Stores and Best Buy.

Privacy supporters know that stores are not public property, but they would still prefer to see some ground rules established, like telling shoppers they are under a mi-⁴⁵ croscope.

But it may already be too late. Paco Underhill, a pioneer in the field of observational customer research pointed out that people are taped dozens of times each day doing routine chores like pumping gas. Cameras, it seems, are everywhere. Stores are merely the latest frontier.

⁵⁰ "We live our lives surrounded by them," he said. *(599 words)*

Text based on: Stephanie Rosenbloom: In Bid to Sway Sales, Cameras Track Shoppers.
(March 19, 2010) © The New York Times

Aufgabenstellung

▶ Entscheiden Sie, ob die folgenden Aussagen zum Text richtig oder falsch sind, und begründen Sie Ihre Entscheidung.

▶ Schreiben Sie Ihre Antworten auf Deutsch in ganzen Sätzen auf separates Prüfungspapier.

1. Video surveillance helps to improve customers' shopping experience.
2. Analyzing the video tapes can reveal needs of different customers such as arranging a corner with chairs to take a rest.
3. Shops use monitoring technology to observe their customers' habits.
4. Facial recognition technology has already added to the loss of privacy.
5. Depending on their age and gender shoppers react differently to merchandise.
6. People buy more when they think that nobody is looking.
7. Stores have to invest a lot of money in customer surveillance because it requires highly advanced technology.
8. Stores find the public's objections justified.
9. The big chains of department stores are particularly keen on monitoring customers.
10. The stores have to inform their customers that they are recorded while shopping.

Aufgabe 3 – Textproduktion: Bildvorlage mit Bezug zum Text von Aufgabe 2

(10 VP: 4 VP Inh./6 VP Spr.)

© Chappatte

Aufgabenstellung
- First describe the picture.
- Then analyze its meaning referring to the text "Stores take close look at habits of customers".
- Use your own words.

Aufgabe 4 – Textproduktion

Choose between Part A **or** Part B.

Part A

Composition 1 *(15 VP: 5 VP Inh./10 VP Spr.)*
Choose either composition 1 a **or** 1 b.

1. a) The staging of a big international sports event like the Olympic Games is often a very controversial issue in the host country.
   Discuss the pros and cons of such a mega event.

   or:

   b) These days more and more employees are expected to work abroad. Is a globalized job market a curse or a blessing?
   Discuss this question.

Composition 2 *(15 VP: 5 VP Inh./10 VP Spr.)*
Choose either composition 2 a **or** 2 b.

2. a) Describe the picture and analyze its message.

© WWF, www.panda.org

b) Describe the cartoon and analyze its message.

© Seppo Leinonen, www.seppo.net

Part B

Textproduktion: Materialgestützter Aufsatz   *(30 VP: 10 VP Inh./20 VP Spr.)*

- Write a composition about the topic "Mother Nature has to pay the price for man's mobility".
- Use the information of at least three of the given materials.
- Name which ones you are using.
- You can add your own ideas.
- Do not write three separate compositions but one covering all the materials chosen.

Material 1

Unbearable lightness?

When it comes to motor vehicles there is widespread belief that bigger is not only better, but safer, too.

But weight is the enemy of fuel economy. Adding air bags, anti-lock braking systems (ABS) and stability control has saved countless lives, but it has increased vehicle weights disproportionately. Cars and light trucks today are 30 % heavier than they were in the mid-1980s.

It therefore comes at no surprise that the White House's pronouncement – that cars and trucks sold in America from the 2016 model year onwards will have to achieve a fleet-wide average of 6.6 litres/100 km – has awoken fears about vehicles becoming smaller and less safe in order to meet the latest fuel-sipping standards.

Text based on: Unbearable lightness? To make cars frugal, they will have to become lighter – and more expensive. (April 9, 2010) © The Economist

Material 2

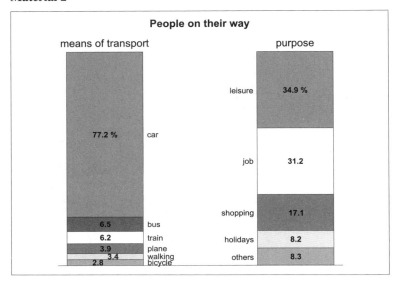

© *OECD*

Material 3

© *Chappatte*

Material 4

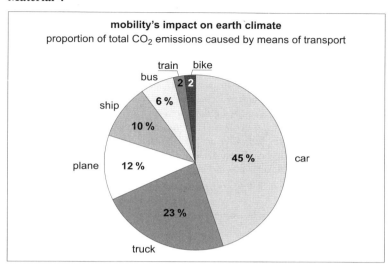

© HWWI

Material 5

Ökos belasten die Umwelt stärker

Gutverdiener mit ökologischen Einstellungen verschmutzen die Umwelt sogar stärker mit Klimagasen als ärmere Bürger ohne ausgeprägtes Umweltbewusstsein. Für Jochen Flasbarth, Chef des Umweltbundesamts, ist das zunächst leicht zu erklären: Sie haben schlicht mehr Geld für Flugreisen oder Autos. Die Deutschen tendieren aber auch dazu, den Handlungsbedarf eher bei anderen als bei sich selbst zu sehen.

So sagen 62 Prozent der Befragten, der Staat tue nicht genug für den Umweltschutz. Bezogen auf die Industrie sagen das sogar neun von zehn Befragten. 85 Prozent glauben beispielsweise, dass die Automobilindustrie mehr für den Umwelt- und Klimaschutz tun kann durch die Produktion und Bereitstellung umweltfreundlicherer Autos. 82 Prozent der Deutschen wollen, dass die Politik mehr Druck auf die Wirtschaft ausübt, damit sie genau diese Umwelt- und Klimaschutzbeiträge erfüllt. Dreiviertel der Befragten erwarten strengere Gesetze und den Abbau umweltschädlicher Subventionen.

© *Sabine Kinkartz, Deutsche Welle*

Lösungsvorschläge

Aufgabe 1 – Mediation

- *Bei dieser Aufgabe sollen Sie einen Schülerzeitungsartikel über die neuesten Entwicklungen auf dem Buchmarkt und ihre Auswirkungen schreiben. Achten Sie darauf, dass Ihre Lösung ein Zeitungsartikel ist, der in der Regel eine Überschrift und oft auch einen Untertitel hat. Verfassen Sie keinen Zeitungartikel, bekommen Sie keine Punkte, da Sie die Aufgabe nicht wie angegeben gelöst haben.*
- *Als Vorlage für Ihren Text dient der Artikel "The future of publishing". Entnehmen Sie diesem die wesentlichen Informationen und verwenden Sie diese für Ihren Schülerzeitungsartikel. Vergessen Sie bei Ihrem Artikel nicht, eine Überschrift einzufügen.*
- *In einem Einleitungssatz führen Sie dann auf das Thema hin, bevor Sie die neuesten Entwicklungen in eigenen Worten erläutern.*

(Überschrift)
Ist das gute alte Buch noch zu retten? – Neue Trends und Entwicklungen aus der Welt des Buches

(Einleitungssatz)
In diesem Jahr war die SMV auf der Buchmesse, auf der es viel über die neuesten Entwicklungen auf dem Buchmarkt und deren Auswirkungen auf die Verlage zu erfahren gab.

(Inhalte des Artikels)
Der Buchmarkt befindet sich derzeit in einem völligen Umbruch. In den USA z. B. werden nur noch weniger als die Hälfte der Bücher noch im Buchladen gekauft. Die meisten Bücher werden bei Online-Händlern wie Amazon bestellt oder bei großen Einzelhändlern wie Wal-Mart gekauft. Der Online-Handel nimmt dabei stark zu und dem guten alten Buch droht nun weitere Konkurrenz durch digitale Bücher, die sogenannten E-Books.
Es wird damit gerechnet, dass das E-Book in den USA innerhalb von drei bis fünf Jahren einen Marktanteil von 25 % erreichen wird. Die Voraussetzung dafür ist, dass sich Smartphones wie das iPhone und Tabletcomputer wie das iPad weiter verbreiten und Leseprogramme bzw. Apps für Bücher immer billiger werden.
Der Marktführer im Bereich E-Books ist derzeit der Online-Händler Amazon, der die Preise niedrig hält, weil der Konkurrenzdruck v. a. von Sony und Apple groß ist und auch bald Google in das Geschäft einsteigen wird. Mehr Anbieter bedeuten auch niedrigere Preise, die die Kunden auch erwarten und zwar auf alle Arten von Büchern.
Die Gewinnspanne bei digitalen Büchern ist auch kaum größer als bei gedruckten Büchern. Bei E-Books entstehen zwar keine Druck- und Versandkosten, jedoch muss die Branche in Datenspeicherung, Datenbereitstellungs- und Sicherheitssysteme gegen Produktpiraterie investieren.
Ein paar Verlage versuchen ihre Umsatzzahlen zu steigern, indem sie sich mit speziellen Webseiten gezielt an bestimmte Gruppen, z. B. Science-Fiction-Fans, wenden.

Einige Verlage stecken auch viel Geld in E-Books mit Bonusmaterial. Dies sind Bücher z. B. mit zusätzlichem Audio- und Videomaterial, die einen höheren Verkaufspreis rechtfertigen sollen.
Viele Verleger hoffen, dass das E-Book dem Lesen wieder zu neuem Aufschwung verhilft, andererseits aber auch, dass der Übergang vom gedruckten zum digitalen Buch langsam verläuft, damit sie mehr Zeit haben, sich daran anzupassen.

Aufgabe 2 – Leseverstehen: Beurteilen von Aussagen zum Text

Bei dieser Aufgabe müssen Sie entscheiden, ob Aussagen zum Text richtig oder falsch sind. Die Aussagen sind in der Regel chronologisch geordnet. Markieren Sie im Text die zur Aussage passende Textstelle und vergleichen Sie die Textstelle mit der Aussage. Treffen Sie dann ihre Entscheidung und begründen Sie diese mit der sinngemäßen Wiedergabe der Textstelle auf Deutsch. Ohne Begründung gibt es keinen Punkt, da man sonst auch raten könnte. Vergessen Sie bei Ihrer Begründung die Zeilenangabe nicht! Die Textstellen selbst müssen Sie jedoch nicht zitieren. Sie sind in dieser Lösung noch zusätzlich zur Veranschaulichung aufgeführt.

1. Die Aussage ist richtig. Die Läden versuchen, den Einkauf für die Kunden angenehmer zu gestalten. Siehe Z. 7: *"[...] stores that are trying to engineer a better experience for the customer [...]"*

   oder:

   Durch die Videoüberwachung können Probleme erkannt und schließlich behoben werden. So werden z. B. Regale niedriger angebracht, damit die Kunden leichter an die Ware kommen. Siehe auch Z. 9–12:
   "[Clips] can help them find solutions to problems in their stores [...] by lowering shelves so that merchandise is within somewhat of an easier reach."

2. Die Aussage ist richtig. Durch die Videoüberwachung kann man die Bedürfnisse der Kunden erkennen. So werden z. B. Sitzgelegenheiten und Spielecken für Kinder eingerichtet. Siehe Z. 9/10: *"[...] they can help find solutions to problems in stores by installing seating and activity areas for children [...]."*

3. Die Aussage ist richtig. Viele Läden nutzen die Geräte, um das Verhalten der Kunden zu analysieren und zu steuern. Siehe Z. 15/16:
   "Many stores [...] are using the appliances [...] to analyze and manipulate the behavior of consumers."

4. Die Aussage ist falsch. Die Gesichtserkennung hat noch nicht zur verstärkten Verletzung der Privatsphäre beigetragen, da die Technik noch in den Kinderschuhen steckt. Allerdings gibt es Bedenken, dass es dazu kommen wird.
   Siehe Z. 18–20: *"[...] the practices will lead to an even greater invasion of privacy, particularly facial recognition technology, which is already in the early stages of development."*

5. Die Aussage stimmt. Firmen nutzen die Technik, um herauszufinden, wie Menschen unterschiedlichen Alters und Geschlechts auf verschiedene Produkte reagieren. Siehe Z. 21–23:
   "[this technology] is used strictly to determine characteristics like age and gender, which they say help them discover how different people respond to various products."
6. Die Aussage ist falsch. Kunden verhalten sich zwar anders, wenn sie beobachtet werden, aber sie kaufen deshalb nicht mehr. Siehe Z. 27/28:
   "When someone's watching me, I'm going to act differently than when I think I'm alone."
7. Die Aussage ist falsch. Läden verwenden bereits bestehende Systeme oder installieren neue. Dass sie viel Geld investieren müssen, steht nicht im Text. Siehe Z. 30/31:
   "Some stores use existing security systems for such monitoring and others have installed entirely new systems."
8. Die Aussage ist falsch. Die Firmen, die die Systeme installieren und die Videos analysieren, halten die Bedenken größtenteils für überzogen. Außerdem wird die Ansicht der Läden selbst nicht erwähnt. Siehe Z. 34/35:
   "The companies [...] say that they are sensitive to privacy issues but that the concerns are mostly overblown."
9. Die Aussage stimmt. Fast jede große Handelskette war oder ist Kunde bei den Videoüberwachungsfirmen. Siehe Z. 42/43:
   "Video analysis companies said nearly every major chain was or had been a client [...]."
10. Die Aussage ist falsch. Befürworter der Privatsphäre wünschen sich zwar, dass bestimmte Regeln eingehalten werden, doch ist dies schwer durchzusetzen, weil Läden keine öffentlichen Orte sind. Siehe Z. 44–46:
    "Privacy supporters know that stores are not public property, but they would prefer to see some ground rules established like telling customers that they are under the microscope."

Aufgabe 3 – Textproduktion: Bildvorlage mit Bezug zum Text von Aufgabe 2

- Bei dieser Aufgabe sollen Sie zunächst das Bild allgemein und im Detail beschreiben.
- Im Anschluss soll die Bedeutung des Bildes im Hinblick auf den Text von Aufgabe 2 erschlossen werden. Sie sollen diese Aufgabe in eigenen Worten bewältigen und auch nicht aus dem Text zitieren. Es wird von Ihnen keine Einleitung und auch keine eigene Stellungnahme am Ende erwartet. Sie erhalten 4 Punkte (VP) für den Inhalt, das sind die Bildbeschreibung und die Bildanalyse (Verbindung Bild und Text) und 6 Punkte (VP) für die Qualität der Sprache.

The cartoon shows a security check at the airport. On a conveyor belt leading into the security check for hand luggage there is a briefcase and a pair of shoes. They belong to a businessman who can be seen in the centre of the picture standing in a body scanner, which is part of the security check at some airports. From his facial expression we can see that he is feeling uncomfortable because the security officers in the right part of the picture can see what he is wearing under his suit. One of the officers is sitting behind a monitor, looking at the screen and is making a humorous remark about the man's underwear. The other security officer is standing behind his colleague and can also see the scan on the monitor. In the foreground on the left there is a young lady, who will be the next to be body-scanned – and whose scan will be seen by the male officers.

What relates the cartoon to the text is that the cartoon is also about the topic of individual privacy. In the cartoon the privacy of people is violated because of public security interests. The security check reveals a person's intimate parts for strangers to see. This can be very embarrassing for the person undergoing the check as he or she is literally stripped of his or her privacy.

In the text, people are supervised and filmed in shops by video cameras, which also can be seen as a loss of privacy. Filming people in shops, however, is often not only there to detect shoplifters, for example, but to monitor customers' shopping behaviour to make them buy more.

Both examples of surveillance measures are officially done for the benefit of people. They show how far surveillance has already gone and what this means for privacy.

Aufgabe 4 – Textproduktion

Part A

Composition 1

1. a) *Für diese Aufgabe können Sie bis zu 5 Punkte für den Inhalt und 10 Punkte für die Sprache erhalten. Achten Sie darauf, nicht nur die Vor- und Nachteile im Allgemeinen zu erörtern, sondern beziehen Sie diese auf das Gastgeberland. Geben Sie, wenn möglich, auch konkrete Beispiele an und legen Sie am Schluss noch einmal Ihre Meinung dar. Der folgende Text ist nur eine mögliche Lösung.*

    Mega events like the Olympic Games or the Football World Cup are very popular with many people all over the world. But what does such an event mean for the host country?

    First of all, the host country needs a lot of money to build new stadiums, sports arenas and infrastructure for the event. This is a problem for poorer countries, in particular, so many host countries end up in debt. In the end, it is often the sports organisation that nominated the host country which makes the profit. However, after the event the infrastructure like new train stations and the stadiums are there for the people of the host country to use. On the other hand, when poor or even developing countries are hosts of mega events, they often don't have any use for the sports arenas and stadiums after the event any more, as was the case with the football arenas in South Africa, host of the FIFA World Cup 2010.

The host countries also hope that mega events will boost tourism in their country because people come here to watch the events or watch them on TV and become curious to visit the country. This is especially important for countries which are poor and need tourists to improve their financial situation. More jobs in tourism would help many people to get out of poverty because they can find work, even if it is only for a limited period of time.

Furthermore, the image of a country can be improved by being a good host of the event and by organising the event well as it happened in Germany during the FIFA World Cup 2006. However, mega events also take place in dictatorial regimes which abuse the event to show their power and distract the world from the violation of human rights in their country such as happened at the Olympic Games in Peking in 2008.

The atmosphere at a mega event is usually very cheerful and happy. Many people of different nations meet in the sports arenas to celebrate. But still there is the danger of violence and hooliganism when so many people meet. Because of the masses of people assembled in one place mega events are also an easy target for terrorists planning an attack.

Security is therefore an important issue. All in all, however, I would say that mega events usually have more positive effects on the host countries than negative effects. I think most countries would be happy to stage a mega event because of the big chances it offers. *(426 words)*

b) *Für diese Aufgabe können Sie bis zu 5 Punkte für den Inhalt und 10 Punkte für die Sprache erhalten. Achten Sie darauf, nicht allgemein über die Vor- und Nachteile der Globalisierung zu schreiben, sondern speziell auf den globalisierten Arbeitsmarkt und seine Bedeutung für die Arbeitnehmer einzugehen. In einer Hinführung zum Thema können Sie kurz erläutern, was mit dem Begriff „globalisierter Arbeitsmarkt" gemeint ist. Am Ende beschließt eine persönliche Stellungnahme die Composition, in der Sie Ihre eigene Meinung darlegen.*

Globalisation has lead to the liberalisation of markets and discussions have been going on about whether this is good or bad for people in different countries. More and more people leave their home countries to work abroad because they have to, or because they seek better job opportunities.

One negative aspect of a globalised job market is that people, especially in developed countries, can easily lose their jobs when their companies shift their production into countries where the cost of labour is lower than at home because companies care mostly about costs and profit. The employers can always threaten to shift jobs abroad if the workers want more money than the company is willing to pay.

In a globalised market employees must be increasingly mobile and flexible in order to keep their jobs because people in other parts of the world are becoming more and more qualified, which makes the job market more competitive. This is not easy for employees who are bound to their countries because they have families, for example. On the other hand, people often have a better chance to get a job if they are prepared to go to a country where their skills are needed. This can be very important if you can't get a job in your own country like a lot of people in southern Europe. If you have worked abroad it can also be much easier to find employment in your own country afterwards because some companies would prefer you to other workers who haven't had work experience abroad.

If you work for an international company, for example, you are almost always required as an employee to work abroad. This is often not an easy step as you leave your friends and sometimes your family behind (although an employee's family usually accompanies him or her to the new country). The employee also has to adapt to a new culture. Therefore, it is essential to learn the language of the country you work in or it will be hard to get into contact with people outside work.

However, going abroad offers an opportunity to broaden one's mind. You can, for example, improve your language skills. You will usually become more tolerant and open-minded towards people when you work together with people from a different country who have another culture and/or religion. So working abroad often makes people more open for other ways of thinking and doing things.

To conclude, I think that the arguments in favour of a globalized job market are much stronger than the ones against it. However, being flexible and mobile isn't easy for everyone, but I would say that a globalized job market is more of a blessing than a curse. *(453 words)*

Composition 2

2. a) *Bei dieser Aufgabe sollen Sie nach einer Einleitung das Thema benennen sowie das dargestellte Problem. Beschreiben Sie dann das Bild und arbeiten Sie seine Botschaft heraus. Die Bildbeschreibung sollten Sie mit einer kurzen persönlichen Stellungnahme abschließen.*

The picture deals with the topic "environment" and is about the dangers of rare species becoming extinct. It is an advertisement by the World Wildlife Fund (WWF) whose logo, the panda bear, is in the top right corner of the picture. You might see this picture on billboards or printed in magazines.

In the foreground you can see two leopards walking behind each other through the savannah. The bigger leopard seems to be the mother of the cub. They both have a size label on their backs, which reads XL on the big leopard and S on the baby leopard. In a drastic way this shows that the fur of these beautiful animals could be used for a fur coat of size XL and size S respectively.

The facial expression of the mother tells us that she is very concentrated and looks very serious, being determined to protect her cub from danger. And indeed, the slogan at the top right of the picture says: "Fashion claims more victims than you think". So this time the danger is not from other animals but human beings. The slogan is to remind us that many rare species often become victims of the fashion industry that uses their furs to make expensive clothes.

The poster wants to make people aware of the fact that rare animals are often killed for fashion and so are in danger of becoming extinct because of this greed for extravagance. So the message of this advertisement is clear: Stop the fashion industry hunting animals for their fur.

I agree with this message because nowadays nobody needs the fur of animals to keep warm in winter as there are so many other materials apart from the skin of animals we can use for this purpose. *(295 words)*

b) *Auch bei dieser Aufgabe sollen Sie nach einer Einleitung das Thema benennen sowie das dargestellte Problem. Beschreiben Sie dann das Bild und arbeiten Sie seine Botschaft heraus. Schließen Sie die Bildbeschreibung mit einer kurzen persönlichen Stellungnahme ab.*

The cartoon is about the topic "health", especially about the problem of health tourism to countries where operation costs are lower than in one's home country.

In the picture you can see an elderly man with a broken leg, standing in front of a signpost. He is walking on crutches and his right leg is in plaster. He seems to be in a bad condition. Obviously, he wanted to come to the hospital to get medical treatment, but from his facial expression you can guess that he is quite surprised to find a large sign where the hospital used to be. The sign says that the clinic has moved to China to cut costs and that he should take a ticket for his flight coupon from a machine next to the signpost. The coupon is sticking out of the machine. In the background there is a water tap still dripping and some other remnants, presumably from the hospital that has been pulled down. Above the sign there is a bird flying over the ruins of the hospital like a vulture.

The cartoonist points out that in many developed countries even tasks and jobs that require top qualifications are shifted to places where labour is cheaper in order to save money. By exaggerating he is mocking this trend and showing us at the same time the dangers of outsourcing by depicting a helpless elderly man who is in need of vital services and doesn't get treatment.

I agree with the message of the cartoon. Outsourcing is a very popular way of lowering costs but I'm afraid that by doing this the quality of products and services will decline. *(277 words)*

Part B

Bei dieser Aufgabe müssen Sie einen Aufsatz über ein vorgegebenes Thema schreiben, wobei Ihnen fünf verschiedene Materialien als Grundlage für Ihren Aufsatz zur Verfügung stehen. Davon müssen <u>mindestens drei</u> inhaltlich in Ihren Aufsatz einfließen. Geben Sie in Ihrem Text an, welchem Material Sie Ihre Informationen entnommen haben. Sie können natürlich auch vier oder alle fünf Materialien verwenden und auch eigene Kenntnisse einbringen. Achten Sie darauf, die Informationen in <u>einem</u> Aufsatz unterzubringen. Es empfiehlt sich, zunächst alle fünf Materialien zu sichten.
Insgesamt können Sie maximal 10 Inhaltspunkte und 20 Sprachpunkte erreichen.

Mother Nature has to pay the price for man's mobility

We all know that most people prefer to have their own cars because of the freedom it gives them to drive wherever they want anytime. Many people also don't think twice when using a plane to reach far away, and not so far away, destinations. However, this is a losing game for the environment.

An OECD study of 2008 *(Material 2)* shows that nearly 80 per cent of all journeys are made by car. People prefer using their own cars to all other means of transport like trains, buses and planes, not to mention riding a bike or walking. The study also reveals that most people leave their homes for private purposes like leisure time activities, for shopping or going on holidays. Only about one third of all trips are because they are part of their jobs.

A study published by Berenberg Bank *(Material 4)* says how much the different means of transport affect the world's climate. The statistics show that about 45 % of the CO_2 emissions are produced by cars and another 23 % by trucks. All other means of public and private transport together don't even produce one third of all carbon emissions. So we can conclude that motor vehicles are the culprits most responsible for air pollution and for climate change.

People are often not aware of these facts and the problems they cause by using their cars. A cartoon *(Material 3)* shows how naïve we really are. In the centre of the cartoon is a globe, representing planet earth, and a family driving on it. The car has circled the earth and is leaving a huge trail of exhaust fumes behind it. The family is leaning out of the car, frantically pointing at a huge cloud of smoke above them, not realizing the smoke is caused by their own car. It looks as if the smoke will cover the whole planet and wrap it up in smoke. The cartoonist's message is to point out that people often don't see or don't want to see that they themselves cause the pollution by their behaviour.

However, even if people have realized that their behaviour has a negative impact on the environment, this doesn't mean that they affect the environment less, as a text from Germany says. *(Material 5)* On the contrary, wealthy people who are environmentally conscious can be worse for Mother Earth than poorer people who don't care about the environment. Well-off people simply have more money to travel by plane and are able to afford more and bigger cars. Germans tend to give the state or industry the blame if not enough is done to protect the environment.

With cars being responsible for most of the CO_2 emissions, something must be done about it. In order to reduce exhaust emissions we must reduce the amount of fuel a car uses. The easiest way of doing that would be to reduce the weight of the cars because 30 years ago cars were much lighter than they are now. An English newspaper text *(Material 1)* says that safety systems like ABS and airbags have added to the weight as well as the size of the cars. Many people feel safer when they have a bigger car, but these cars need more petrol than smaller ones. However, it is a problem to skip safety in order to consume less petrol and produce fewer CO_2 emissions.

To sum up we must admit that Mother Nature does pay the price for our mobility. Most people in the industrialised world want to be independent and have a car of their own. However, we often don't want to see that our way of living is harmful to the environment. Emerging countries like India and China also want to have that lifestyle and so add to pollution.

Everyone of us has to contribute their share to less pollution. If we only took the car when it is really necessary or if we drove smaller cars, we could save a lot of petrol. If we don't get this message, we won't have the chance to enjoy Mother Nature for much longer. *(687 words)*

Fachhochschulreife Englisch (Berufskolleg Baden-Württemberg)
Hörverstehenstest 2012

Aufgabe 1: Satzergänzung *(8 VP)*

Bei einem Kneipenbesuch unterhalten sich zwei Kollegen über ihre Arbeit.
- Hören Sie aufmerksam zu und vervollständigen Sie auf Deutsch die unten stehenden Sätze.
- Sie hören das Gespräch zweimal. Während des Hörens dürfen Sie sich Notizen machen.

1	Dominic denkt, dass Großraumbüros sinnvoll sind, weil …

(2 VP)

2	Beide sind sich darüber einig, dass das Nennen des Vornamens am Telefon von Vorteil ist, da …

(2 VP)

3	Dominic findet informelle Kleidung in Ordnung, wenn …

(2 VP)

4	Beide stimmen aber überein, dass Dresscodes …

(2 VP)

Aufgabe 2: Offene Fragen *(7 VP)*

Im britischen Radiosender *FreshAir* geht es in der Sendung *Current Issues* um Jugendgewalt in Großbritannien. Moderatorin Anne Baker spricht darüber mit John Stuart, dem Leiter einer Polizeiabteilung in Glasgow.

▶ Hören Sie aufmerksam zu und beantworten Sie die Fragen in ganzen Sätzen oder verständlichen Stichworten auf Deutsch.
▶ Sie hören das Gespräch zweimal. Während des Hörens dürfen Sie sich Notizen machen.

1	Wo und wie organisieren sich die Jugendgangs?
	(1 VP)
2	Wodurch wird das gewaltbereite Verhalten britischer Jugendlicher noch unterstützt?
	(1 VP)
3	Welche Ursachen nennt Herr Stuart für die Probleme mit den Jugendlichen?
	(2 VP)
4	Worin liegt das Hauptproblem nach Aussage von Herrn Stuart?
	(1 VP)
5	Wie sieht die Realität für arme Kinder aus?
	(1 VP)
6	Wie und in welchem Zeitraum möchte die Regierung die Situation für Kinder, die in Armut aufwachsen, ändern?
	(1 VP)

Aufgabe 3: Mediation *(10 VP)*

Einer Ihrer Freunde überlegt, ob er ein Sabbatjahr, also eine berufliche Auszeit, nehmen soll. Im Web hören Sie im englischen Radiosender *Channel 4U* die Sendung *People and Places,* in der Moderator Paul Smith sich über dieses Thema mit Laura Male unterhält. Frau Male ist Produktmanagerin bei der Firma *Go Travel.*

▶ Schreiben Sie (auf Deutsch) Ihrem Freund eine E-Mail in einem zusammenhängenden Text
  – mit den Gründen für ein solches Sabbatjahr und
  – was **er** bei der Durchführung beachten muss.
▶ Sie hören das Gespräch zweimal. Während des Hörens dürfen Sie sich Notizen machen.

Lösungsvorschläge

Aufgabe 1: Satzergänzung

Transcript:

DOMINIC: Talking about formality in the workplace, I think that open plan offices really improve the working environment and make people not only talk about the job and about problems among themselves but also to the boss who is sitting in the same office with them.

SUE: I, personally, wouldn't be able to concentrate.

DOMINIC: Well, it depends on the individual, I suppose. But it works for me.

SUE: But these days with email and all these other ways of communicating, I can't see any advantage in having open plan offices.

DOMINIC: That's hardly an argument against them. Everyone wants a more informal atmosphere these days.

SUE: Another aspect of being less formal is calling your colleagues by their first names. Where I work, the managers want to be called Mr and Mrs, but the rest of us all call each other by our first names. Does your company have any rules for that?

DOMINIC: We are trying to go for polite informality. I answer the phone and introduce myself as Dominic Greenfield, not Mr Greenfield. So, everyone calls me Dominic and that's a good start. It really helps to make a conversation pleasant.

SUE: I'm sure you're right, because you're immediately breaking the ice. You can do business more easily than if you sound too formal.

DOMINIC: Yes, that's right. And what about wearing casual clothes at work? My boss has changed his mind and now he thinks that it's acceptable. What do you think?

SUE: I'm for it in the right environment. Maybe you work in a very young environment, not an old-fashioned workplace like mine. Then it's probably fine as long as it doesn't get too sloppy – people might work better, because they feel more comfortable. However, if there is no dress code at all, it just tends to encourage people to be lazy.

DOMINIC: I understand what you're saying and maybe wearing a nice shirt and a tie is important in order to impress your customers. But when you have a day without any official meetings or when you are stuck in an overheated office, I prefer casual clothes, which are more comfortable.

SUE: Hmm, but modern offices usually have air-conditioning nowadays.

DOMINIC: Yes, OK, but one thing we should also keep in mind is that the way you dress may create an unspoken hierarchy that doesn't really exist. Imagine, for example, employees who're maybe all on the same level. If one of them wears designer clothes, even if they're casual clothes, that person will automatically be seen as being more important. So, in this case, you see that dress code can make people more equal in an environment where they need to concentrate on work and not on their looks.

SUE: I take your point there.

DOMINIC: Hey, your glass is empty. Can I get you another drink?
SUE: Yes, thanks, why not? The next one's on me then!
DOMINIC: Sounds good! Do you fancy another beer, or should we go for something a little stronger?
SUE: Uh ... I have to get up at six in the morning so I think I'd better stick to beer, please!
DOMINIC: Coming up!

http://www.ih.hu/exercises/upper_int/l2.htm

Bei dieser Aufgabe sollen Sie die vorgegebenen Satzanfänge auf Deutsch vervollständigen. Sie hören den Text zweimal. Lesen Sie sich die vier Satzanfänge genau durch, bevor Sie sich die Radiosendung dazu anhören. Die Sprechgeschwindigkeit ist recht schnell. Schreiben Sie nicht alles auf, was Sie verstehen, sondern machen Sie sich während des Hörens gezielt Notizen, die sich auf den jeweiligen Punkt beziehen. Insgesamt erhalten Sie für diese Aufgabe 8 Punkte. Das bedeutet, dass Sie für jede Satzergänzung jeweils zwei Informationen erfassen müssen, für die Sie jeweils einen Verrechnungspunkt erhalten. Nutzen Sie die zweiminütige Pause zwischen dem ersten und zweiten Vorspielen sowie die Pause nach dem zweiten Vorspielen zum Ergänzen der Satzanfänge. Die vorgegebene Lösung enthält mehr als die verlangten zwei Ergänzungen. Führen Sie in der Prüfung jedoch nicht mehr als zwei Informationen auf.

1	Dominik denkt, dass Großraumbüros sinnvoll sind, weil ... • sie das Arbeitsumfeld verbessern, indem ... • die Kollegen nicht nur über die Arbeit, sondern untereinander auch über Probleme reden. / die Leute auch mit dem Chef reden, der im selben Büro sitzt. / die Kollegen leichter miteinander kommunizieren können.
2	Beide sind sich darüber einig, dass das Nennen des Vornamens am Telefon von Vorteil ist, da ... • so gleich eine angenehme Gesprächsatmosphäre entsteht ... / man schnell das Eis bricht, wenn man sich z. B. nicht mit Mr Greenfield, sondern mit Dominic vorstellt ... • und man auch leichter Geschäfte machen kann, (wenn man nicht zu formal erscheint).
3	Dominic findet informelle Kleidung in Ordnung, wenn ... • man sich nicht mit Kunden treffen muss ... • und keine offiziellen Besprechungen anstehen. / man in einem überhitzten Büro sitzen muss.

| 4 | Beide stimmen aber überein, dass Dresscodes ...
- eine versteckte Hierarchie schaffen, die nicht wirklich existiert ... / mehr Gleichheit unter den Arbeitnehmern schaffen.
- in Ordnung sind, weil die Kleidung dann nicht mehr im Vordergrund steht ...
- und bewirken, dass die Leute sich mehr auf die Arbeit als auf das Aussehen konzentrieren. |

Aufgabe 2: Offene Fragen

Transcript:

ANNE: Hello and welcome to *Current Issues* here on *FreshAir*. My name is Anne Baker. Our guest today is Chief Superintendent John Stuart, the head of Glasgow's Police Violence Reduction Unit. He will be explaining his views on violent youngsters and how he believes the community should tackle this problem. Thanks so much for being with us, John.

JOHN: Thanks for having me on your programme.

ANNE: Last year more than a fifth of Britons didn't risk going out after dark because they were afraid of experiencing a new form of terror: child gangs. Are the British frightened of their own youngsters?

JOHN: In a way "yes", and it's easy to see why. One Glasgow youth explained it to me like this: "It usually starts outside McDonald's – that's the hot spot. You might go down there with one mate, then you get a phone call. After one hour, there'll be 10 of us there, with nothing to do. Frightening people gives you something to do, a way of getting kicks. Like, 'Oh my God, did you see how they ran away?'

ANNE: What, in your opinion, triggers such behaviour?

JOHN: The boys and girls who casually pick fights are often fuelled by cheap booze. British youngsters drink their Continental European counterparts under the table. A study published in 2008 showed that 27 % of British 15-year-olds had been drunk 20 times or more, compared with 12 % of youngsters in Germany, 6 % in the Netherlands and only 3 % of youngsters in France.

ANNE: These figures are really worrying. It looks as if the behaviour of British kids is going from bad to worse.

JOHN: And there is more worrying news, I'm afraid. For example, last September, 29-year-old Gavin Richardson died after being attacked by two boys. The attack was recorded on a cell phone by a 15-year-old girl. And in January this year, three teenagers from the northwest of England kicked 47-year-old Garry Green to death after he tried to stop them vandalizing his car.

ANNE: All over the world, teenagers are giving their parents headaches. Why are the headaches caused by British kids felt across the whole of Britain?

JOHN: One of the reasons may be that parents aren't always around to help socialize their children. Compared to other countries, British kids are less integrated into the adult world and spend more time in their peer group. Kids who try to integrate into the adult world often feel rejected. Sometimes I get the feeling that Britain is not the most child-friendly of cultures.

ANNE: What, in your opinion, is the root of the problem?

JOHN: Well, I think that kids who are born into poverty start life with a serious disadvantage. There are many people in Britain who believe that poor people just need a kick up the backside in order to break out of poverty.

ANNE: And what is life really like for poor kids in Britain?

JOHN: Well, they will probably live in an area where unemployment is very high. There's probably nowhere to play, and home may not provide much of a refuge. Such conditions breed trouble. Children who try to stay on the right side of the law find it very difficult to resist the growing influence of gangs.

ANNE: And what is the government doing to tackle child poverty?

JOHN: There is an ambitious government plan to halve child poverty by 2020. Its aim is to make Britain the best place in the world for children and young people by investing 53.5 million pounds in playgrounds and youth clubs.

ANNE: Is it true to say that Britain will have to acknowledge the roots of the problem if it really is to become a better place for its children?

JOHN: Yes, that's true. The government must focus on helping kids more than on punishing them. We can help them by providing education in their early years and by offering help to their parents. This will help young people to develop skills which will, in turn, allow them to get jobs and deal with their lives effectively. It's a huge challenge and I'm not saying it's going to be easy, but we must make a start and in some respects it doesn't matter where we start, but start we must.

ANNE: Thank you very much for being here, John.

JOHN: It was my pleasure.

ANNE: Coming up next is a special treat for lovers of Pat Metheny's famous sound ...

eigene Zusammenstellung nach: Time Magazine, URL:
http://www.time.com/time/magazine/article/0.9171.1725547-4.00.html

Bei dieser Aufgabe sollen Sie sechs Fragen in ganzen Sätzen oder in verständlichen Stichworten auf Deutsch beantworten. Sie hören das Interview zweimal. Machen Sie sich während des Hörens Notizen. Sie erhalten für diese Aufgabe insgesamt 7 Punkte.
Achten Sie darauf, dass in einer Frage auch nach mehr als einer Information gefragt werden kann (z. B. „Wo und wann ..." oder „Wann und wie ...").
Notieren Sie gezielt diejenigen Informationen, die sich auf die Frage beziehen. Beim zweiten Hören können Sie noch Informationen hinzufügen, die Ihnen beim ersten Hören entgangen sind. Nutzen Sie wiederum die Pausen zwischen dem ersten und zweiten Hören sowie nach dem zweiten Hören zum Beantworten der Fragen mithilfe Ihrer Notizen.

1	Wo und wie organisieren sich die Jugendgangs?	
	• Man trifft sich z. B. zu zweit bei McDonalds. (0,5)	
	• Dann erhält einer der beiden einen Telefonanruf und eine Stunde später sind 10 gelangweilte Jugendliche dort versammelt. (0,5)	
2	Wodurch wird das gewaltbereite Verhalten britischer Jugendlicher noch unterstützt?	
	• Das gewaltbereite Verhalten wird durch das Trinken billigen Alkohols unterstützt. (1)	
3	Welche Ursachen nennt Herr Stuart für die Probleme mit den Jugendlichen?	
	• Die Eltern versäumen es oft, sich um die Erziehung ihrer Kinder zu kümmern. (1)	
	• Britische Kinder fühlen sich von den Erwachsenen oft abgelehnt. / Sie sind oft kaum in die Erwachsenenwelt integriert und verbringen daher viel Zeit in ihrer Peergroup (Gruppe von Gleichaltrigen). (1)	
	(• Großbritannien ist nicht das kinderfreundlichste Land.)	
4	Worin liegt das Hauptproblem nach Aussage von Herrn Stuart?	
	• Das Hauptproblem ist die Kinderarmut. (0,5)	
	• Kinder, die in die Armut hineingeboren werden, finden auch nur schwer wieder aus ihr heraus. (0,5)	
5	Wie sieht die Realität für arme Kinder aus?	
	• Sie leben in Vierteln mit hoher Arbeitslosigkeit, in denen es außerdem kaum Möglichkeiten zum Spielen gibt. (0,5)	
	• Zudem bietet ihnen ihr Zuhause keine Zuflucht. (0,5)	
6	Wie und in welchem Zeitraum möchte die Regierung die Situation für Kinder, die in Armut aufwachsen, ändern?	
	• Bis zum Jahr 2020 soll die Kinderarmut halbiert werden, (0,5)	
	• indem 55,3 Millionen Pfund in Spielplätze und Jugendhäuser investiert werden. (0,5)	

Aufgabe 3: Mediation

Transcript:

PAUL: Good morning, on today's show I'm speaking to Laura Male, brand manager of *Go Travel*, a British company that organizes travel for adults taking sabbatical time out. Thank you for coming, Laura.

LAURA: Thank you for inviting me.

PAUL: So, can you start by telling us what exactly motivates people to take sabbaticals?

LAURA: Well, often, people taking a sabbatical see it as the gap year they never experienced as a youngster. Taking a sabbatical is also a great way of finding new motivation by experiencing new cultures, people and places. Also, the fact that you will have to face new challenges and learn new skills is really exciting.

PAUL: I see. So what would you say is the best time to take a sabbatical?

LAURA: There's no real answer to this question. It varies from person to person, depending on what else is going on around you at the time.

PAUL: Can you give an example?

LAURA: Yes, of course. Clearly, if there is a lot of reorganization going on at your place of work, for example, if there is a new boss, or if you are up for promotion, then it may be best to postpone the plan.

PAUL: What practical things should you think about before going abroad on your sabbatical?

LAURA: Obviously, there's a lot of planning to be done for a sabbatical. You may need to decide whether to rent out your house or flat or, perhaps, even sell it. And, of course, you have to organize your finances so that you don't run out of money during your time out.

PAUL: What you're saying is that you have to organize things at home first. But for me, the most important point is how to organize the trip. Can you give us any advice for this, Laura?

LAURA: Yes, certainly. There are many things to consider. The most important points are the duration of your trip and the budget. People should plan very carefully how long they would like to stay away and whether they can afford a sabbatical. Also, deciding on a destination is a crucial point. Don't try to squeeze in too many countries or activities. Your trip might become too stressful and not allow you enough time for relaxation.

PAUL: Oh, that sounds as if a lot of decisions need to be made. How can I find out what would be the best trip for me?

LAURA: Well, think about the things and places you have always wanted to see. Make a list of them and loosely plan your journey around them. I recommend having some fixed dates for your trip as a guideline, but you should remain flexible as well. You never know who, or what, you may discover on your trip that could just change your plans.

PAUL: Well, that certainly might help in planning the trip. There's one last thing I'd like to know. Have you ever met people who felt that doing a sabbatical was a mistake?

LAURA: In my experience, people found their trips to be life-changing, positive experiences. Remember that there is no set time for a sabbatical. Even taking just a few weeks off from work can allow you to have an incredible experience.
PAUL: Thank you Laura, it's been a pleasure having you here today.
LAURA: Thank you, Paul, my pleasure, too.
PAUL: Coming up next after the music is a story you've all probably heard of before: Lost luggage …

*eigene Zusammenstellung nach: Margaret Davis: I'll be off, then.
In: Business Spotlight 1/2010*

Mithilfe der Informationen, die Sie aus einem Radiointerview gewonnen haben, sollen Sie in dieser Mediationsaufgabe eine E-Mail an einen Freund verfassen, der ein Sabbatjahr plant. Sie hören das Radiointerview zweimal. Machen Sie sich während des Hörens Notizen und erstellen Sie eine Checkliste. Schreiben Sie dann mithilfe der Checkliste die E-Mail. Vergessen Sie dabei nicht die Anrede sowie einen Einleitungs- und Schlusssatz mit Verabschiedung. Falls man nur Stichpunkte aufgeschrieben hat, kann höchstens die halbe Punktzahl erreicht werden.

Checkliste für den Inhalt

Gründe für ein Sabbatjahr:
- eine Auszeit nehmen, falls man dies als junger Mensch nicht gemacht hat
- neue Kulturen, Leute und Orte kennenlernen und daraus neue Motivation schöpfen
- sich neuen Herausforderungen stellen müssen / neue Fähigkeiten und Fertigkeiten erlernen
- lebensverändernde, positive Erfahrung

Was sollte man bei der Durchführung beachten?
- Verschieben der Reise bei Umstrukturierung am Arbeitsplatz, neuem Chef oder einer Beförderung
- Haus oder Wohnung: vermieten oder verkaufen?
- Finanzen überprüfen: genug Geld für das Sabbatjahr einplanen
- Festlegung von Reiseziel(en) und Reisedauer: nicht zu viele Länder, da sonst keine Entspannung
- Flexibel bleiben: nur ein paar feste Termine setzen

E-Mail (Lösungsbeispiel):

Hallo Josef,

ich habe gerade im Radio ein Gespräch über das Thema „Sabbatjahr" angehört, das dich sehr interessieren wird, da du ja vorhast, demnächst eine berufliche Auszeit zu nehmen.

Als möglicher Grund für so ein Jahr wurde unter anderem genannt, dass viele das Auslandsjahr nachholen, das sie als Jugendliche nicht gemacht haben. Manche erhoffen sich neue Motivation durch das Kennenlernen von anderen Kulturen und

Menschen. Andere suchen nach neuen Herausforderungen und haben dabei die Erwartung, weitere Fähigkeiten und Fertigkeiten zu erlernen.

Allerdings gibt es viele Dinge zu planen und zu beachten. Der richtige Zeitpunkt für ein Sabbatjahr ist von Person zu Person verschieden. Ein ungünstiger Zeitpunkt dafür wäre aber, wenn am Arbeitsplatz Umstrukturierungen im Gange sind, ein neuer Chef kommt oder man vor einer Beförderung steht.

Was man unbedingt vorher klären sollte, ist die Frage, ob man sein Haus oder seine Wohnung vermieten oder verkaufen sollte.

Die wichtigsten Punkte sind die Dauer der Reise sowie die eigene finanzielle Situation, d. h., ob und wie lange man sich eine Auszeit leisten kann.

Ein weiterer wichtiger Punkt ist das Festlegen der Reiseziele. Dabei sollte man sich eine Liste von den Ländern und Dingen machen, die man schon immer einmal sehen wollte. Auf jeden Fall sollten nicht zu viele Ziele und Aktivitäten eingeplant werden, um Stress zu vermeiden. Man sollte also nur einen groben Zeitplan entwerfen, damit man flexibel auf das reagieren kann, was man entdeckt und was evtl. zu Planänderungen führen kann.

Als Ermutigung zum Schluss: Es wurde auch gesagt, dass die Auszeit für alle, die sie genommen haben, eine lebensverändernde, positive Erfahrung war und es bislang keiner bereut oder als Fehler angesehen hat.

Ich beneide dich heute schon um diese Erfahrung.

Dein

Hans Georg

Fachhochschulreife Englisch (Berufskolleg Baden-Württemberg)
Schriftliche Hauptprüfung 2012

Aufgabe 1 – Mediation (10 VP)

Aufgabenstellung

Als Mitglied der Umweltgruppe „Rettet die natürlichen Ressourcen" bereiten Sie sich auf eine Präsentation für Ihre Mitschüler über den Zusammenhang zwischen Wasserknappheit und weggeworfenen Lebensmitteln vor.

- Entwerfen Sie zu diesem Zweck ein Handout.
- Entnehmen Sie dem vorliegenden Zeitungsartikel die entsprechenden Informationen.
- Formulieren Sie ganze deutsche Sätze.

Don't waste the world's water!

As consumers throw millions of tonnes of uneaten food into the bin each year, few give a thought to the hidden costs of such waste – the water that it took to grow the food. But new research shows that we throw away, on average, twice as much water per year in the form of uneaten food as we use for washing and drinking.

5 What is worse, increasing amounts of our food comes from countries where water is scarce, meaning the food we dump has a huge hidden impact on valuable water resources across the world.

The first extensive study into the impact of the "embedded water" in the UK's food waste on world water supplies was carried out by the government's Waste and
10 Resources Action Programme (WRAP). It shows that the water used to produce food thrown away by households in the UK amounts to about 6.2 billion cubic metres a year. That represents 6 % of the UK's total water <u>footprint</u>, which includes water used in industry and agriculture. About a quarter of the water used to grow and process the wasted food comes from the UK, but much of it from countries that are al-
15 ready experiencing water stress.

For years green campaigners have called for more attention to be paid to "hidden" or "embedded" water – water that is used in the production of all sorts of goods, from food and clothing to cars and furniture, and which represents hidden costs on exports.

20 As more countries suffer from water shortage, these exports can further reduce natural resources and cause environmental problems such as <u>salination</u> – which can make land unsuitable for growing crops – and higher prices for water to poorer consumers.

Food waste carries further environmental costs: it accounts for about 3 % of the
25 UK's annual greenhouse gas emissions, equivalent to the amount generated by

7 million cars each year. That is enough to neutralize the greenhouse gases which British households save each year by their recycling efforts.

Liz Goodwin, chief executive at WRAP, said: "These figures are quite shocking. Although greenhouse gas emissions have been widely discussed, the water used to produce food and drink has been overlooked until recently. However, worries over the availability of water in the UK and abroad, and security of the supply of food are growing. Therefore it is vital we understand the connections between food waste, water and climate change." *(413 words)*

Abridged and adapted from: © Fiona Harvey, in: Guardian.co.uk, 22 March 2011

Wortangaben:
l. 12: footprint: *hier:* Verbrauch
l. 21: salination: Versalzung

Aufgabe 2 – Leseverstehen: Beurteilen von Aussagen zum Text *(10 VP)*

New film uncovers racism in Germany

Is Germany a racist country? That is what a new documentary, 'Black on White', is trying to find out. Its findings are shocking.

For more than a year, journalist Gunter Wallraff travelled across Germany wearing a dark-haired curly <u>wig</u> and with his white skin painted black. Equipped with a secret camera, and calling himself Kwami Ogonno, he went to mainly white areas to see how a black man with a foreign accent is treated. The experience, he said, was even more depressing than he had expected. "I hadn't known what we would discover. I had thought maybe the story will be what a tolerant and accepting country Germany has become," said Mr Wallraff after a screening of the film 'Black on White' in Berlin. "Unfortunately, I was wrong." He was almost beaten up by neo-Nazis after a football match in eastern Germany. And outside a small-town nightclub he was told by a skinhead: "Europe for whites, Africa for monkeys."

But the film's most disturbing aspect is not the well-known racism of right-wing extremists, but rather the secretly-filmed reactions of everyday people – the landlady who says she could not possibly rent out a flat to a black person, or the shop owner who will not let "Kwami" try on an expensive watch, but willingly hands over the same watch to the next customer who is white.

For black people in certain parts of Germany such experiences as described in the film are commonplace, believes Sven Mekarides, general secretary of the Africa Council in Berlin. Mr Mekarides left his home country Cameroon in 1991 and came to study in a small town in eastern Germany. After his arrival he and his fellow African students experienced racist attacks and abuse every day. They were spat at, shouted at and beer bottles were thrown at them.

The worst attack took place in the eastern Berlin district of Lichtenberg in 2004, when Mr Mekarides and his girlfriend were surrounded by seven young men armed with knives. Since then the situation has not got much better. According to the Amadeu Antonio Foundation there have been 138 racially-motivated murders in Germany since 1990. And last year police registered 140 race attacks in Berlin. "Those are only the most extreme cases the police know about," said Mr Mekarides. "Every day we get calls from black people who have been falsely accused of stealing something or insulted on the street."

Although Mr Mekarides welcomes the discussion about racism the film has started, he believes the filmmaker's exaggerated disguise confirms Europeans' worst stereotypes of an African. "He just doesn't look like an African," said Mr Mekarides. "The wig, the make-up and the brightly-coloured shirt are all so over the top, he looks like he's a clown in a carnival. After he has washed his skin, he can forget the problem. But black people have this problem every day."

However, the film has won praise for starting a debate about racism in Germany. After a Q & A session with Mr Wallraff in a Berlin cinema, one young black woman said the film was "interesting, helpful and needed for Germany". She said: "I've lived here all my life, and this is the first time I've ever seen an audience like this discussing this issue."

Gunter Wallraff's film has already done a lot to provoke discussion about racism. With an ageing population, Germany is now having to come to terms with being a country of immigration. Clearly the debate is just beginning. *(579 words)*

Abridged and adapted from: © BBC News, http://news.bbc.co.uk, 6 November 2009

Wortangabe:
l. 4: wig: Perücke

Aufgabenstellung

▶ Entscheiden Sie, ob die folgenden Aussagen zum Text richtig oder falsch sind, und begründen Sie Ihre Entscheidung.

▶ Schreiben Sie Ihre Antworten auf Deutsch in ganzen Sätzen auf separates Prüfungspapier.

1. A new black and white documentary on racism by G. Wallraff is now showing in German movie theatres.
2. Mr Wallraff was not surprised by the experience he made when doing research for his project.
3. He was often attacked by neo-Nazis after football matches.
4. He experienced racism not only in the ultra-right scene but also with normal members of society.
5. Mr Mekarides and his girlfriend were even injured by knives.
6. It is a common experience for blacks to be charged with criminal acts.
7. Mr Wallraff's disguise reflects the common prejudices Europeans hold towards the way Africans dress and look like.
8. A viewer of the film considered the documentary necessary to be watched by foreigners in Germany.
9. People have been talking about racism in Germany for quite a long time now.
10. All in all, the article comes to the conclusion that racism isn't really an important issue in Germany.

Aufgabe 3 – Textproduktion: Bildvorlage mit Bezug zum Text von Aufgabe 2

(10 VP: 4 VP Inh. / 6 VP Spr.)

© Johnathan West/cartoonstock.com

Aufgabenstellung
- First describe the picture.
- Then analyze its meaning with reference to the text "New film uncovers racism in Germany".
- Use your own words.

Aufgabe 4 – Textproduktion

Choose between Part A **or** Part B.

Part A

Composition 1 *(15 VP: 5 VP Inh. / 10 VP Spr.)*
Drug-taking and drug abuse are issues that affect both
ordinary people and celebrities from film, music and sports.
Discuss possible reasons for drug-taking. What are the consequences?

Composition 2 *(15 VP: 5 VP Inh. / 10 VP Spr.)*
Describe the cartoon and analyze its message.

© *Jeff Danziger, NY Times Syndicate*

Part B

Textproduktion: Materialgestützter Aufsatz *(30 VP: 10 VP Inh. / 20 VP Spr.)*

- Write a composition about the topic "Serious accidents involving young drivers are a burning issue. Explain why. What can be done to limit the risks?"
  Use the information of at least three of the given materials.
- Name which ones you are using.
- Do not write three separate compositions but one covering all the materials chosen.
- You can add your own ideas.

Material 1

© Department of Transport, UK

2012-19

Material 2

Unfallursachen 18- bis 24-Jähriger (alle Unfälle)	2008 in %
Nicht angepasste Geschwindigkeit	21,0 %
Abstandsfehler	11,0 %
Vorfahrt-/Vorrangfehler	10,0 %
Abbiegefehler	10,0 %
Alkoholeinfluss	4,2 %
Falsche Straßenbenutzung	3,6 %
Fehler beim Überholen	2,7 %

© *Statistisches Bundesamt, Hrsg. Verkehrswacht*

Material 3
Unfallrisiko junger Fahrer durch sichere Autos und „Begleitetes Fahren" minimieren

Das Risiko junger Fahrer zwischen 17 und 24 Jahren, bei einem Unfall verletzt oder getötet zu werden, liegt – sowohl auf den Anteil an der Bevölkerung als auch auf die Fahrleistung bezogen – mehr als doppelt so hoch als bei der Gruppe der 25- bis 54-Jährigen. Diese seit vielen Jahren unveränderte und inakzeptable Tatsache konnte bisher mit keiner im Bereich Fahrkönnen und Fahrverhalten angesiedelten Maßnahme wirkungsvoll beeinflusst werden.

Deshalb hat die Unfallforschung der Versicherer (UDV) auf dem 48. Deutschen Verkehrsgerichtstag in Goslar nochmals die seit Jahren formulierte Forderung unterstrichen, nur Fahrzeuge mit Systemen zu kaufen, die Fahrfehler korrigieren können. Dies trifft vor allem auf ESP zu, das nun spätestens ab Ende 2014 in jedem verkauften Neufahrzeug eingebaut sein muss.

Die UDV ist überzeugt, dass mit dem „Begleiteten Fahren" (Führerschein mit 17) erstmals eine Maßnahme existiert, die auch auf der Verhaltensseite Erfolge zeigt. Alle bisher bekannten Evaluationen und Zwischenergebnisse – auch der Versicherer – weisen für die 18-jährigen in diesem Modell ausgebildeten Fahrer gegenüber der Vergleichsgruppe einen günstigeren Schadensverlauf auf.

© *Unfallforschung der Versicherer; GDV*

Material 4

Material 5

Teenagers Road Accident Group (T.R.A.G.) – Drive 4 Life

We have developed an innovative program aimed at highlighting the awareness of young people to the dangers of modern driving. Our group consists of firefighters, ambulance and police officers, and those who have first-hand experience with road trauma. Our goal is to raise the awareness of young adults to their responsibilities when they get behind the wheel of a motor vehicle.

T.R.A.G. has produced a 45-minute presentation targeting students in years 10, 11 & 12. Initially a short 3-minute video places the audience at the scene of several serious accidents.
- An ambulance officer – usually the first to arrive at an accident scene, details the type of devastation he encounters.
- A firefighter – describes spending sometimes hours cutting open twisted wrecks to release seriously injured victims.
- A police officer – speaks about the pain of attending accidents involving young people, the trauma of telling families and friends that their loved one has been killed or injured, and the responsibility that drivers have in ensuring the safety of their passengers, other road users and themselves.
- Surviving victims and relatives of road accidents tell of the lifelong effects of road trauma.

T.R.A.G. is of the opinion that if this program saves one life then we have achieved our goal. We want young people to drive safely and responsibly but more importantly – DRIVE 4 LIFE.

Abridged and adapted from: Teenagers Road Accident Group – TRAG Mornington Peninsula Inc. Victoria Australia © 1999. URL: http://www.trag-vic.org/; http://www.trag-vic.org/program.html

Lösungsvorschläge

Aufgabe 1 – Mediation

Bei dieser Aufgabe sollen Sie den Zusammenhang zwischen Wasserknappheit und weggeworfenen Lebensmitteln in einem Handout für eine Präsentation darlegen. Achten Sie darauf, dass Ihre Lösung in jedem Fall ein Handout ist, das in der Regel eine Überschrift hat und im Hauptteil auch Untertitel haben kann. Ist Ihre Lösung kein Handout, erhalten Sie keine Punkte, weil Sie die gestellte Aufgabe nicht gelöst haben. Auch dürfen Sie Teile des vorliegenden Zeitungsartikels nicht einfach übersetzen, da Sie für eine reine Übersetzung keine Punkte erhalten. Von Ihnen ist vielmehr eine Mediation gefordert, also die sinngemäße Wiedergabe des Inhalts auf Deutsch. Sie müssen die wichtigsten Inhaltspunkte des Textes, in der Regel sind es mindestens 10 Punkte, in eigenen Worten und in gut verständlichem Deutsch wiedergeben. Der Zeitungsartikel dient Ihnen dabei als Vorlage, aus der Sie Ideen und Fakten für Ihr Handout herausholen.

Insgesamt gibt es 10 Verrechnungspunkte (VP) für diese Aufgabe, wobei Inhalts- und Sprachpunkte gemeinsam gewertet werden, d. h. es gibt keine getrennte Wertung von Inhalts- und Sprachpunkten.

Das Handout sollten Sie folgendermaßen strukturieren:
- *Überschrift*
- *Einleitungssatz, der zu den inhaltlichen Informationen hinführt*
- *Hauptteil mit passenden Informationen zum Thema aus dem Zeitungsartikel*
- *Abschlusssatz: an die Adressaten gerichteter Appell, oder: Fazit als Zusammenfassung*

Wassermangel durch Lebensmittelverschwendung

Jedes Jahr werfen wir Millionen Tonnen Lebensmittel einfach weg. Dadurch werden nicht nur Nahrungsmittel verschwendet, sondern auch das Wasser, das zum Wachsen der Nahrung benötigt wurde.

Problem:
Durch die nicht verzehrten Lebensmittel verbrauchen wir jedes Jahr doppelt so viel Wasser, wie wir zum Waschen und Trinken benötigen. Da auch immer mehr Nahrungsmittel aus Ländern kommen, in denen Wassermangel herrscht, wirkt sich das Entsorgen von Lebensmitteln auch in besonderem Maße auf die weltweiten Wasserreserven aus.
Seit Jahren fordern Umweltaktivisten daher, dem Trinkwasser, das zur Produktion von Gütern, Lebensmitteln, Kleidung und Möbeln verwendet wird, mehr Beachtung zu schenken.

Fakten:
Die erste ausführliche Studie über die Auswirkungen der „versteckten" Wasserverschwendung durch die britische Regierung belegt, dass ...
– ... 6,2 Milliarden m^3 Wasser zur Herstellung derjenigen Lebensmittel verbraucht werden, die in Großbritannien pro Jahr weggeworfen werden.

- ... dies 6 % des gesamten Wasserverbrauchs in Großbritannien entspricht.
- ... nur ein Viertel des Wassers, das zur Herstellung der weggeworfenen Lebensmittel benötigt wird, aus Großbritannien selbst kommt, der Großteil der Nahrungsmittel aber aus Ländern eingeführt wird, in denen Wasserknappheit herrscht.

Folgen:
- Immer mehr Länder leiden an Wassermangel, sodass diese Exporte die natürlichen Wasserreserven weiter reduzieren und Umweltprobleme wie die Versalzung der Böden verursachen. Auch kann Wasserknappheit zu höheren Wasserpreisen in ärmeren Ländern führen.
- Nahrungsmittelverschwendung verursacht weitere Umweltkosten und ist verantwortlich für etwa 3 % der jährlichen Treibhausgasemissionen in Großbritannien, was ungefähr dem Schadstoffausstoß von 7 Millionen Autos jährlich entspricht.

Fazit:
Wenn man den Zusammenhang zwischen Nahrungsmittelverschwendung, Wassermangel und Klimawandel erkannt hat, sollte man in Zukunft möglichst keine Lebensmittel mehr wegwerfen!

Aufgabe 2 – Leseverstehen: Beurteilen von Aussagen zum Text

Bei dieser Aufgabe müssen Sie entscheiden, ob Aussagen zum Text richtig oder falsch sind. Die Aussagen sind in der Regel chronologisch geordnet. Markieren Sie im Text die zur Aussage passende Textstelle und vergleichen Sie die Textstelle mit der vorgegebenen Aussage. Treffen Sie dann Ihre Entscheidung und begründen Sie diese mit der sinngemäßen Wiedergabe der Textstelle auf Deutsch. Ohne Begründung gibt es keinen Punkt, da man sonst auch raten könnte. Vergessen Sie bei Ihrer Begründung die Zeilenangabe nicht! Die Textstellen selbst müssen Sie jedoch nicht zitieren. Sie sind in dieser Lösung noch zusätzlich zur Veranschaulichung aufgeführt.

1. Die Aussage stimmt nicht, denn in Zeile 1 steht, dass der neue Dokumentarfilm den Titel „Black on White" hat und nicht, dass es sich um einen Schwarz-Weiß Dokumentarfilm handelt: *"That is what a new documentary, 'Black on White', is trying to find out."*
2. Die Aussage stimmt nicht, da in Zeile 6 f. steht, dass die Erfahrung viel schlimmer war, als er es erwartet hatte: *"The experience, he said, was even more depressing than he had expected."*
3. Die Aussage trifft nicht zu, denn in Zeile 9 f. steht, dass er nach einem Spiel beinahe zusammengeschlagen wurde: *"He was almost beaten up by neo-Nazis after a football match in eastern Germany."*
4. Die Aussage stimmt, weil in Zeile 13 f. steht, dass der beunruhigendeste Aspekt des Films nicht der bekannte Rassismus der Rechtsextremen war, sondern die Reaktionen der gewöhnlichen Leute: *"But the film's most disturbing aspect is not the well-known racism of right-wing extremists, but rather the secretly-filmed reactions of everyday people. (...)"*

5. Die Aussage trifft nicht zu, da in Zeile 25 f. steht, dass er und seine Freundin von mehreren mit einem Messer bewaffneten Männern eingekreist worden sind, aber es wird nicht erwähnt, ob sie verletzt wurden: *"(...) Mr Mekarides and his girlfriend were surrounded by seven young men with knives."*
6. Die Aussage ist richtig, denn in Zeile 29 ff. steht, dass Herr Mekarides täglich Anrufe von Menschen mit dunkler Hautfarbe erhält, die fälschlicherweise beschuldigt werden, etwas gestohlen zu haben. *"Every day we get calls from black people who have been falsely accused of stealing something (...)."*
7. Die Aussage stimmt, denn in Zeile 33 f. steht, dass Wallraffs übertriebene Verkleidung die schlimmsten Vorurteile der Europäer gegenüber Afrikanern bestätigen würde: *"(...) the filmmaker's exaggerated disguise confirms Europeans' worst stereotypes of an African."*
8. Diese Aussage stimmt nicht, denn in Zeile 39 f. steht, dass der Film interessant, hilfreich und notwendig für die Deutschen ist: *"(...) the film was interesting, helpful and needed for Germany."*
9. Die Aussage stimmt nicht, denn in Zeile 40 ff. steht, dass es die Zuhörerin das erste Mal erlebt, dass vor einem Publikum über dieses Thema gesprochen wird: *"I've lived here all my life and this is the first time I've ever seen an audience like this discussing this issue."*
10. Die Aussage stimmt nicht, denn der Artikel an sich belegt, dass Rassismus in Deutschland ein großes Problem darstellt. In Zeile 44 f. wird angemerkt, dass Deutschland damit klarkommen muss, ein Einwanderungsland zu sein: *"(...) Germany is now having to come to terms with being a country of immigration."*

Aufgabe 3 – Textproduktion: Bildvorlage mit Bezug zum Text von Aufgabe 2

Beschreiben Sie den Cartoon zunächst allgemein und dann im Detail. Arbeiten Sie anschließend die Aussage des Bildes heraus sowie seinen Bezug zum Text in Aufgabe 2. Schreiben Sie darüber, was das Bild mit dem Text gemeinsam hat und was anders ist. Sie sollten diese Aufgabe in eigenen Worten bewältigen und nicht aus dem Text zitieren. Es wird von Ihnen jedoch keine Einleitung und auch keine eigene Stellungnahme am Ende erwartet.

Sie erhalten bis zu 4 Verrechnungspunkte (VP) für den Inhalt, das sind die Bildbeschreibung und die Bildanalyse (mit Verbindung Bild und Text), und bis zu 6 VP für die Qualität der Sprache.

The cartoon shows an interrogation after an offence has been committed. In the centre of the picture there is a policeman standing in a garden next to a tree in front of a fence. He is taking notes and is questioning an eye-witness.
The policeman is interviewing a young boy about the possible offender. From the policeman's facial expression we can see that he is very serious. The boy is standing next to the policeman on the left and is looking as if he is a bit intimidated by the policeman as he has his eyes wide open and his mouth shut.

Below the picture you can read what the policeman is saying to the little boy: "This giant, Jack, are you sure he wasn't a dark gentleman?" From this statement you can gather that the boy has mentioned a "giant" but hasn't said anything about the colour of the skin of this "giant". Still the policeman suggests, by making his statement, that the culprit must have been a black man.

This matches Mr Wallraff's experience in the text that racism does not only occur with right wing radicals but is also widespread among ordinary people – and, as the cartoon tries to illustrate, also with authorities like the police. As the text shows, it is often hidden behind side remarks or can be detected in a different behaviour towards foreigners or people with a different skin colour.

And another thing is similar; in the text it is said that black people are often falsely accused of committing offences and this is what the policeman in the cartoon also does by trying to suggest that it was "a dark gentleman", using politically correct language, but taking it for granted that the offender must have been black.

The difference between the text and the picture is that the cartoon scene takes place in Britain as there is a policeman depicted in a Bobby uniform, whereas the text is about racism in Germany. *(330 words)*

Aufgabe 4 – Textproduktion

Beim Verfassen Ihrer Texte können Ihnen die Redewendungen behilflich sein, die in den Hinweisen und Tipps aufgelistet sind.

Part A

Composition 1

Bei dieser Aufgabe können Sie 5 Verrechnungspunkte (VP) für den Inhalt und 10 VP für die Sprache erhalten. Die Textlänge soll dabei ca. 200 bis 300 Wörter betragen.
Denken Sie auch an eine Einleitung und die persönliche Stellungnahme am Schluss.
Führen Sie dann mindestens fünf Gründe für den Gebrauch von Drogen aus und erläutern Sie auch die Folgen des Drogenmissbrauchs. Vergessen Sie nicht, Ihre Ausführungen mit Beispielen zu illustrieren. Achten Sie auch auf die sprachliche Qualität des Textes, da Sie für die Sprache mehr Punkte erhalten als für den Inhalt.

We hear a lot about stars taking drugs at parties and of athletes taking drugs in order to win, but there are also many ordinary people who can't get away from their addiction. So the question comes up why do people, not only stars, take drugs and what are the consequences of this habit for them and for society.

An important reason why people take drugs is that they can make them feel better for a while. You can forget about your problems as long as you are on drugs. Drugs are also taken by people who work very hard and who are under pressure. They want the drugs to help them reduce stress and make them able to work long hours without getting tired.

The reason why many young people take drugs or drink alcohol, which is also a drug, is peer pressure. They feel if they don't take part in drug-taking or drinking, they wouldn't be part of the group any more to which they want to belong. Often young people also take drugs out of curiosity because they want to try them out in order to share the experience with others, or they try drugs because they are bored.

A grave consequence of drug taking is that you can easily get addicted and you simply can't stop. That's because your body, mind and soul have got used to getting their drug every day. The drugs occupy your thoughts day and night. The worst impact of drugs, which is connected with the aspect of addiction, is that drugs usually destroy your health and often lead to death. Users of so called hard drugs, for example, often die of overdoses.

One point which shouldn't be forgotten is that drugs, especially illegal drugs, cost a lot of money when you are addicted. Many long-time addicts have lost their money and even some stars have got into financial difficulties because of their drug consumption. That's why addicts who are poor often turn to crime or prostitution to get the money they need. The only one to profit from drug addiction is organized crime that earns huge sums from dealing in drugs.

To sum up we can say that drugs have so many damaging effects on people that they should be avoided or, in the case of alcohol, consumed in a reasonable way.

(391 words)

Composition 2

Bei dieser Aufgabe sollen Sie nach einer Einleitung, zu der die Angabe des Themas oder des dargestellten Problems gehört, erst das Bild beschreiben und dann dessen Botschaft herausarbeiten. Die Bildbeschreibung sollten Sie mit einer persönlichen Stellungnahme abschließen.

Sie erhalten für diese Aufgabe insgesamt 15 Verrechnungspunkte (VP), 5 VP für den Inhalt und 10 VP für die Sprache, auf die Sie also besonders achten sollten. Für eine gute Leistung sollte der Umfang Ihres Textes 200 bis 300 Wörter betragen. Der Lösungsvorschlag ist etwas umfangreicher.

(Einleitung)
The picture deals with the effects of globalisation, especially with the effects it has on jobs and life in the developed and the developing countries. The cartoon consists of two pictures. Above the left picture we can read "USA" and above the right picture the caption says "Indonesia".

(Beschreibung)
In the cartoon on the left there is a boy leaning against a wall. He has his hands in his pockets as if he has nothing to do. And indeed he has no job as the caption next to the boy says. From his facial expression you can see that he feels cool. He is dressed in a fashionable way with baggy pants, baseball cap and expensive trainers which cost $ 150 as you can see from the caption in front of his legs.

In the right picture there is a girl sitting behind an old sewing machine. She is sewing a shoe which looks like the expensive one of the boy on the left. She is wearing a simple black dress and has no shoes, which is also written under the sewing machine in front of her legs. From her facial expression you can see that she isn't happy as she has a lot of work to do, which the caption above the sewing machine says. She is sweating because of the hard work. In the background you can see a stack of shoe boxes all having the Nike logo printed on them.

(Botschaft)
The cartoonist is showing the huge gap between the life and work of people in developed and in developing countries. In rich countries, people, even if they are out of work, can afford expensive clothing, for example, whereas the people in poor countries who produce these goods and work hard can't even afford the most basic things of life like a pair of shoes or enough to eat. By contrasting the hard-working girl with the lazy boy the cartoonist makes his point clear. He also criticizes the fact that goods are often produced as cheaply as possible under bad working conditions, with the workers not getting enough money to make ends meet, not to mention making a decent living.

The cartoon also conveys the message that if you are lucky to be born in a rich country you can have quite a carefree life and enjoy the positive effects of globalisation, whereas people in poorer countries don't profit from globalisation although they produce the goods for the world market.

(persönliche Stellungnahme)
I agree with the message of the cartoon as I have seen reports about the appalling working conditions in the big sweatshops of Asian companies where most multinationals like H & M produce their clothes. *(435 words)*

Part B

Bei dieser Aufgabe müssen Sie <u>einen</u> Aufsatz über ein vorgegebenes Thema schreiben, wobei Ihnen fünf verschiedene Materialien als Hilfestellung für den Inhalt zur Verfügung stehen. Von diesen <u>Materialien</u> müssen Sie <u>mindestens drei inhaltlich auswerten</u>. Sie können natürlich auch vier oder alle fünf Materialien verwenden und auch noch eigenes Wissen in Ihren Aufsatz einfließen lassen. Daher empfiehlt es sich, zunächst alle Materialien zu sichten und auf Englisch stichpunktartig zu notieren, um was es im jeweiligen Material geht, bevor Sie sich entscheiden, wie und in welcher Reihenfolge Sie die Materialien in den eigenen Aufsatz einbringen. Sie haben für diese Aufgabe 90 Minuten Zeit und können maximal 10 Inhaltspunkte und 20 Sprachpunkte bekommen. Achten Sie also besonders auch auf die Qualität Ihrer Sprache.
Die Textmenge für eine gute Leistung umfasst in der Regel 300 bis 400 Wörter.
Schreiben Sie eine Einleitung, bevor Sie im Hauptteil Informationen aus den Materialien einfließen lassen und am Ende die Ergebnisse zusammenfassen. Sie können auch mit einer persönlichen Stellungnahme abschließen, in der Sie Ihre eigene Meinung einbringen, diese erklären und mit einem Beispiel ausführen. Der Lösungsvorschlag ist etwas ausführlicher, da er alle fünf Materialien erhält.

Serious accidents involving young drivers are a burning issue. What can be done to limit the risks?

(Einleitung)
Often we read or hear about terrible accidents in which young people are involved. The risk of being injured or killed in an accident is twice as high for people between 17 and 24 years compared to those between 24 to 50 years of age. *(Material 3)* Many of the young people are severely injured or lose their lives. So the question arises what could be done to limit the number of serious accidents.

(Hauptteil)
Statistically, the main cause for accidents involving young people is speeding, which means driving too fast. Surprisingly, the number of accidents caused by driving under the influence of alcohol is relatively small, but it is still a problem. *(Material 2)* That is why there are campaigns to make young drivers aware of the dangers of speeding and drunk driving. There are ads, for example, that show in a drastic way that the faster you drive the higher the risk to cause a fatal accident. *(Material 4)* An ad with the caption "Who's taking you home tonight" shows three options for young people to get home after a night out: a police car, an ambulance or a taxi. The message is that "Drinking and driving wrecks lives", which means that if you drink and drive you can easily have an accident and you and/or your passengers are not taken home but to the hospital in an ambulance. You can also be taken to the police when you are caught while driving under the influence of alcohol. The best way to get home when you have drunk alcohol is to get a taxi. *(Material 1)*
All in all, however, measures to reduce the numbers of accidents haven't been effective so far. But new technical devices like EPS, which can correct driving mistakes, will be included in every new car from 2014 onwards. However, according to the statistics of insurance companies, supervised driving at the age of 17 has already enhanced driving security. *(Material 3)* Another effective way to promote safe driving is a programme by the Teenager Road Accident Group (TRAG). They visit schools and show a film to older pupils about the consequences of driving. In the film, policemen, ambulance officers, firefighters and survivors of accidents tell about their experiences. Their shocking reports are supposed to make the pupils aware of what could happen if they drive too fast or if they drink and drive. *(Material 5)*

(Zusammenfassung)
To sum up it can be said that there are many campaigns and measures to reduce the number of serious accidents, and we can only hope that these will reach young drivers and make them drive more carefully.

(438 words)

Fachhochschulreife Englisch (Berufskolleg Baden-Württemberg)
Hörverstehenstest 2013

Aufgabe 1: Satzergänzungen *(8 VP)*

Elizabeth Aldrigde vom Magazin *Teenage Consumer* befragt vier englische Jugendliche zum Thema „Jugendarbeitslosigkeit".

▶ Hören Sie aufmerksam zu und vervollständigen Sie auf Deutsch die unten stehenden Sätze. Entnehmen Sie den Aussagen je zwei Aspekte.

1	Linda begründet die hohe Zahl jugendlicher Arbeitsloser damit, dass ...
	(2 VP)
2	John bezweifelt, dass die unterschiedlich hohe Jugendarbeitslosigkeit auf zwei Ursachen zurückzuführen ist, nämlich ...
	(2 VP)
3	Laut Jill ist die Jugendarbeitslosigkeit in Ländern wie Deutschland und den Niederlanden geringer, weil ...
	(2 VP)
4	Die zwei Maßnahmen, die Michael vorschlägt, um jugendliche Langzeitarbeitslose zu unterstützen, sind ...
	(2 VP)

Aufgabe 2: Offene Fragen (7 VP)

Melissa Block vom Sender NPR News befragt für die Sendung *All things considered* einen Journalisten, der einen Fernsehbericht über die Bekämpfung von Armut in den USA gemacht hat.

▶ Hören Sie aufmerksam zu und beantworten Sie die Fragen auf Deutsch in verständlichen Stichworten.

Wortangaben:
non-profit making organisation: gemeinnützige Organisation, die von Spenden lebt
warehouse: Lagerhaus
start-up support: Unterstützung zur Existenzgründung

1	Wie unterstützt die Organisation *Opportunity House* einkommensschwache Familien? (2 Nennungen)	
		(1 VP)
2	Warum steht die Hilfsorganisation *Opportunity House* zunehmend unter Druck? (2 Gründe)	
		(2 VP)
3	Weshalb bedauert Präsident Fiume die Entlassungen seiner langjährigen Mitarbeiter? (1 Grund)	
		(1 VP)
4	Wie hilft die *St. Vincent Society* einkommensschwachen Mitbürgern? (2 Beispiele)	
		(1 VP)
5	Welche Veränderungen sind geplant, damit die Organisation *Opportunity House* in Zukunft überleben kann? (2 Nennungen)	
		(2 VP)

Aufgabe 3: Mediation (10 VP)

Christine Martin vom englischen Radiosender *Channel4U* spricht in ihrer Sendung „Technology Report" mit Jim Barry über neue Tablet-PCs.
Ihre Freundin Ina möchte sich einen Tablet-PC kaufen. Raten Sie ihr aufgrund des gehörten Interviews zum Kauf eines iPads, indem Sie ihr die Vorteile des Geräts im Vergleich zu Amazons *Kindle Fire* nennen. Formulieren Sie Ihre Antwort auf Deutsch in Form einer E-Mail in einem zusammenhängenden Text.

Lösungsvorschläge

Aufgabe 1: Satzergänzungen

Transcript:

LINDA (1): I think it's a fact that in GB you can link the causes of youth unemployment to problems with the British education system. On the one hand, the system does not ensure that the young people leave school as fully-formed "job-ready" employees. That's the way it should be. On the other hand, the UK's education system is to blame that it is not producing enough young people who are sufficiently prepared for the world of work.

JOHN (2): To me it's a big surprise that there are such huge differences in levels of youth unemployment across Europe. Are the work skills of young people in Germany or the Netherlands, where youth unemployment stands at less than 10 %, significantly stronger than in the UK, where it pushes towards 22 %? Or is it a problem of culture in countries like Greece and Spain that is the reason for youth unemployment rates of 50 %? It's really hard to believe that.

JILL (3): To my mind, we need to step back and look at how the education systems in the European countries help or don't help young people in entering the world of work. In countries with low levels of youth unemployment, there is a great support for young people to make the switch from school to work. In Germany and the Netherlands, apprenticeships and other vocational qualifications provide structured ways into skilled work, opening up strong career and earning prospects for young people who do not go to university.

MICHAEL (4): If you ask me, youth unemployment is the worst thing I have ever experienced. I was unemployed for some time. That was hard. Being unemployed for longer periods of time can have a lasting impact on young people's employment and earning prospects. If young people who have been out of work for more than a year were given a job guarantee, a generation of young people would not be "lost" to poverty and unemployment. Additionally, the introduction of some unemployment pay is absolutely necessary. *(325 words)*

Bei dieser Aufgabe sollen Sie die vorgegebenen Sätze auf Deutsch vervollständigen. Den Text hören Sie dabei zweimal. Lesen Sie sich die Aufgabenstellung, d. h. die vier unvollständigen Sätze, genau durch, bevor Sie sich die Kommentare der englischen Jugendlichen anhören. Während des Hörens dürfen Sie sich Notizen machen. Notieren Sie sich in Stichpunkten die Informationen, die zur Vervollständigung der Sätze wichtig sein können. Die Sprechgeschwindigkeit ist relativ schnell, sodass nicht viel Zeit zum Nachdenken besteht.

Sie erhalten für diese Aufgabe insgesamt 8 Punkte. Pro Kommentar müssen Sie je zwei Aspekte bzw. Gesichtspunkte nennen. Für jede richtige Information erhalten Sie einen Verrechnungspunkt. Die vorgegebene Lösung enthält manchmal verschiedene Lösungsvarianten.

Nutzen Sie zum Vervollständigen der Sätze vor allem die Pause zwischen dem ersten und zweiten Vorspielen sowie nach dem zweiten Vorspielen des Textes, weil Sie in dieser Zeit keine Informationen versäumen. Versuchen Sie während des Hörens bereits gezielt die zum jeweiligen Satz passenden Informationen in Stichpunkten zu notieren.

Linda (1)	Linda begründet die hohe Zahl jugendlicher Arbeitsloser damit, dass … • die Jugendarbeitslosigkeit mit den Problemen des britischen Bildungssystems in Verbindung steht. • das Schulsystem nicht sicherstellt, dass die Jugendlichen als voll ausgebildete, arbeitsbereite Arbeitnehmer die Schule verlassen. / das Bildungssystem nicht genug junge Leute ausreichend auf die Arbeitswelt vorbereitet.
John (2)	John bezweifelt, dass die unterschiedlich hohe Jugendarbeitslosigkeit auf zwei Ursachen zurückzuführen ist, nämlich … • auf die (vermeintlich) besseren beruflichen Fähigkeiten z. B. der Deutschen und der Niederländer • sowie auf ein kulturelles Problem z. B. in Griechenland und Spanien, wo die Jugendarbeitslosigkeit sehr hoch ist.
Jill (3)	Laut Jill ist die Jugendarbeitslosigkeit in Ländern wie Deutschland und den Niederlanden geringer, weil … • die Jugendlichen dort besser unterstützt werden, um den Wechsel von der Schule in die Berufswelt zu schaffen./ es dort Ausbildungsberufe und andere Möglichkeiten der beruflichen Ausbildung gibt. • sich dort auch gute Karriere- und Verdienstaussichten für junge Leute eröffnen, die nicht auf die Universität gehen.
Michael (4)	Die zwei Maßnahmen, die Michael vorschlägt, um jugendliche Langzeitarbeitslose zu unterstützen, sind … • eine Beschäftigungsgarantie für Jugendliche, die über ein Jahr arbeitslos sind • sowie die Einführung von Arbeitslosengeld.

Aufgabe 2: Offene Fragen

Transcript:

MELISSA BLOCK: Hello, and good afternoon. My name is Melissa Block. As we continue our series on poverty this week, we return to Reading, Pennsylvania, which has been labeled the poorest city in America. People there are really suffering. Opportunity House is a non-profit organization whose aim is to help. It provides low-income families in Reading with day care for kids, housing and emergency shelter. Unfortunately, Opportunity House itself is also in trouble. With me on today's show is Andrew Jacobs, who did a television report on the activities of Opportunity House. Andrew, could you please describe the situation in Reading.

ANDREW JACOBS: Hello Melissa. Well, many families in Reading rely on Opportunity House, people like Tracy Boggs, for example, a single mother of two. She lost her full-time job a few years ago. Now she is trying to survive by cleaning stores. Opportunity House helps her with housing and day care. She says that if they weren't there, she wouldn't know what to do. She would feel kind of lost.

MELISSA BLOCK: But is Opportunity House itself also feeling the increasing pressure, just like Tracy?

ANDREW JACOBS: Yes, Pennsylvania has cut its budget, and as a non-profit group it now gets less money to provide round-the-clock child care for parents who might otherwise not be able to work. To make matters worse, the number of volunteers has fallen constantly.

MELISSA BLOCK: How did the management of Opportunity House react?

ANDREW JACOBS: Well, Mr. Fiume, who is the president of the organization, recently had to do something he hoped he'd never have to do: he had to dismiss 20 percent of his staff. For Mr. Fiume this was a terrible experience because, as low-wage workers, they will have a hard time finding other jobs. He feels especially sorry for them since these people had worked for Opportunity House for quite a number of years.

MELISSA BLOCK: Let's talk about the services Opportunity House had to cut.

ANDREW JACOBS: Well, they had to stop offering day care on Sundays, all to make up for a $335,000 deficit. Donations and volunteers can fill some of the gaps but not nearly enough. So, like many non-profit organizations they've desperately been looking elsewhere for help.

MELISSA BLOCK: In your report, you described efforts to keep services for the poor by collecting junk or waste. How exactly does that work?

ANDREW JACOBS: Well, at the moment Mr. Terry Brown is talking to Opportunity House and Reading officials about how they might get into the trash recycling business. Brown's full-time job is director of the St. Vincent Society in Oregon. It's a non-profit-making organization that provides a wide range of services such as meals on wheels for tens of thousands of low-income residents. It's also the largest bicycle recycler in the country, providing jobs for many workers. With two factories in Oregon, Brown recycles about 17,500 bicycles a year. And now Opportunity House is interested in doing the same in Reading. Mr. Fiume thinks that this could bring jobs – meaningful jobs – that offer a proper, not a minimum wage, of maybe $ 12 or 13 an hour, including health benefits.

MELISSA BLOCK: I think that would make a great difference in a city that's been losing jobs for years. And it could make Opportunity House less dependent on donations and government funds.

ANDREW JACOBS: That's right. If you want to survive as a non-profit-making organization, and if you want to continue to meet the needs of people who are most in need of support, then you have to change things. Opportunity House has to find a warehouse, technical equipment and start-up support. For a non-profit-making organization that has been used to helping the poor instead of running a business, it's a whole new world.

MELISSA BLOCK: Thank you Andrew for this really interesting interview. *(639 words)*

adapted from: Pam Fessler: Cycle Of Poverty Hard To Break In Poorest U.S. City. In: NPR.org July 10, 2012.

Bei dieser Aufgabe sollen Sie die unten stehenden fünf Fragen in ganzen Sätzen oder in verständlichen Stichworten auf Deutsch beantworten. Sie hören das Interview insgesamt zweimal. Während des Hörens dürfen Sie sich Notizen machen. Sie erhalten für diese Aufgabe insgesamt 7 Punkte. Für jede richtige Antwort erhalten Sie einen Punkt, bei Frage 2 und 5 jeweils zwei Punkte. Werden bei einer 1-Punkt-Frage zwei Antworten verlangt, erhält man für jede richtige Antwort 0,5 Punkte. In den folgenden Lösungen sind manchmal auch mehr Lösungen als nötig angegeben.

Notieren Sie sich in Stichpunkten die Informationen, die zur Beantwortung der Fragen wichtig sein können. Zeit zum Nachdenken besteht während des Interviews nicht, da Sie sonst weitere Informationen verpassen. Nutzen Sie wiederum die Pausen zwischen dem ersten und zweiten Anhören der Kurzberichte sowie nach dem zweiten Anhören zum Verfassen der Antworten.

1	Wie unterstützt die Organisation *Opportunity House* einkommensschwache Familien? **Sie hilft, indem sie …** • **eine Tagesbetreuung für Kinder,** • **Wohnungen / Wohnraum und** • **Notunterkünfte bereitstellt.**
2	Warum steht die Hilfsorganisation *Opportunity House* zunehmend unter Druck? • **Sie erhält weniger Geld, weil der Bundesstaat Pennsylvania die Zuschüsse gekürzt hat.** • **Die Zahl der freiwilligen Helfer nimmt immer mehr ab.**

3	Weshalb bedauert Präsident Fiume die Entlassungen seiner langjährigen Mitarbeiter?
	• Als Geringverdiener werden sie es schwer haben, eine andere Arbeit zu finden.
	• Es tut ihm besonders leid, weil sie viele Jahre für die Organisation gearbeitet haben.
4	Wie hilft die *St. Vincent Society* einkommensschwachen Mitbürgern?
	• Sie bietet Essen auf Rädern für zehntausende Bürger an.
	• Sie recycelt Fahrräder und schafft somit Arbeitsplätze.
5	Welche Veränderungen sind geplant, damit die Organisation *Opportunity House* in Zukunft überleben kann?
	• Sie muss ein Lagerhaus/eine Lagerfläche finden.
	• Sie muss sich technische Ausrüstung besorgen.
	• Sie braucht (finanzielle) Unterstützung für die Existenzgründung.

Aufgabe 3: Mediation

Transcript:

CHRISTINE: This is the *Channel4U* Technology Report. I'm Christine Martin. Amazon has launched a new Kindle, the Kindle Fire, which is no longer just an e-reader. The new Kindle is, in actual fact, a tablet which offers many possibilities which customers usually connect with Apple's iPad. So now there's plenty of debate and confusion about which to buy – a Kindle Fire or an iPad. So, let's ask Jim Barry, the spokesman for the Consumer Electronics Association, what he would buy if we gave him $ 500.

JIM: Well, Christine, my first instinct would be to choose the new Kindle Fire tablet. The 7-inch tablet is a handy, comfortable size, whereas the 10-inch screen of the iPad is quite difficult to read books with and a little bit too big to travel with if you're also taking along a laptop. And, last but not least, $ 199 is a fantastic price.

CHRISTINE: True, the iPad for example costs $ 499 to $ 829, but the iPad beats the Kindle Fire on most levels, don't you think?

JIM: Well, not necessarily, it all depends on what you want to do with it. On the whole, productivity is probably the biggest difference between the two. Its small screen makes the Kindle unsuitable for many of the tasks people usually want to do on a tablet, like writing e-mails or editing photos. All this is no problem with an iPad. We all know that the capabilities of the iPad are fantastic. As I already said, the screen is bigger, which means you can do much more with it. I think it's one of the best tools I've found because its display is big enough to look at together with other people.

CHRISTINE: But what can the Kindle Fire be used for?

JIM: I must say the Kindle Fire can handle about 80 % of what I want to do on an iPad for 40 % of the price. Mainly, it is a device for reading books and watching videos and can also be used for e-commerce. That's why Amazon is getting involved in this business. The Kindle Fire does a good job accessing all of Amazon's products (books, movies, TV shows, newspapers, and magazines etc.) and downloading and displaying them quickly.

CHRISTINE: However, other than that, the Kindle Fire doesn't offer any apps worth mentioning, does it?

JIM: No, you're right. In contrast, the iPad offers multiple software options. Think of the wide range of apps that are available on the market, such as games and quick links to many web pages.

CHRISTINE: Does the iPad have any other advantages?

JIM: Well, the iPad has a higher storage capacity compared with the Kindle Fire. You can store more movies, music, and pictures on the Apple device. Some people might also miss a camera on the Kindle Fire, which is a standard feature of the iPad.

CHRISTINE: So, Jim, to sum up, which would you say is the best buy?

JIM: Well, it all depends on what you want your tablet to do and how much you want to pay. While the iPad is, without a doubt, the best performing and the most multifunctional tablet on the market, the Kindle Fire is a very solid tablet for the price.

CHRISTINE: Thank you Jim. It's been a pleasure having you here today.

JIM: Thank you, Christine, it's been my pleasure.

(559 words)

Bei dieser Aufgabe sollen Sie einer Freundin zum Kauf eines iPads raten, indem Sie ihr die Vorteile des Geräts im Vergleich zu Amazons Kindle Fire nennen. Die Antwort muss in der Form einer E-Mail als zusammenhängender Text verfasst werden.

Sie können sich während des Hörens und in den Hörpausen bereits die Vorteile des iPads in Stichpunkten notieren.

Checkliste für die E-Mail
- Hauptunterschied: Leistungsfähigkeit

Vorteile des iPads:
- ausreichend großer Bildschirm ≠ Kindle Fire: ungeeignet für E-Mails, Fotos
- vielseitiger nutzbar
- große Anzahl von lohnenswerten Apps ≠ Kindle Fire
- unzählige Softwareanwendungen ≠ Kindle Fire
- größere Speicherkapazität für Musik, Filme und Bilder
- Kamera ≠ Kindle Fire
- leistungsfähigstes und multifunktionalstes Tablet

E-Mail (Lösungsbeispiel):

Liebe Ina,

wie ich weiß, willst du dir ein Tablet kaufen und bist dir nicht sicher, ob du einen Kindle Fire von Amazon oder ein iPad von Apple kaufen sollst.

Ich habe im Radio ein Interview gehört, in dem es um den Vergleich zwischen den beiden Geräten ging. Ich würde dir zum Kauf des iPads raten, obwohl es das viel teurere Gerät ist.

Seine Leistungsfähigkeit und die vielen Anwendungsmöglichkeiten sprechen für das iPad. Der kleinere Bildschirm des Kindle macht das Gerät zwar handlicher, es ist aber nicht geeignet, um E-Mails zu schreiben oder Bilder zu bearbeiten. Das ist auf dem iPad kein Problem.

Außerdem bietet das iPad viel mehr Apps und es ist vielseitiger nutzbar als der Kindle Fire, mit dem man höchstens einen guten Zugang zu den Amazon-Produkten hat.

Der Kindle hat auch viel weniger Speicherkapazität. Er hat nicht einmal eine Kamera, die beim iPad zur Standardausstattung gehört.

Das iPad ist das leistungsfähigste und vielseitigste Gerät auf dem Markt. Es ist meiner Meinung nach das beste Gerät.

Ich hoffe diese Fakten haben dich überzeugt und helfen dir bei deiner Entscheidung.

Liebe Grüße

Dein/Deine ...

Fachhochschulreife Englisch (Berufskolleg Baden-Württemberg)
Schriftliche Hauptprüfung 2013

Aufgabe 1 – Mediation *(10 VP)*

Aufgabenstellung

Als Mitglied der Schülerzeitung Ihrer Schule sollen Sie einen Artikel zu der Themenreihe „Unsere Erde: der Einfluss des Menschen auf die Umwelt" verfassen. Ihr aktueller Beitrag soll sich mit dem Thema „Lärm macht uns Menschen krank – wie, warum und was können wir dagegen tun?" beschäftigen.

▶ Entnehmen Sie dem vorliegenden Zeitungsartikel die entsprechenden Informationen.
▶ Formulieren Sie ganze deutsche Sätze.

Noise pollution: why the silence?

No other pollutant ruins nearly as many lives in Britain and other industrialised countries as noise – yet few receive so little public attention. Green pressure groups are almost silent about it. Virtually no governments, anywhere in the world, seem to be prepared to tackle the problem.

5   Yet two thirds of Europeans – 450 million people – are exposed every day to noise levels that the World Health Organisation (WHO) says are unacceptable.

The most annoying noises come from machines. Particularly disturbing – as a new book by one of Britain's leading environmental campaigners, John Stewart, points out – is the low-frequency noise produced by aircraft, wind turbines and many
10 household appliances such as washing machines and air conditioners. Additionally, more people say they hate piped music in shops, restaurants and public buildings more than they like it.

As a consequence, one in every eight American youngsters, aged 6 to 19, has been found to have noise-related hearing loss, while Stewart predicts: "Within a dec-
15 ade or two, the iPod in the ear could be replaced with the hearing aid." Learning can be affected. A study in a Manhattan school found that children in classrooms beside a busy train track learned how to read 11 months later than their counterparts on the quiet side of the building. When measures were taken to reduce the noise, they caught up.

20 Noise also raises blood pressure and increases heart rates, especially at night, leading to heart and other diseases, as well as affecting sleep. The WHO calculated this year that Europeans collectively lose at least a million years of healthy living as a result.

Wildlife, which relies on sound to communicate, is affected, too. It's most obvi-
25 ous in the oceans, where underwater noise is estimated to have doubled each decade over the past 50 years – shipping has grown, oil and gas prospectors use loud blasts

from "airguns" to scan the sea bed, and ships increasingly rely on sonar. Whole populations of whales and dolphins are potentially threatened, and the amount of fish caught has fallen.

Many of the solutions are known: traffic noise could be cut by 70 per cent; shipping could be made much quieter; good insulation in homes could reduce neighbour noise; and piped music could be simply turned off.

In Britain, political interest has faded. The government repeatedly promised to publish a national noise strategy, but never did so. And the EU's record is little better: it has neither carried out a study on the impacts of noise nor set targets for its reduction – as it has with air pollution.

One way or another, it is time to make a lot more noise about noise.   *(448 words)*

Abridged and adapted from: © Lean Geoffrey, in: The Telegraph

Aufgabe 2 – Leseverstehen: Beurteilen von Aussagen zum Text *(10 VP)*

Gangless in Glasgow

When he was 12, William Palmer joined a gang without even realizing it. He was just hanging out with his big brother and their friends in their Easterhouse neighbourhood in Glasgow. At first, he stood and watched as his friends defended their 200 m² territory from rivals. Lining up like soldiers, someone, usually drunk, started the fight. By the time he was 20, Palmer was selling drugs – mostly ecstasy – to younger kids in his neighbourhood. Now 29, Palmer regards himself lucky to have survived his youth. Palmer was in prison for two years after attacking a rival. Today he looks after kids at risk of joining gangs, even though the charity for which he works still has to carefully smuggle him through enemy lines – five years after he left his gang. He is also wanted by the Glasgow police, but in a good way. They regularly ask Palmer to talk with new police officers about how to get in contact with gang members. This swapping of roles amuses him. "We used to phone them up just to play with them so we could get them to chase us," he says of the police, "Now they're phoning me up for advice."

As London and other English cities experienced riots for several days in August 2011, Glasgow, once a centre of gang violence, remained remarkably peaceful. If the riots had happened five years ago, there would have been a good chance that gangs in the city and in the surrounding region would have been as violent as their southern counterparts. Instead, as Britain's politicians and police chiefs analyse what went so terribly wrong in the capital, they're asking, "Can Glasgow's lessons be applied to London?" Prime Minister David Cameron thinks they can. "I want us to use the record of success against gangs by the police in Scotland who have done this by engaging the police, the voluntary sector and the local government," he told Parliament after the riots. "I want this to be a national priority." Glasgow suffers from the greatest economic differences in Western Europe. It also has a hard-earned reputation for violence and criminality. But only in 2004, when a U.N. study showed that Glasgow had the highest murder rate in Western Europe local police realized this fact. Then a police official started the police department's violence-reduction unit (VRU) in 2005 which co-ordinated the efforts of existing charities, the courts and the police to create a broader approach to treating youths. The effort, funded by the city council and the Scottish parliament, spent millions of pounds on programs starting in kindergarten and focused on self-esteem and zero-tolerance. In one of the projects, kids and their mothers are taught to bond, to play, to enjoy each other. The programs have had astonishing results. Violent crime has decreased by 49.2 % in the past two years. Although Glasgow still has the fifth highest murder rate in Western Europe, it is still much lower than that of comparable U.S. cities.

Not all the programs that have worked in Glasgow can be applied to London: the two cities differ in many important aspects. Scotland's gang members, for example, are almost all white, so police there don't have to deal with ethnic and racial tensions.

Even so, English police chiefs believe they can learn from their Glaswegian counterparts, who borrowed policing tactics that worked in US cities such as Boston and New York. The main point: never stop communicating with youngsters, especially with those who are already in trouble. *(583 words)*

Abridged and adapted from: Jay Newton-Small: Gangless in Glasgow: The City Famed for Youth Violence Is Keeping the Kids Clean. In: TIME Magazine, October 1st, 2011

Aufgabenstellung
- Entscheiden Sie, ob die folgenden Aussagen zum Text „Gangless in Glasgow" richtig oder falsch sind, und begründen Sie Ihre Entscheidung.
- Schreiben Sie Ihre Antworten auf Deutsch in ganzen Sätzen auf separates Prüfungspapier.

1. In his early youth William and his gang were protecting their area against competitors.
2. When he was older, he became involved in crime.
3. Today he still has problems with the police.
4. In the period of gang violence in summer 2011 Glasgow was heavily affected.
5. Prime Minister Cameron thinks that London can learn from Glasgow.
6. For a long time Glasgow wasn't aware of leading the crime statistics in Western Europe.
7. The newly-founded VRU launched a campaign to reduce youth crime.
8. Since the campaign against crime was introduced Glasgow has no longer been confronted with a high rate of serious crimes.
9. London police has been able to use the Scottish program completely.
10. The US police have copied the strategy of the Glasgow police.

Aufgabe 3 – Textproduktion: Bildvorlage mit Bezug zum Text von Aufgabe 2

(10 VP: 4 VP Inh./6 VP Spr.)

© Stacy Curtis/The Times of Northwest Indiana

Aufgabenstellung
- First describe the picture.
- Then analyze its meaning with reference to the text "Gangless in Glasgow".
- Use your own words.

Aufgabe 4 – Textproduktion

Choose between Part A **or** Part B.

Part A

Composition 1 *(15 VP: 5 VP Inh. / 10 VP Spr.)*

Facebook parties have become more and more trendy.
Private party-throwers and party goers spread an invitation as a "public event", maybe on purpose or by accident and thus cause chaos.
What are reasons for organizing parties via Facebook and what are possible consequences?

Composition 2 *(15 VP: 5 VP Inh. / 10 VP Spr.)*

Describe the cartoon and analyze its message.

Londons Times Cartoons. Artist: David Sullivan. Rick London/Writer Concepts

Part B

Textproduktion: Materialgestützter Aufsatz *(30 VP: 10 VP Inh. / 20 VP Spr.)*

980 million people worldwide went on holiday in 2011. Some consider this enormous travel activity a huge problem, others see benefits in travelling. What do you think?

Write a composition about the topic.

- ▶ Use the information of at least three of the given materials.
- ▶ Name which ones you are using.
- ▶ Make use of your own ideas.
- ▶ Do not write three separate compositions but one covering all the materials chosen.

Material 1

Haupturlauberströme 2010 – Reiseziele deutscher Touristen 2010

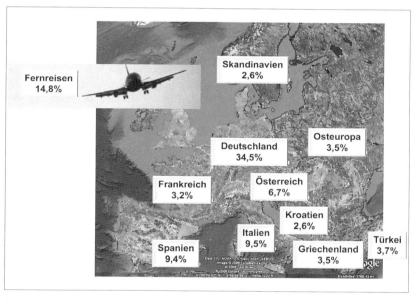

© ADAC Reise-Monitor 2010

Material 2

1. "Tourism is not only an important economic activity, it is also about the millions of conversations and interactions that take place every day as visitors and host communities come together. And it is because tourism means exchanging ideas and beliefs that it can be one of the most effective tools to promote mutual understanding, tolerance and peace."
   © *Taleb Rifai, Secretary-General of the UNWTO (World Tourism Organisation der UN)*

2. "Real is when your rusty bus breaks down somewhere in Tibet and you have to fix it quickly or freeze to death. Real is learning to track a family of bears across magnificent landscapes in Central Sweden or climbing a beautiful (and not too dangerous) mountain or just cycling down an English country lane ..."
   © *Stephen Keeler, in: BBC Learning English, Column 24 Sept 2007*

Material 3

Aus: Das kleine ABC des sanften Tourismus – Ratgeber für umweltbewusstes Reisen

Der wachsende Tourismus bringt aber auch vielfältige Probleme mit sich. Suchen zu viele Menschen am gleichen Ort Ruhe und Natur, zerstören sie häufig, was sie suchen. Naturparadiese verlieren oft ihre Attraktivität bzw. Existenzgrundlage, wenn sie vorwiegend auf Masse statt auf Klasse setzen. Ein Problem unter mehreren, das der Natur zusetzt, ist z. B. die unzureichende Wasserversorgung.

Es muss eine Umkehr vom unkontrollierten Massentourismus hin zum „verantwortungsvollen Tourismus" erfolgen. Die Erhaltung des ökologischen Reichtums einer Region bildet die Grundlage für deren touristische Zukunft. Zahlreiche Wintersportorte sind Beispiele dafür, welche schädigenden Auswirkungen der Massentourismus verursachen kann, denn viele der früher intakten Naturgebiete sind heute dort zerstört. Immer mehr drängt der Tourismus auf der Suche nach neuen attraktiven Gebieten in die letzten Naturareale vor. Meist in „strukturschwachen" Gebieten gelegen, erhoffen sich die Bewohner einen wirtschaftlichen Aufschwung für die Region. Naturschutz spielt angesichts der wirtschaftlichen Probleme nur eine untergeordnete Rolle. Dadurch entsteht eine einseitige Abhängigkeit, da bei zu viel Tourismus Urlauber abgestoßen werden bzw. Umweltprobleme auftauchen, die den Urlaub beeinträchtigen. Beides führt zum Rückgang der Gästezahlen und somit zu sinkenden Einkommen.

© *Gläser, Christian: Das kleine ABC des sanften Tourismus. Ratgeber für umweltbewusstes Reisen. AUbE Umweltakademie, Bielefeld 2009, S. 6f.*

Material 4

© Klaus Pitter/Wien

Material 5

Getting to know the Culture

Responsible travel involves more than just being a passive observer. Try to get to know the culture you are visiting, both for your own personal enrichment and to avoid accidentally insulting those around you with different beliefs and views.

A good way to get to know a culture better is to try and learn some of its language. A simple 'hello' and 'thank you' can go a long way to breaking down barriers.

Also take note of the local ways of dressing. In many cultures women are required to cover up from top to toe. As a general rule, dressing smartly shows more respect.

A rich westerner who dresses sloppily in dirty clothes can be considered as insulting in the face of a poorer tribe in Africa, which despite their poverty make an effort to appear smart. Before taking pictures, ask first, and do not treat people as objects. A township in Soweto, South Africa may be a million miles from your home, but poverty is poverty and making those 'gritty and real' pictures of people begging on the street just for your photo album isn't really a good idea.

http://www.responsible-travel.org

Lösungsvorschläge

Aufgabe 1 – Mediation

Bei dieser Aufgabe sollen Sie als Mitglied der Schülerzeitung einen Artikel verfassen, der sich mit den schädlichen Auswirkungen des Lärms auf Mensch und Tier befasst. Die Grundlage für Ihren Artikel bildet der Ihnen vorliegende englische Text. Achten Sie darauf, dass Ihre Lösung in jedem Fall ein Zeitungsartikel ist, der eine Überschrift haben muss und oft auch einen Untertitel hat. Ist Ihre Lösung kein Zeitungsartikel, erhalten Sie keine Punkte, weil Sie die gestellte Aufgabe nicht gelöst haben. Sie dürfen den englischen Text allerdings auch nicht einfach übersetzen, da eine reine Übersetzung ebenfalls mit null Punkten bewertet wird. Gefordert ist hier eine Mediation – in diesem Fall eine sinngemäße Zusammenfassung der wesentlichen Inhalte auf Deutsch. Dabei müssen Sie die wichtigsten Inhaltspunkte des Textes, in der Regel sind es etwa 10 Punkte, in eigenen Worten und in gut verständlichem Deutsch wiedergeben. Erstellen Sie einen zusammenhängenden Text und übersetzen Sie nicht einfach 10 Sätze aus der Vorlage. Der englische Text bietet Ihnen die Ideen und Fakten, die Sie sinnvoll in Ihren Artikel einbauen sollen.

Insgesamt gibt es 10 Verrechnungspunkte (VP) für diese Aufgabe, wobei Inhalts- und Sprachpunkte gemeinsam gewertet werden, d. h., es gibt keine getrennte Wertung von Inhalts- und Sprachpunkten.

Ihren Artikel sollten Sie folgendermaßen strukturieren:
- *Überschrift, evtl. mit Untertitel*
- *Einleitungssatz, der zu den inhaltlichen Informationen hinführt*
- *Hauptteil mit passenden Informationen zum Thema aus dem Zeitungsartikel*
- *Abschlusssatz: an die Adressaten gerichteter Appell, oder: Fazit als Zusammenfassung*

(Überschrift)
Lärm macht uns Menschen krank – wie, warum und was können wir dagegen tun?

(Untertitel)
Aus der Themenreihe „Unsere Erde: der Einfluss der Menschen auf die Umwelt"

(Einleitungssatz)
Obwohl Lärmbelästigung das Leben der Menschen in den Industrieländern stark beeinträchtigt, findet dieses Problem in der Öffentlichkeit kaum Beachtung. Deshalb befassen wir uns heute in unserer Themenreihe mit diesem vernachlässigten Thema.

(Inhalte des Artikels)
Etwa zwei Drittel aller Europäer sind täglich einer hohen Lärmbelastung ausgesetzt, was laut Weltgesundheitsorganisation (WHO) nicht mehr vertretbar ist.
Was sind die Ursachen und wie sieht die alltägliche Lärmbelastung aus?
Die schlimmsten Geräusche werden von Maschinen erzeugt, wobei besonders der Lärm von Flugzeugen, Windkrafträdern und Haushaltsgeräten wie Waschmaschinen und Klimaanlagen störend ist. Die meisten Leute empfinden zudem die Musikberieselung in Kaufhäusern, Restaurants und öffentlichen Gebäuden als nervend.

Was sind die Folgen der alltäglichen Lärmbelastung?
Eine Folge davon ist, dass z. B. Jugendliche immer schlechter hören. Jeder achte amerikanische Jugendliche erleidet einen so großen Hörverlust, dass irgendwann ein Hörgerät benötigt werden wird.
Auch das Lernen wird durch Lärm negativ beeinflusst, wie eine amerikanische Studie belegt. An einer Schule in Manhattan benötigten Kinder in einem Klassenzimmer, das an eine Eisenbahnlinie angrenzt, 11 Monate länger, um das Lesen zu lernen, als Kinder in einem ruhigeren Bereich des Gebäudes.
Außerdem erhöht der Lärm, besonders in der Nacht, Blutdruck und Herzfrequenz. Dies kann zu Herz- und Kreislauferkrankungen führen und sich auf den Schlaf auswirken.
Wildtiere, die sich mithilfe des Klangs untereinander verständigen, sind ebenfalls betroffen. Beispielsweise ist der Geräuschpegel im Meer durch Öl- und Gasbohrungen sowie den Schiffsverkehr so sehr gestiegen, dass Wale und Delfine bedroht sind und der Fischbestand abgenommen hat.
Wie könnte man das Lärmproblem lösen?
Der Verkehrslärm könnte um 70 % reduziert werden, die durch die Schifffahrt verursachten Geräusche könnten gedämpft und der Nachbarschaftslärm könnte durch bessere Isolierung der Häuser verringert werden. Die Musikberieselung könnte man auch einfach ganz abschalten.
Und wieso passiert nichts?
Das politische Interesse an dem Thema hat abgenommen. So gibt es weder offizielle Untersuchungen über die Auswirkungen des Lärms noch Ziele für die Lärmreduzierung.
(Fazit/Appell)
Es ist nun wirklich an der Zeit, dass mehr Lärm um den Lärm gemacht wird!

Aufgabe 2 – Leseverstehen: Beurteilen von Aussagen zum Text

Hier müssen Sie entscheiden, ob die zum Text angegebenen 10 Aussagen richtig oder falsch sind. Die Aussagen sind in der Regel chronologisch geordnet. Markieren Sie im Text die zur Aussage passende Textstelle und vergleichen Sie die Textstelle mit der vorgegebenen Aussage. Treffen Sie dann Ihre Entscheidung und begründen Sie diese mit der sinngemäßen Wiedergabe der Textstelle auf Deutsch. Ohne die Begründung gibt es keinen Punkt, weil man sonst auch geraten haben könnte. Vergessen Sie bei Ihrer Begründung die Zeilenangabe nicht. Bei falscher Entscheidung, aber richtiger Begründung mit Zeilenangabe erhält man einen halben Punkt. Die Textstellen selbst müssen Sie jedoch nicht zitieren. Sie sind in dieser Lösung noch zusätzlich zur Veranschaulichung aufgeführt.

1. Die Aussage stimmt nicht, denn in Zeile 3 f. steht, dass William am Anfang abseits stand und beobachtete, wie seine Freunde ihr Gebiet gegen Rivalen verteidigten: *"At first he stood and watched as his friends defended their 200 m² territory from rivals."*

2. Das ist richtig, denn in Zeile 4 ff. steht, dass er mit 20 Jahren in der Nachbarschaft Drogen verkaufte: *"By the time he was 20, Palmer was selling drugs – mostly ecstasy – to younger kids in his neigbourhood."*

3. Die Aussage ist falsch. Heute bittet die Polizei ihn um Rat oder Hilfe, wenn es darum geht, Kontakt mit Gangmitgliedern aufzunehmen (siehe Z. 9 ff.): *"He is also wanted by the Glasgow police, but in a good way. They regularly ask Palmer to talk with new police officers about how to get in contact with gang members."; "Now they're phoning me up for advice."*

4. Die Aussage ist falsch, weil es in Glasgow, das einstmals eine Hochburg der Bandenkriminalität war, erstaunlich friedlich blieb (siehe Zeile 16): *"Glasgow, once a centre of gang violence, remained remarkably peaceful."*

5. Die Aussage ist richtig, denn Premierminister Cameron glaubt, dass die erfolgreiche Vorgehensweise der Polizei von Glasgow auch auf London übertragen werden kann (siehe Zeile 20 ff.): *"'Can Glasgow's lessons be applied to London?' Prime Minister David Cameron thinks they can. 'I want us to use the record of success against gangs by the police in Scotland ...'"*

6. Die Aussage ist richtig, denn erst als eine UN-Studie im Jahr 2004 zeigte, dass Glasgow die höchste Mordrate Westeuropas hatte, wurde diese Tatsache der Polizei vor Ort bewusst (siehe Zeile 26 ff.): *"But only in 2004, when a U.N. study showed that Glasgow had the highest murder rate in Western Europe local police realized this fact."*

7. Die Aussage trifft zu, denn in Z. 28 ff. steht, dass die VRU die Arbeit von Wohlfahrtsorganisationen, Gerichten und Polizei koordinierte: *"... the police department's violence-reduction unit (VRU) in 2005 which co-ordinated the efforts of existing charities, the courts and the police to create a broader approach to treating youths."*

8. Die Aussage ist falsch, denn Glasgow hat immer noch die fünfthöchste Mordrate in Westeuropa (siehe Z. 35): *"Although Glasgow still has the fifth highest murder rate in Western Europe ..."*

9. Die Aussage ist falsch. Nicht alle Programme konnten übernommen werden, da die beiden Großstädte sich in vielen wichtigen Aspekten unterscheiden (siehe Z. 37 f.): *"Not all the programs that have worked in Glasgow can be applied to London: the two cities differ in many important aspects."*

10. Die Aussage ist falsch. Vielmehr hat die Polizei von Glasgow Polizeistrategien, die in den USA funktionierten, übernommen (siehe Z. 40 ff.): *"English police chiefs believe they can learn from their Glaswegian counterparts, who borrowed policing tactics that worked in US cities such as Boston and New York."*

Aufgabe 3 – Textproduktion: Bildvorlage mit Bezug zum Text von Aufgabe 2

Bei dieser Aufgabe sollen Sie das Bild zunächst allgemein und dann auch im Detail beschreiben. Danach sollen Sie die inhaltliche Verbindung des Bildes mit dem Text von Aufgabe 2 herausarbeiten. Schreiben Sie dabei in eigenen Worten und zitieren Sie nicht aus dem Text. Es wird von Ihnen keine Einleitung und am Ende auch keine eigene Stellungnahme erwartet.
Sie erhalten 4 Verrechnungspunkte (VP) für den Inhalt, das sind die Bildbeschreibung und die Bildanalyse (Verbindung Bild und Text), und 6 VP für die Sprache bzw. deren Qualität.

The cartoon shows a scene in the street. A mother and a father are on the left hand side of the picture. They are well-dressed and they look rather conservative: the woman is wearing a dress and the man a suit and a bow tie. The man is also wearing a hat and he is smoking a pipe. He is leaning against a tree and seems to be rather relaxed. The parents are looking at their son who is standing in front of them. The woman is patting his head and her facial expression shows that she is happy with him. She says to her boy: "Don't ever join a gang ... Not that there are any of them in our fine town".

The boy in the picture is still quite small. On his cheeks there are some freckles. He is dressed like an ordinary pupil, wearing a casual pair of trousers and an oversized jumper. He must be on his way to school because he is holding a stack of books under one arm. The boy is looking towards a group of hooligans on his right.

On the right side of the picture there are three hooligans, who are depicted as weird and evil-looking. The gang member in front is moving his index finger as if to lure the boy to come over to them. He has the haircut of a punk and is wearing an oversized sleeveless shirt. On his left arm there is a tattoo and in his right earlobe there is an earring. The guy behind him has a skull on his shirt and a knife between his teeth. In his left hand he is holding a pistol. The tallest one of them is bending his body forward and is staring at the boy like a vulture watching his prey.

The problem the cartoon wants to illustrate is one of parents trying to protect their kids from evil, e. g. gangs, while their kids are in danger of becoming part of a gang as soon they are out of their parents' reach.

The link between the text and the picture is the danger of youngsters becoming part of gangs and organized crime. In the picture, the parents play down the situation by telling their son that there are no gangs in their town. In reality, however, as shown in the text, crime is a major problem, especially in big cites. If the parents in the picture keep on ignoring the danger, their son could one day become the member of a gang. This is what happened to William Palmer in the text. He was 12 when he joined a gang and gave up the chance of growing up like a normal boy.

In the text, the police finally took action when a study showed that Glasgow was the town with the highest murder rate in Western Europe. The parents in the cartoon will finally realize that there are gangs in their town, when their son becomes a member of one. Like the city of Glasgow in the text they would need to take action then – or should have done before. *(524 words)*

Aufgabe 4 – Textproduktion

Beim Verfassen Ihrer Texte können Ihnen die Redewendungen behilflich sein, die in den Hinweisen und Tipps aufgelistet sind.

Part A

Composition 1

Bei dieser Aufgabe können Sie bis zu 5 Punkte für den Inhalt und 10 Punkte für die Sprache erhalten. Achten Sie darauf, nicht nur mögliche Gründe, Partys über Facebook zu organisieren, aufzuführen, sondern auch die möglichen Folgen und Auswirkungen eines solchen (unfreiwillig) öffentlichen Events für die Betroffenen und die Allgemeinheit aufzuzeigen.
Führen Sie in einer Einleitung auf das Thema hin. Stellen Sie dann im Hauptteil die Gründe für die Organisation von Partys über Facebook den möglichen (negativen) Folgen gegenüber. Geben Sie auch konkrete Beispiele an und legen Sie zum Schluss Ihre eigene Meinung dar. Der folgende Text ist nur eine mögliche Lösung. Er ist etwas länger als die 200 bis 300 Wörter, die Ihr Text umfassen soll.

(Einleitung)
Every now and then you can read in the press about parties that had been organised through Facebook and went terribly out of hand, causing a lot of trouble to police and neighbours. So what are the reasons why Facebook is used to organize parties and what could be the consequences for the organizers and the public?

(Hauptteil: Gründe)
One reason for using Facebook to organize an event is that it is an easy and simple way of inviting your friends. It is much quicker than writing invitation cards or sending e-mails or text messages. You write one invitation and make it public to your Facebook friends with a click. As most young people are on Facebook, almost all the people you want to invite can be reached easily.
Another advantage of inviting people via Facebook is that you can invite a lot of people at the same time. Many youngsters think the more people come the better the party will be and if there are a lot of people celebrating the event it will be remembered for a very long time. There are also people who want to be at the centre of attention in order to feel like a star. Others do it out of curiosity, because they want to find out how many people will turn up at their party.

(Hauptteil: mögliche Folgen)
Sometimes, however, things go wrong and people forget to send the invitation only to their friends and so make it visible for everyone on Facebook. It can thus happen that many people they don't know feel invited and turn up, causing a lot of chaos and confusion. Then the party usually gets out of control and they need to call the police. In the end the house or flat and the area around it are left in a total mess. Neighbours could also be disturbed by the noise and the cars parking everywhere, as well as by the rubbish that is left in their gardens or in the street. Many party-goers also drink

too much alcohol and get violent or vandalise a place so that there is a lot of damage in the end. If they made the party public on Facebook, it can be very expensive for the organizers to pay for the police operation and the damages.

(Abschluss mit persönlicher Stellungnahme)
To sum up, I can say you should think twice before organizing a party via Facebook as things can get out of control if the party is made public either on purpose or by accident. So you should make sure that the invitation can only be seen by your friends.

(429 words)

Composition 2

Bei dieser Aufgabe sollen Sie nach einer Einleitung das Thema sowie das dargestellte Problem benennen. Falls dies für die Analyse von Belang ist, können Sie auch den Autor des Cartoons und den Ort seiner Veröffentlichung angeben.
Im Hauptteil sollen Sie sowohl das Bild beschreiben als auch dessen Funktion oder Botschaft herausarbeiten. Die Bildbeschreibung und Analyse sollten Sie mit einer persönlichen Stellungnahme abschließen. Sie erhalten für diese Aufgabe insgesamt 15 Verrechnungspunkte (VP), fünf VP für den Inhalt und 10 VP für die Sprache. Ihr Text soll 200 bis 300 Wörter umfassen.

(Einleitung)
The cartoon deals with the topic "environment and its destruction". It consists of two illustrations, the first one depicting woodcutters in front of a forest, the other one showing an audience at an "Earth Day concert".

(Beschreibung)
In the first picture you can see woodcutters in the foreground. They are wearing working clothes and safety helmets and are carrying chainsaws. The woodcutters are about to cut down the trees that can be seen in the background and are listening to their boss. He has a sheet of paper, probably with instructions, in his hand and is telling his men: "All these trees have to go. Big concert is Saturday."
In the picture at the bottom we can see the same location as in the first picture, but it looks different now. There is a concert taking place with a large audience. Where the forest used to be there is now a big stage with a band performing on it. Above the stage you can see a banner saying "Earth Day Concert". So the concert probably takes place to raise money for the protection of the environment and wants to make aware of its destruction.

(Botschaft des Cartoons und eigene Meinung)
What the cartoon wants to show is that the concert is meant to raise money for the protection of the environment, but in fact it contributes to its destruction, because a forest has been cut down for the concert. It is therefore ironic that an event for a good purpose has the contrary effect. The cartoonist uses the stylistic device of exaggeration to make us understand his point.
I agree with the message of the cartoon. Most people want the environment to be protected, but it isn't always easy to act appropriately. Even if you think that you do the right thing it can have negative effects you often aren't aware of.

(310 words)

Part B

- *Hier sollen Sie <u>einen</u> Aufsatz über ein vorgegebenes Thema schreiben, wobei Ihnen fünf verschiedene Materialien als Grundlage für Ihren Text zur Verfügung stehen. Von diesen <u>Materialien</u> müssen Sie <u>mindestens drei verwenden</u>. Sie können natürlich auch vier oder alle fünf Materialien verwenden und noch eigenes Wissen in Ihren Aufsatz einfließen lassen. Es empfiehlt sich daher, zunächst alle Materialien zu sichten und den Inhalt auf Englisch stichpunktartig zu notieren. So können Sie leichter entscheiden, welche Materialien Sie in Ihren Aufsatz integrieren wollen. Sie haben für die Aufgabe 90 Minuten Zeit und Sie können maximal 10 Inhaltspunkte und 20 Sprachpunkte bekommen. Achten Sie also besonders auf die Qualität Ihrer Sprache.*
- *Die Textmenge für eine gute Leistung umfasst in der Regel 300 bis 400 Wörter.*
- *Schreiben Sie eine Einleitung, bevor Sie im Hauptteil Informationen aus den Materialien einfließen lassen. Sie sollen Ihren Aufsatz auch mit einer <u>persönlichen Stellungnahme</u> abschließen, in die Sie Ihre eigene Meinung einbringen. Der Lösungsvorschlag ist etwas ausführlicher, da er alle fünf Materialien enthält.*

(Einleitung)
Many people enjoy going on holiday and so each year millions of people travel to places all over the world. On the one hand, travelling is a real burden for our environment. On the other hand, there are also positive aspects of tourism.

(Hauptteil)
The Germans are often called the "travel champions". According to a study made by the ADAC in 2010, most of them spend their holiday in Germany. The most popular destinations in Europe are Italy and Spain. About 15 % of German travellers fly off to far-away countries. Most people go on holiday by car or plane, with the plane doing much more damage to the environment because of its huge CO_2 emissions.
(Material 1)
In many countries tourism is an important economic factor. It can also promote tolerance as encounters between visitors and hosts can lead to the exchange of ideas and thus better mutual understanding. Travelling also makes it possible for us to have special and challenging experiences which will last a lifetime. *(Material 2)* It can also broaden your horizon as you get to know ways of life different from your own. You should always show respect and tolerance for other cultures – and learning a bit of the host country's language helps to get in touch with the locals. *(Material 5)*
However, tourism also causes a lot of problems. In many poor countries with a dry climate, for example, tourism contributes to water shortages. Often tourists are ignorant and don't care about the effects the wasting of water has on the everyday lives of the locals who don't have enough water for themselves. *(Material 4)* Another negative effect of mass tourism on the host countries is the destruction of the environment. As poor countries, in particular, often depend on the money generated by mass tourism, places of natural beauty are often turned into tourist spots. However, this can have an adverse effect as many people look for peace and quiet in unspoiled scenery and they will stay away when they can't find the natural environment they are looking for any more. *(Material 3)*

(Abschluss)
To sum up, travelling can have positive effects for travellers and locals alike, although we shouldn't forget that mass tourism causes a lot of problems in the host countries. But if we travel in a responsible way, visitors and hosts can both profit from tourism and learn from each other.   *(401 words)*

Fachhochschulreife Englisch (Berufskolleg Baden-Württemberg)
Schriftliche Hauptprüfung 2014

Teil A: Hörverstehen

Aufgabe 1a – Satzergänzungen *(8 VP)*

Radio *FreshAir* hat bei Teenagern eine E-Mail-Umfrage zum Thema Waffenkontrolle gemacht. Einige der Beiträge werden im Radio vorgestellt.

▶ Hören Sie aufmerksam zu und vervollständigen Sie auf Deutsch die unten stehenden Sätze. Entnehmen Sie den Aussagen je zwei Aspekte.

(1) Tom	Laut Tom haben Waffen und Autos ein unterschiedliches Gefahrenpotential, da …
(2) Peter	Peter zufolge gibt es für das Waffenproblem in Amerika zwei Ursachen, nämlich …
(3) Abigail	Abigail meint, dass kein Waffenverbot Amokläufer aufhalten kann, weil …
(4) Don	Don wundert sich darüber, dass sich Leute über Waffen aufregen, aber nicht über …

2014-1

Aufgabe 1b – Offene Fragen (7 VP)

Kim Sandfort vom Onlinemagazin *travelling2report.com* berichtet in einem Podcast über die Probleme der Intha-Bevölkerung am Inle-See in Burma.

▶ Hören Sie aufmerksam zu und vervollständigen Sie auf Deutsch in verständlichen Stichworten.

1	Beschreiben Sie die touristischen Attraktionen des Inle-Sees.

(2 VP)

2	Erklären Sie, inwiefern das hohe Touristenaufkommen ein Problem für den Tomatenanbau darstellt.

(2 VP)

3	Nennen Sie die zwei Ursachen für die Trinkwasserverschmutzung.

(2 VP)

4	Nennen Sie die Internetadresse, wo sich künftige Besucher über Umweltschutz am Inle-See informieren können.

(1 VP)

Teil B: Leseverstehen

Aufgabe 2 – Mediation   *(15 VP)*

Sie machen ein Praktikum in der Personalabteilung eines IT-Unternehmens, das schon längere Zeit Probleme hat, qualifizierte Fachkräfte für sich zu gewinnen. Daher bittet Ihr Chef Sie, ihm ein Informationsblatt darüber zu erstellen, welche innovativen zusätzlichen Leistungen Unternehmen und Dienstleister in Silicon Valley ihren Mitarbeitern bieten.
- Entnehmen Sie dem vorliegenden Zeitungsartikel die dafür notwendigen Informationen.
- Formulieren Sie ganze deutsche Sätze.

Housecleaning, then dinner? Silicon Valley perks come home

SAN FRANCISCO – Phil Libin, chief executive of Evernote, turned to his wife last year and asked if she had suggestions for how the software company might improve the lives of its employees and their families. His wife, who also works at Evernote, didn't hesitate: housecleaning.

Today, Evernote's 250 employees – every full-time worker, from receptionist to top executive – have their homes cleaned twice a month, free.

It is the latest innovation from Silicon Valley: the employee perk is moving from the office to the home. Facebook gives new parents $4,000 in spending money. Stanford School of Medicine is piloting a project to provide doctors with housecleaning and in-home dinner delivery. Genentech offers take-home dinners and helps employees find last-minute baby-sitters when a child is too sick to go to school.

These kinds of benefits are a departure from cafeteria meals, massages and other services intended to keep employees happy and productive while at work. And the goal is not just to reduce stress for employees, but for their families, too. If the companies succeed, the thinking goes, they will minimize distractions and sources of tension that can disturb concentration and creativity.

Now that technology has allowed work to enter home life, it seems that companies are trying to address the impact of home life on work.

There is, of course, the possibility that relieving people of chores at home will simply free them up to work more. But David Lewin, a compensation expert and management professor at the University of California, Los Angeles, said he viewed the perks as part of a growing effort by American business to reward people with time and peace of mind instead of more traditional financial tools, like stock options and bonuses.

At Deloitte, the consulting firm, employees can get a backup care worker if an aging parent or grandparent needs help. The company subsidizes personal trainers and nutritionists, and offers round-the-clock counseling service for help. Deloitte executives, and other experts, said they believe that such benefits were likely to spread.

"The workplace was built on the assumption that there was somebody at home dealing with the home front," said Anne Weisberg, a longtime human resources executive who helped write a book about new kinds of workplace policies. Not only is that no longer the case, she said, but the work-life pressures seem to be building.

Hannah Valantine, a cardiologist and professor at the Stanford School of Medicine, said the university's experiment with helping out at home was part of a broader
35 effort to support doctors, given their hectic pace of life. "If you're coming home at the end of the day exhausted and you have a pile of cleaning to do, it's the kind of thing that leads rapidly to burnout, and burned-out physicians don't give the best care," Dr. Valantine said. "We're trying to send a very strong message that the institution cares about you and about your life."
40 Mr. Libin, from Evernote, also gives employees $1,000 to spend on vacation, but it has to be 'a real vacation'. "Happy workers make better products," he said. "The output we care about has everything to do with your state of mind."

At Facebook, employees can take home a free dinner or, if working late, their families can come in to eat with them, leading to a regular sight of children in the
45 campus cafeteria. The company also pays $3,000 per family in child care expenses. Slater Tow, a Facebook spokesman, said the company was not trying to be New Age but simply strategic. "We don't want to give aromatherapy for your dog," he said. "We want things that are practical for you and your family."   *(621 words)*

Matt Richtel: Housecleaning, Then Dinner? Silicon Valley Perks Come Home. From The New York Times, 19 Oct 2012 © 2012 The New York Times. All rights reserved. Used by permission and protected by the Copyright Laws of the United States. The printing, copying, redistribution, or retransmission of this Content without express written permission is prohibited.

Teil C: Textproduktion

Aufgabe 3 – Materialgestützter Aufsatz   *(30 VP: 10 VP Inh./20 VP Spr.)*

Choose between composition 1 or composition 2.

Write a composition about the chosen topic.

- ▶ Use the information of at least three of the given materials.
- ▶ Name which ones you are using.
- ▶ Make use of your own ideas.
- ▶ Do not write three separate compositions but one covering all the materials chosen.

Composition 1

Everywhere we go, we are constantly confronted with advertising.
Discuss how advertising influences consumers' way of thinking and behaviour.

Material 1

Werbung: Eine Milliarden-Investition

Für die Werbeindustrie ist das Fernsehen eine Goldgrube und die Zuschauer ein gefundenes Fressen. Alleine in den letzten 24 Stunden hatten wir 2 000 bis 3 000 Werbeimpulse – auch wenn man das jetzt vielleicht nicht für möglich hält, aber es stimmt. 1990 warben 2 000 Marken im TV, heute sind es rund 5 000. Über 7 000 Werbespots laufen täglich im Fernsehen. Stündlich werden, über alle TV-Sender verteilt, 290 Spots ausgestrahlt, mit insgesamt 2 700 Werbeminuten. Das heißt: täglich läuft im Fernsehen 45 Stunden lang Werbung. Auch wenn sich nur acht Prozent der Zuschauer an einen Werbespot erinnern können – sie haben ihn doch gesehen.

Die Werbeindustrie steckt jährlich tausende Euros in ihre Spots, um neue Konsumenten unter den Fernsehfreaks zu gewinnen: Im Jahr 2012 wurden 30,78 Milliarden Euro alleine in Deutschland in Werbung investiert. Die Werbeanzeigen werden sowohl vom Sender als auch vom Werbetreibenden sorgfältig geplant. Das Erreichen einer bestimmten Zielgruppe zu bestimmten Uhrzeiten, und das möglichst ohne Streuverluste, ist das angestrebte Ziel. Deshalb müssen wir uns zwischen dem Vorspann und dem Beginn einer Serie auch noch schnell einen 20-Sekunden-Spot anschauen, und wenn die Gäste bei Stefan Raabs „TV-Total" das Studio verlassen, wird auf einem Viertel des Bildschirms ganz beiläufig das neueste Handy angepriesen.

© Politik-Ressort Studiengang Online-Redakteur/Institut für Infomationswissenschaft FH Köln, in: http://dein-konsum.de/freizeit_e2.html

Material 2

"Actually, Mama was her third word. *Buy Now* were her first two."

© T. McCracken, www.mchumor.com

Material 3

Brand bullying growing, warn teachers

Children who cannot afford the latest brands and fashions face bullying or exclusion by their peers, teachers warned yesterday. A desire to fit in plays a huge role in the products children want to own, a poll by the Association of Teachers and Lecturers
5 (ATL) found. Almost half of the teachers questioned said young people who cannot afford the fashionable items owned by their friends have been excluded, isolated or bullied as a result.

Dr Mary Bousted, ATL general secretary, said: "Bullying of this kind can be quite insidious: it can just be a look that a child is given. Children feel under
10 immense pressure to look right and having the key brands is part of that."

The poll found 85 % of teachers believe possession of fashionable goods is important to their pupils, with 93 % saying brands are the top influence on what children buy. The influence of advertising and marketing is much more significant now, with more than 70 % of teachers saying it has increased from 10 years ago. Almost all (98 %)
15 believe advertising directly targets children and young people. Bousted added: "Advertising and marketing have made our society increasingly image conscious and our children are suffering the consequences."

© *Press Association, in: The Guardian, 11. 08. 2008*

Material 4

Quotes regarding honesty in advertising

1. "The most powerful element in advertising is the truth."
   Bill Bernbach, amerikanischer Kommunikations- und Werbemanager

2. "Facts are irrelevant. What matters is what the consumer believes."
   Seth Godin, amerikanischer Unternehmer und Bestsellerautor

3. "I am one who believes that one of the greatest dangers of advertising is not that of misleading people, but that of boring them to death."
   © *Leo Burnett*

   Leo Burnett, Gründer einer der größten Werbeagenturen Amerikas

Material 5

Which form of advertising do people trust in most?

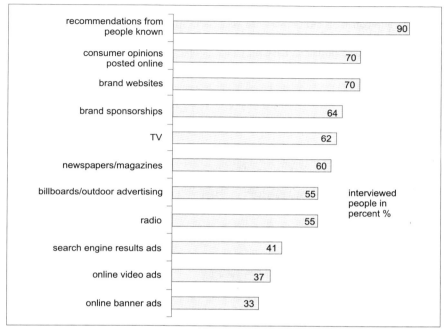

Nielsen Global Survey, April 2009

Composition 2

Approximately 30 million American children participate in competitive sports, others don't do any sports at all.
Some people consider sports a way to success in life, while others are critical about possible negative physical and mental consequences.
Discuss the impact sports can have on young people's lives.

Material 1

Baby: © Can Stock Photo Inc./luiscar; Hanteln: © BMCL.Shutterstock

* Aus urheberrechtlichen Gründen wurde hier ein von der Prüfung abweichendes Bild verwendet.

Material 2

"Gold medals aren't really made of gold. They are made of sweat, determination and a hard-to-find alloy called guts."
Dan Gable (wrestler)

"Champions aren't made in the gym. Champions are made from something they have deep inside them – a desire, a dream, a vision. They have to have the skill, and the will. But the will must be stronger than the skill."
© *Muhammad Ali*

Muhammad Ali (boxer)

"The more difficult the victory, the greater the happiness in winning."
Pelé (footballer)

Material 3

Are Competitive Sports Bad for Kids?

Each year more than 30 million American children participate in organized sports, according to Children's Hospital Boston. Sports give children an outlet for physical activity and can teach valuable lessons about sportsmanship and listening. However, sports participation, particularly for competitive sports such as football, soccer and basketball, can sometimes prevent kids from being kids. While competitive sports are not always bad for kids, there are some instances where they are too intense for a young child.

When children begin competitive sports at too young an age or feel pushed to excel, a condition known as "burnout" can occur. This shows that the child is experiencing significant amounts of stress and no longer enjoys the activity. This commonly occurs around the age of 13. However, children also experience positive effects, including building confidence and physical fitness, meeting new friends and learning about winning and losing.

Children who play competitive, physical sports too early may be at risk for injuries that can plague them for a lifetime. An estimated 3 million athletes under the age of 14 are injured annually while playing an organized sport or recreational activity, according to Children's Hospital Boston.

Adapted from: http://everydaylife.globalpost.com/sports-injuries-affecting-children-teens-17488.html; http://everydaylife.globalpost.com/age-should-child-start-playing-sports-4035.html

Material 4

IFMA – International Federation of Muaythai Amateur

Material 5

80 Prozent der Jugendlichen sind Sportmuffel

Radfahren, Joggen, Fußballspielen – eigentlich Dinge, die Kinder und Jugendliche gerne machen. Doch nun zeigt eine Studie, nur die wenigsten der 11- bis 15-Jährigen bewegen sich überhaupt genug.

Bewegungsdrang ist typisch für junge Menschen. Kinder rennen begeistert durch die Gegend, Jugendliche treiben sich am liebsten auf Fußballplätzen und in Fitnesscentern herum. Denkt man. Doch das ist offenbar ein Irrglaube, wie eine neue Studie nun zeigt.

Mehr als 80 Prozent der deutschen Jugendlichen bewegen sich zu wenig. Vor allem zwischen dem 11. und 15. Lebensjahr steigt der Anteil der Bewegungsmuffel drastisch. Das konnten Wissenschaftler der Universität Bielefeld in einer umfangreichen Studie nun nachweisen.

Demnach bewegen sich bei den Elfjährigen noch jeder vierte Junge und jedes fünfte Mädchen ausreichend. Bei den 15-Jährigen sind es nur noch 13,6 Prozent der Jungen und 8,6 Prozent der Mädchen.

Die Untersuchung ist Teil einer umfassenden Studie der Weltgesundheitsorganisation (WHO) zum Gesundheitsverhalten von Schulkindern in rund 40 Ländern. Laut internationalen Empfehlungen sollten sich Jugendliche täglich 60 Minuten so bewegen, dass der Pulsschlag erhöht ist und sie ins Schwitzen kommen.

© ph/AFP, in: Die Welt, 12. 03. 2013

Lösungsvorschläge

Teil A: Hörverstehen

Aufgabe 1a – Satzergänzungen

Transkript:

Hello and welcome to *Current Issues* here on *FreshAir*. My name is Ron Clover and today our topic is gun control in the US. Recently, the National Rifle Association, the NRA, reported that gun sales have hit an all-time high a year after the horrific elementary school massacre in Newtown, Connecticut. Since then, President Obama has announced stricter gun laws. We've asked our listeners to comment on this issue. Let's see what they have to say:

Here's Tom's email. He's from Dayton, Ohio.

(1) Tom	It is not the weapons that kill; it's the people that use them. Nonetheless, there must be laws to prevent people from acquiring these weapons. How else can this be done unless there is a general ban on weapons? The tragedy at Newtown elementary school could perhaps have been avoided if a complete ban on rifles in the USA had been in place. The weak argument of the gun lobby that guns don't kill people, people kill people, is illogical: what do people use guns for? Unlike motor vehicles, which, if misused, can cause fatal accidents too, guns are made for one purpose only, and that is to kill.

Rhode Island resident Peter has quite an interesting point of view:

(2) Peter	The US is one of the major gun states in the world. Fact is, we Americans are the biggest manufacturers of guns and also supply other nations and countries with weapons. For me, the real problem is written down in our constitution which makes it legal for every citizen to carry a weapon. Plus, the USA has been at war too many times in the last decade. This kind of war-like mentality encourages people to carry a gun. The parents of this kind of society already teach their young children how to fire a gun.

We've now got Abigail on the phone. Hi Abigail (Abigail: Hi Ron) What do you think about the issue?

(3) Abigail	Disturbed people might commit mass killings. They want the world to pay attention to their final act of revenge as it never did to their miserable and lonely lives. Their decision to act out their sick fantasies has nothing to do with the availability of guns. They could also use firebombs, explosives, or poison. The extreme preventive control which would be required to eliminate guns in the US would be a terrible burden on all citizens, and killers, drug dealers, and frustrated psychos won't ever follow such laws anyway.

Our final email is from Don from California. He says:

(4) Don	The real problem is our society, and not the guns. We even teach small kids about violence; we allow them to watch hour upon hour of violent TV programmes and let them play video games that promote killing. This crap is placed in their minds from a very early age. It's strange how Hollywood doesn't mind making millions of dollars producing movies that promote killing and violence, yet they say they want gun control. On the other hand, over 25,000 people die each year in the U.S. from alcohol-related accidents and I don't see any protesters marching to ban alcohol.

Vervollständigen Sie die vorgegebenen Satzanfänge auf Deutsch. Sie hören den Text zweimal. Lesen Sie sich die Aufgabenstellung und die vier Satzanfänge genau durch, bevor Sie sich die Kommentare aus der Radiosendung anhören. Sie dürfen sich während des Hörens Notizen machen. Notieren Sie in Stichpunkten die Informationen, die Sie für die Vervollständigung der Sätze brauchen. Die Sprechgeschwindigkeit ist relativ schnell – notieren Sie deshalb erst einmal alles, was Ihnen wichtig erscheint.
Sie erhalten für diese Aufgabe insgesamt 8 Punkte. Pro Kommentar sollten Sie also zwei Informationen erfassen. Für jede richtige Satzergänzung erhalten Sie einen Verrechnungspunkt. In der folgenden Lösung sind teilweise mehrere Lösungsmöglichkeiten angegeben.
Nutzen Sie zum Vervollständigen der Satzanfänge v. a. die Pausen zwischen dem ersten und zweiten Vorspielen, sowie nach dem zweiten Vorspielen des Textes, weil Sie in dieser Zeit keine Informationen versäumen.

(1) Tom	Laut Tom haben Waffen und Autos ein unterschiedliches Gefahrenpotential, da ...
	• Menschen zwar auch durch Autounfälle ums Leben kommen können,
	• Waffen jedoch nur zu einem Zweck hergestellt werden, und zwar zum Töten.
(2) Peter	Peter zufolge gibt es für das Waffenproblem in Amerika zwei Ursachen, nämlich ...
	• dass die USA der größte Waffenhersteller der Welt sind und auch andere Länder mit Waffen beliefern. /
	• dass es laut Verfassung legal ist, Waffen zu besitzen und sie zu tragen. /
	• die Tatsache, dass die USA in den letzten zehn Jahren zu oft Krieg geführt haben und so eine Mentalität entstanden ist, die die Leute ermutigt eine Waffe zu tragen. /
	• dass Eltern ihren Kindern schon in jungen Jahren beibringen, wie man mit Waffen umgeht.
(3) Abigail	Abigail meint, dass kein Waffenverbot Amokläufer aufhalten kann, weil ...
	• die Umsetzung ihrer kranken Fantasien nichts mit der Verfügbarkeit von Waffen zu tun hat. /
	• sie anstatt Waffen z. B. auch Brandbomben, Sprengstoffe oder Gift verwenden würden. /
	• Kriminelle und Psychopathen sich ohnehin nicht an Gesetze halten.
(4) Don	Don wundert sich darüber, dass sich Leute über Waffen aufregen, aber nicht über ...
	• die Gewalt in Videospielen sowie in Film und Fernsehen, der schon kleine Kinder ausgesetzt sind.
	• durch Alkohol verursachte Unfälle, bei denen jährlich 25 000 Leute sterben.

Aufgabe 1 b – Offene Fragen

Transkript:

The country Burma, Asia's newest tourist hotspot, is experiencing an extreme rise in the number of foreign visitors eager to visit places that have been closed-off for decades. Burma's scenic Inle Lake is considered a jewel of Asia.

Here, a steady stream of foreign tourists comes to visit the swimming villages of the Intha people who live in bamboo huts built on poles above the water and also to explore the unique ecosystem around the 110 square kilometer freshwater reservoir with its numerous rare plants and animal species. Although this means big business for some, many locals say they are losing out.

The main income of the Intha people is farming. They plant crops on beds which float on the water. Floating tomato gardens are the primary cash crop in this area, comprising more than 60 percent of the local agriculture. Farmer Mee Intara says he welcomes foreign visitors, but not the increase in traffic. "The constant waves from the increase in motor boats are destroying my crops on the lake," states Intara.

As unregulated development and business moves forward, local environmentalists are also worried about an even bigger potential environmental disaster – the contamination of freshwater supplies.

The residue of the diesel fuel from the motor boats, together with large amounts of pesticides already used by the farmers, are threatening drinking supplies. Khin Moe Khao says his family and others living on the shores of the lake must now fetch clean water from elsewhere.

Andrew Jenkings, an environmentalist with the Pa-Oh Youth Organization, says that waste water from an open coal mine, 13 kilometers away, is also ending up in Inle Lake's watershed, making matters even worse. "Most of the people in the villages who rely on the upper Tigyit Creek use the water for bathing and drinking, so it is very dangerous for them because of the water pollution caused by the mining. This is now affecting Inle Lake too," says Jenkings.

Future visitors of Inle Lake might want to support this youth organization's online donation campaign. If so, please visit their webpage on paoh-intha.com/tigyit (P-A-O-H minus I-N-T-H-A dot com slash T-I-G-Y-I-T) to get further information about the organization's activities to protect the environment of Burma's second largest freshwater lake.

* Bei dieser Aufgabe sollen Sie in verständlichen Stichworten auf Deutsch antworten.
* Sie hören die Kurzberichte zweimal. Lesen Sie die Aufgabe genau durch und machen
* Sie sich dann während des Hörens gezielt Notizen. Nutzen Sie wiederum die Hör-
* pausen zum Schreiben. Für diese Aufgabe erhalten Sie insgesamt 7 Punkte. Pro Satz
* bzw. Stichpunkt wird ein Punkt vergeben. In der folgenden Lösung sind teilweise
* mehr als zwei Antwortmöglichkeiten angegeben.

1	Beschreiben Sie die touristischen Attraktionen des Inle-See.
	• **Schwimmende Dörfer, bestehend aus Bambushütten, die auf Pfählen im Wasser stehen**
	• **Einzigartiges Ökosystem rund um den See /**
	• **Zahlreiche seltene Pflanzen und Tiere**
2	Erklären Sie, inwiefern das hohe Tourismusaufkommen ein Problem für den Tomatenanbau darstellt.
	• **Durch die vielen ausländischen Touristen hat der Motorbootverkehr zugenommen.**
	• **Die von den Motorbooten verursachten Wellen zerstören die Tomaten, die auf dem See angebaut werden.**
3	Nennen Sie zwei Ursachen für die Trinkwasserverschmutzung.
	• **Rückstände des Diesels von den Motorbooten /**
	• **Große Menge an von den Bauern verwendeten Pestiziden /**
	• **Schmutzwasser aus einer offenen Kohlemine gelangt in den See.**
4	Nennen Sie die Internetadresse, wo sich künftige Besucher über Umweltschutz am Inle-See informieren können.
	• **(www) paoh-intha.com/tigyit**

Teil B: Leseverstehen

Aufgabe 2 – Mediation

Bei dieser Aufgabe sollen Sie, ausgehend von den Informationen im vorliegenden Zeitungsartikel, einen eigenen Text in Form eines Informationsblattes erstellen. Achten Sie darauf, in ganzen Sätzen zu schreiben. Vergessen Sie auch nicht die Überschrift und einen auf das Thema hinführenden Satz. Geben Sie dann eine Übersicht über die zusätzlichen Leistungen, die Unternehmen im Silicon Valley anbieten. Schließen Sie Ihren Text mit einem Fazit ab. Der folgende Text ist eine Beispiellösung.
Es gibt insgesamt 15 Verrechnungspunkte (VP) für diese Aufgabe, wobei Inhalts- und Sprachpunkte gemeinsam gewertet werden, d. h., es gibt keine getrennte Wertung von Inhalts- und Sprachpunkten. Die volle Punktzahl bekommen Sie, wenn Sie die wesentlichen Punkte aufgelistet haben, und Ihr Text in gutem Deutsch geschrieben ist (Sprache, Stil, Rechtschreibung und Zeichensetzung).

(Überschrift)
Informationsblatt zu innovativen Zusatzleistungen für Mitarbeiter

(Einleitungssatz)
Das folgende Informationsblatt enthält neuartige Ideen und Vorschläge, die Unternehmen und Dienstleister im Silicon Valley ihren Angestellten bieten, damit diese zufrieden und produktiv sind.

(Informationen aus dem Text)
Die Firmen im Silicon Valley bieten verstärkt Dienstleistungen an, um ihre Mitarbeiter zu entlasten. Eine Firma z. B. lässt die Häuser und Wohnungen der Vollzeitbeschäftigten zweimal im Monat kostenlos putzen. Auch die Medizinfakultät der Stanford University bietet den Ärzten einen Reinigungsdienst an. Auch können sich die Ärzte das Abendessen nach Hause bringen lassen. Eine andere Firma wiederum bietet ihren Mitarbeitern an, sich ein Abendessen mit nach Hause zu nehmen. Sie hilft auch dabei, kurzfristig Babysitter zu finden, wenn ein Kind krank ist und nicht zur Schule gehen kann.
Bei der Unternehmensberatungsfirma Deloitte können die Angestellten eine Pflegekraft bekommen, wenn Eltern oder Großeltern Hilfe brauchen. Außerdem subventioniert die Firma Privattrainer sowie Ernährungsberater und bietet rund um die Uhr einen Beratungsservice bei Problemen an.
Auch bei Facebook werden insbesondere Familien unterstützt. Junge Eltern bekommen 4 000 Dollar ausgezahlt. Weiterhin zahlt die Firma jeder Familie 3.000 Dollar für die Kinderbetreuung. Bei Facebook können die Familien auch zum Essen in die Firma kommen, wenn es in der Arbeit einmal spät wird.
Eine andere Firma zahlt ihren Mitarbeitern 1 000 Dollar für einen Urlaub, aber nur unter der Bedingung, dann auch wirklich Urlaub zu machen.

(Abschluss)
Soweit einige Beispiele für innovative Zusatzleistungen von Firmen aus dem Silicon Valley. Es ist zu überlegen, ob nicht auch wir die eine oder andere Leistung übernehmen könnten, um qualifizierte Fachkräfte zu halten bzw. für unsere Firma zu gewinnen.

Teil C: Textproduktion

Aufgabe 3 – Materialgestützter Aufsatz

Bei Aufgabe 3 müssen Sie zwischen zwei Themen (Composition 1 oder Composition 2) wählen. Zu einem Thema schreiben Sie einen Aufsatz, in den Sie Informationen aus mindestens drei der vorliegenden Materialien einfließen lassen müssen. Geben sie in Ihrem Text an, welchem Material Sie Ihre Informationen entnommen haben. Sie können natürlich auch Bezug auf vier oder alle fünf Materialien nehmen und eigenes Wissen einbringen. Es empfiehlt sich, zunächst alle Materialien zu sichten und den Inhalt auf Englisch stichpunktartig zu notieren. So fällt es Ihnen leichter zu entscheiden, welche Materialien Sie verwenden wollen. Sie haben für die Aufgabe 90 Minuten Zeit und Sie können bis zu 10 Inhalts- und 20 Sprachpunkte bekommen. Achten Sie also besonders auf korrektes Englisch. Die Textmenge für eine gute Leistung umfasst in der Regel 300 bis 400 Wörter. Einer der folgenden Lösungsvorschläge ist etwas ausführlicher. Schreiben Sie eine Einleitung, bevor Sie im Hauptteil Informationen aus den Materialien einfließen lassen. Schließen Sie ihren Aufsatz auch mit einem Fazit oder einer persönlichen Stellungnahme ab.

Composition 1

Unter Verwendung aller Materialien:

Advertising is everywhere in our lives: on billboards, on TV, on the radio, in newspapers and on the internet. So the question is in what way we are influenced by advertising and how strong its impact is on consumers. In the following this question will be discussed in detail.

Advertising has an impact on our lives from a very early age. This fact is depicted in a cartoon *(Material 2)*, although in an exaggerated way. In the cartoon you can see two women sitting in front of the TV. On the floor in front of them there is a little child also staring at the screen. On the screen you can see the words "Buy now". In the caption below the picture you can read what the mother is saying to the other woman: "Actually Mama was her third word. 'Buy now' were her first two." In this way the cartoonist criticizes the fact that even young children are influenced by slogans in TV commercials.

On German TV, for example, there are thousands of commercials every day *(Material 1)*. The total number per hour is 290 spots and the number is growing. Since 1990 the number of firms advertising their products on TV has risen from 2,000 to 5,000. As companies invest such a lot of money in TV commercials, it can be concluded that TV advertising must be worth the money and have an impact on consumer behaviour. Furthermore, the spots are targeted at specific groups of people and are presented at the time when these potential customers are likely to be watching TV.

An American advertising manager once said that "the most powerful element in advertising is the truth" *(Material 4)*. Statistics *(Material 5)* show what kind of advertising people think is the most truthful. Above all, people trust recommendations from people they know, followed by consumer opinions which are posted online. Only 55 to 62 % believe that TV spots, newspaper ads or radio commercials are trustworthy. Even fewer people trust online banner and video ads or the results of search engines, which involve a lot of advertising.

Massive advertising can have negative effects on youngsters *(Material 3)*. Teachers criticise the fact that a lot of children who do not wear the right brand of clothes, for example, are often excluded by their classmates and become victims of bullying. So children get under pressure to buy and wear trendy clothes. This is becoming even more serious nowadays because advertisers concentrate on children and teenagers, in particular, and target them with their advertising spots. Teachers report that the influence of advertising has increased enormously within the last few decades.

To sum up, it can be said that consumer behaviour is influenced by advertising to a great extent starting at a very young age. The impact of advertising can even lead to peer pressure at school. Most people, however, know that there is often not much truth in advertising and that it is better to ask people they know before buying something so as not to be fooled or manipulated.

(511 words)

Composition 2

Unter Verwendung aller Materialien:

Today most of us would agree that sport has a positive impact on people's lives, but there is also criticism of its negative consequences. In the following the impact sport has on young people is discussed.

We think that doing sports like playing football or riding a bike is natural for children and teenagers. However, as a study by the University of Bielefeld shows, over 80 % of German teenagers do not get enough exercise. At the age of 15, only 13.6 % of the boys and 8.6 % of the girls do sports. These facts are worrying, as according to recommendations young people should do exercise about 60 minutes a day in a way that increases their blood pressure and makes them sweat. *(Material 5)* Other positive aspects of doing sports, apart from physical fitness, would be strengthening one's character *(Material 2, 3)* and keeping young people away from crime, for example *(Material 4)*.

However, too much sport, particularly from an early age, could have negative consequences. One photo *(Material 1)* shows a young child who is dressed up like an adult gymnast. He is doing a press-up next to a pair of dumb-bells. The photo can be seen as a criticism of the way some children are pushed, mainly by their ambitious parents, to do sports in order to be successful at a very early age. Tough physical exercise, however, can be harmful for children and teenagers. Organised competitive sports, which are done by 30 million American children, teaches young people life skills and offers them a way to get rid of aggression and superfluous energy. It also helps them to keep fit and build up confidence, which is important for their future lives. However, when done too excessively, this kind of sport can have negative consequences such as burnout or serious injury. When children start at too young an age, they might also lose interest and stop enjoying the physical exercise. *(Material 3)*

All in all, we can say that sport is good for young people if done in a regular and natural way. They stay fit and they can even develop social skills, such as learning to cooperate with others, learning to lose fairly and accepting the rules of the game. However, if sport is done excessively and at an early age, it can also have negative consequences for children. *(394 words)*

Fachhochschulreife Englisch (Berufskolleg Baden-Württemberg)
Schriftliche Hauptprüfung 2015

Teil A: Hörverstehen

Aufgabe 1a – Satzergänzungen *(8 VP)*

Lebensmittelkennzeichnung

Radio CNB hat bei seinen Hörern eine Umfrage zum Thema Lebensmittelkennzeichnung gestartet. Einige der Beiträge werden im Radio vorgestellt.

▶ Hören Sie aufmerksam zu und vervollständigen Sie auf Deutsch die unten stehenden Sätze. Entnehmen Sie jeder Aussage mindestens **zwei** Aspekte.

(1) Tom	Einem kalorienreduzierten Nahrungsmittel viele Sterne zu verleihen ist fragwürdig, wenn …
(2) Peter	Die Kennzeichnung von Lebensmitteln wäre sinnvoll für all diejenigen, die … (4 Nennungen)
(3) Susan	Wenn Verbraucher weiterhin ungesunde Kaufentscheidungen treffen, geht uns das alle etwas an, weil …
(4) Don	Eine durchdachte Lebensmittel-App wäre die bessere Alternative zur Lebensmittelkennzeichnung, weil …

2015-1

Aufgabe 1 b – Offene Fragen (7 VP)

„Land Grabbing" (Übernahme von Land)

Pam Templeton unterhält sich in ihrer Sendung *Global Issues* mit dem Wissenschaftsjournalisten Fred Pearce über das Thema „Land grabbing".

- ▶ Hören Sie aufmerksam zu und beantworten Sie die Fragen auf Deutsch in Stichworten.

1	Wie erklärt Fred Pearce „Land grabbing"?

(2 VP)

2	Aus welchem Grund begannen Saudi-Arabien und Südkorea in den Jahren 2007 und 2008 mit dem „Land grabbing"?

(1 VP)

3	Warum gibt es keine verlässlichen Angaben über das Ausmaß von „Land grabbing"?

(2 VP)

4	Wer ist von „Land grabbing" betroffen und welche Folgen hat dies für die Betroffenen?

(2 VP)

Teil B: Leseverstehen

Aufgabe 2 – Mediation *(15 VP)*

An Ihrer Schule wird ein Umwelttag veranstaltet, an dem Sie Ihren Mitschülern das Konzept der „Smart City" erläutern. Sie möchten in Ihrer Präsentation auf umweltfreundliche innovative Technologien eingehen.
- Erstellen Sie ein Handout.
- Entnehmen Sie dem vorliegenden Zeitungsartikel die dafür notwendigen Informationen.
- Formulieren Sie ganze deutsche Sätze.

Europe Remains Ahead of U.S. in Creating Smart Cities

Barcelona is among a number of European cities adopting new forms of technology aimed at improving services. More important, the investments, including neighbourhood wide high-speed Internet connections and electricity charge points for cars and motorbikes, offer ways to cut energy use and generate income. Alongside the city's world-famous architecture and beautiful sandy beaches, sensors attached to trash cans now inform the garbage collectors when they need to empty them.

"It's essential that these new technologies are useful to our citizens," Xavier Trias, Barcelona's mayor, said in his stately offices, which date from the 15th century. "It's an important change. We have to create a sustainable system."

This reflects efforts in cities including San Francisco and Boston, which have spent millions of dollars to upgrade their infrastructure. Yet analysts say Europe, despite being hit hard by the recent financial crisis, remains a step ahead of the United States in creating efficient, so-called smart cities. They combine traditional services like electricity networks with 21st-century technology like Internet-connected home appliances, e.g. fridges that automatically send an order to the next supermarket when they need to be refilled.

Mayors in places including Copenhagen and Hamburg hope to cut their cities' energy and water use by upgrading municipal services so that they can monitor how services are delivered and point out where savings can be made.

In Barcelona, where the unemployment rate remains above 20 percent, the city expects to cut its water bill by 25 percent this year after installing sensors in local parks. The irrigation systems built in Barcelona's parks monitor soil moisture and turn on sprinklers when water is needed. The annual savings are expected to total almost $60 million. "We were wasting a lot of water," said Julia Lopez, coordinator of Barcelona's smart city program. "We can now control the system directly from an iPad."

The infrastructure upgrades have led to agreements between cities and some of the world's largest technology companies, including IBM, Hewlett-Packard and General Electric. By applying their technology in citywide pilot projects, these companies say they can test new business models and other services that might have worldwide appeal. In January, Google reached a $3.2 billion deal to buy Nest Labs, which makes energy-saving devices like Internet-connected thermostats and smoke detectors.

Nest Labs says its products, designed by former Apple engineers, can cut household heating and cooling bills by around 20 percent by monitoring people's habits and adjusting thermostats automatically.

The European technology companies Philips and Ericsson, for example, are working with Verizon Wireless on a pilot project in the United States that will combine energy-efficient street lighting with mobile phone infrastructure. This year, Philips and Ericsson plan to start selling their new product to city governments. The idea is to provide cities with a source of income through rentals of streetlights to providers that want to expand their cellphone coverage. The companies also expect that the energy-efficient streetlights, which can be switched on via smartphone, will offer savings of about 50 percent compared with traditional lighting.

While cutting electricity use and garbage collections has environmental benefits, policy makers say that economic profits, not carbon dioxide reductions, are now driving many cities' plans.

Across Europe, cities are opening their infrastructure to companies eager to offer new services that provide income for the city and offer potential environmental benefits. In London, the start-up Citymapper used access to the city's transport data to create a smartphone application that helps people navigate the complicated bus and subway networks. Azmat Yusuf, the company's founder, said that since Citymapper started in 2011, usage of London's red buses jumped significantly, creating additional income for local government and cutting the number of cars on the streets. The app is now available in New York, Berlin and Paris.

Last year Barcelona created a service aimed at making it easier for drivers to find parking spaces. Drivers spent up to 20 percent of their time looking for places to park, even as many spaces across the city remained empty during the day when residents were at work. This system allowed individuals to rent out their private parking spaces by installing sensors that record when they are available. The information is transmitted in real time over local mobile networks, and customers can book the spaces hourly through a smartphone app. So far, 1,500 parking spaces across the city have been signed up, including some at shopping malls and hospitals. This scheme has almost 100,000 users, or roughly 6 percent of Barcelona's total population. As people are driving less to find parking spaces, Barcelona as a city is getting a direct benefit. *(767 words)*

Mark Scott: Old World, New Tech. From The New York Times, Apr 21, 2014
© 2014 The New York Times. All rights reserved. Used by permission and protected by the Copyright Laws of the United States. The printing, copying, redistribution, or retransmission of this Content without express written permission is prohibited.

Teil C: Textproduktion

Aufgabe 3 – Materialgestützter Aufsatz (30 VP: 10 VP Inh./20 VP Spr.)

Choose between Composition 1 or Composition 2.

Write a composition about the chosen topic.
- Use the information of at least three of the given materials.
- Name which ones you are using.
- Make use of your own ideas.
- Do not write three separate compositions but one covering all the materials chosen.

Composition 1

Thousands of African refugees risk their lives on dangerous boats in order to migrate to Europe; around the world approximately 50 million people are fleeing their homelands. A lot of European citizens are afraid of the rising numbers of immigrants. Discuss the dilemma between the immigrants' motivation on the one hand, and the Europeans' fears on the other hand.

Material 1

Die Angst vor den Armen

1 Migrationsängste haben Konjunktur im vermeintlichen Paradies in der Mitte Europas. Neben den „Armutswanderern" aus Bulgarien und Rumänien richten sie sich nach den jüngsten Katastrophen vor Lampedusa wieder verstärkt gegen sogenannte Wirtschaftsflüchtlinge und gegen Asylbewerber vornehmlich aus Afrika, aber auch
5 aus anderen Regionen der Welt.

Opfer werden dabei zu Tätern abgestempelt: Menschen, die wirtschaftlicher Not, Krieg und Unterdrückung in ihren Heimatländern entfliehen wollen, verwandeln sich in den Augen vieler Deutscher und anderer Mitteleuropäer zu einer Bedrohung ihres eigenen Wohlstandes und der Sozialsysteme.

10 Übersehen wird, dass es für Migranten, die aus existentiellen Gründen nach Europa drängen, oft nur die Alternative Flucht oder Verelendung gibt. Und vergessen wird meist auch, dass es all das auch in der deutschen Geschichte massenhaft gab. [...]

Ähnlich ist es auch heute bei den oft menschenfeindlichen Aufwallungen gegen „Wirtschaftsflüchtlinge" und „Armutswanderer" aus Afrika genauso wie aus Rumä-
15 nien oder Bulgarien. Die Ankunft einer jungen Migrantenelite von gut- bis hochqualifizierten Zuwanderern aus den Krisenstaaten im Süden Europas hingegen wurde vor kurzem noch gefeiert, als Bereicherung für das aus demographischen Gründen schrumpfende Arbeitskräfteangebot in Deutschland. Jetzt aber geht wieder die Urangst vor der europäischen Ost-West-Migration und der außereuropäischen Süd-
20 Nord-Wanderung um.

Quelle: Klaus J. Bade, ZEIT Online, 15.10.2013

Material 2

Migrant Flows

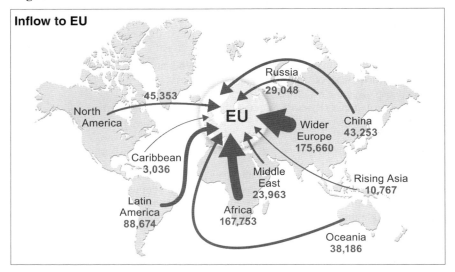

Scale: number of people; arrow width is directly proportional to its value, but lowest numbers are not to scale
Data Source: International Labour Organization

Material 3

"Because of human misery, because of despair, for reasons of persecution in their home countries, these people have nothing else but to take an unseaworthy boat to a European haven," Volker Tuerk, director with the Office of U.N. High Commissioner for Refugees, said. He called on the European Union to stop overcrowded boats leaving Northern Africa and come to the aid of those who put themselves at risk when they do manage to set off.

The search for better jobs and higher incomes still drives much of the human tide across the Mediterranean Sea. But the economic migrants are now joined by growing crowds of Syrians fleeing their civil war-torn country, by Somalis escaping lawlessness and religious conflict, and by political refugees from the "Arab Spring", the pro-democracy movements in the Middle East that have replaced authoritarian rule by near-anarchy in countries such as Libya, Egypt and Yemen.

Carol J. Williams: War, poverty, repression: Why so many Africans risk their lives to migrate. In: Los Angeles Times, Oct 04, 2013. Copyright © 2013 Los Angeles Times. Reprinted with Permission.

Material 4

Quotes about migration

1. "In countries where people have to flee their homes because of persecution and violence, political solutions must be found, peace and tolerance restored, so that refugees can return home. In my experience, going home is the deepest wish of most refugees."
   Angelina Jolie, Schauspielerin
2. "I urge you to celebrate the extraordinary courage and contributions of refugees past and present."
   Kofi Annan, früherer U.N.-Generalsekretär

Material 5

Siham Zebiri / Cartoon Movement

Composition 2

Worldwide trade is on the rise. Consumers in industrialized countries can buy anything from anywhere at any time, while those producing the goods are struggling to make a living.
Discuss why some people see Fairtrade as beneficial, whereas others are very critical about it.

Material 1
Fairtrade accused of failing to deliver benefits to African farmworkers

Sales of Fairtrade-certified products from Uganda and Ethiopia are not benefiting poor farmworkers because profits fail to reach much of the workforce, says a groundbreaking study. The Fairtrade Foundation is committed to "better prices, decent working conditions, local sustainability and fair terms of trade for farmers and workers in the developing world".

But a UK government-sponsored study, which investigated the production of flowers, coffee and tea in Ethiopia and Uganda, found that "where Fairtrade flowers were grown, and where there were farmers' groups selling coffee and tea into Fairtrade certified markets, wages were very low". Christopher Cramer, an economics professor at the University of London and one of the report's authors, said: "Wages in other comparable areas and among comparable employers producing the same crops but where there was no Fairtrade certification were usually higher and working conditions better. In our research sites, Fairtrade has not been an effective mechanism for improving the lives of wage workers, the poorest rural people."

From: Claire Provost & John Vidal, The Observer/Guardian News and Media, May 24, 2014

Material 2
Fairer Handel wächst rasant

Weltweit wächst die Nachfrage nach Schokolade, Kaffee und Co. aus fairem Handel. Starke Zuwächse bei Produkten mit Fair Trade Siegel hätten im vergangenen Jahr zu Einnahmen in Höhe von 5,5 Milliarden Euro weltweit geführt, teilte der Verein Trans-Fair in Bonn mit. Im Vergleich zum Vorjahr mit 4,78 Milliarden Euro bedeute dies einen globalen Zuwachs um 15 Prozent. Der Einzelhandel biete mittlerweile 30 000 Fair Trade Produkte in 125 Ländern an, berichtet die Dachorganisation Fair Trade International. (…)

Deutschland habe im Ländervergleich seine Position auf Platz zwei hinter dem Marktführer Großbritannien ausbauen können, heißt es in dem Jahresbericht. Deutschland verzeichnete demnach Rekordabsätze in Höhe von 650 Millionen Euro und ein Jahreswachstum von 23 Prozent. Marktführer Großbritannien verzeichnete ein Wachstum um zwölf Prozent auf gut zwei Milliarden Euro Einnahmen.

Die Organisation Fair Trade International ist für die Entwicklung der Fair Trade Standards und die Betreuung der Produzenten von fair gehandelten Produkten verant-
15 wortlich. Fair Trade International ist der Dachverband der nationalen Fairhandels-Organisationen, unter anderem von Trans-Fair in Deutschland, und der Produzenten-Netzwerke.

Quelle: dpa, in: Stuttgarter Zeitung, 03. 09. 2014

Material 3

Van Bo Le-Mentzel; https://www.startnext.com/karma-chakhs

Material 4

Quotes about Fairtrade

1. "A bite of Fairtrade chocolate means a lot to farmers in the South. It opens the doors to development and gives children access to healthcare, education, and a decent standard of living."
K. Ohemeng-Tinyase, Geschäftsführer der Kuapa Kokoo Kakaogenossenschaft in Ghana

2. "Before you finish eating your breakfast this morning you've depended on half the world. This is the way our universe is structured. We aren't going to have peace on earth until we recognise this basic fact."
Dr. Martin Luther King, amerikanischer Bürgerrechtler

Andy Singer, Politicalcartoons.com

Lösungsvorschläge

Teil A: Hörverstehen

Aufgabe 1a – Satzergänzungen

Transkript:

Hello and welcome to Current Issues here on CNB. My name is Jane Clover and our topic today is food labelling. The federal government is likely to introduce a star system for food packages next year to help consumers make healthier food choices. The proposed easy-to-understand food labelling system would see healthier choices carrying more stars than less healthy choices. Let's see what our listeners have to say.

Here is our first e-mail. It's from Tom, he's writing us from Perth:

(1) Tom	The whole star rating system assumes that there is one commonly accepted standard of rating something. However, if we give a food lots of stars because it is low in sugar but contains chemical sweeteners, is that a good thing? Studies show that these artificial sweeteners and flavour intensifiers are dangerous for our health. So, if we rate a low-calorie, but sweetened yoghurt with let's say three to four stars, it is misleading!

Let's listen to our first call from Peter. He is from Sydney. Peter, tell us your opinion:

(2) Peter	Star ratings are a good idea but I agree with Tom that it will always be controversial. However, Tom seems to have the time and expertise to work out what is the best solution for his circumstances. Honestly, most people in this world are not so fortunate; they either lack the time, the knowledge, and the experience or just don't care about working these things out. The majority of consumers would be grateful for easy-to-understand food labels.

Now, we've got Susan on the line. She's from Broome in Western Australia and has just successfully finished a bachelor degree. Congrats by the way, Susan.

(3) Susan	Thanks, Jane! Let's make it easy for everyone to make healthy choices. My experience is that consumers for whatever reason seem to make all the wrong choices. The consequence is that we are facing a massive public health problem, which will adversely affect ALL of us if it becomes hard to receive medical attention because others are putting pressure on the health system, and so much of our tax will have to be diverted to looking after people who make poor and hence unhealthy choices.

Thank you, Susan, for your point of view. And finally we've got another call on this topic from Don:

(4) Don	It would be way easier, if the star ratings were put in a sophisticated app that people could use while shopping instead of printing the information on labels because any recommendations by the food companies themselves would be irrelevant. Plus, people could search for products that fit their particular needs. For example, gluten free, or all Australian ingredients, or EXCLUDE something they are allergic to in the ingredients. It would make life so much easier!

Thank you, Don. The response to this topic is amazing. My name is Jane Clover. Thanks a lot for listening …

Based on: Big food fight continues after Senator Fiona Nash controversy. In: Background Briefing, RN Australian Broadcasting Corporation 30 March 2014

Bei dieser Aufgabe sollen Sie die vorgegebenen Satzanfänge auf Deutsch vervollständigen. Sie hören den Text zweimal. Lesen Sie sich die Aufgabenstellung, d. h. die vier Satzanfänge, genau durch, bevor Sie sich die Kommentare aus der Radiosendung anhören. Während des Hörens dürfen Sie sich Notizen machen. Notieren Sie in Stichpunkten, da das Hörverstehen sehr schnell abläuft und wenig Zeit zum Nachdenken bleibt. Sie erhalten für diese Aufgabe insgesamt 8 Punkte. Das bedeutet, dass Sie pro Kommentar mindestens zwei Informationen erfassen müssen. Achtung: bei (2) Peter sind vier Nennungen verlangt, um die 2 Verrechnungspunkte zu erhalten.
Nutzen Sie zum Schreiben vor allem die Pausen zwischen den Hördurchgängen und nach dem Abspielen. Schreiben Sie alles auf, was Ihnen aus dem Gedächtnis heraus einfällt, da es manchmal nur die zwei geforderten Informationen gibt. In dieser Musterlösung sind z. T. mehr als zwei Antwortmöglichkeiten angegeben.

(1) Tom	Einem kalorienreduzierten Nahrungsmittel viele Sterne zu verleihen ist fragwürdig, wenn … • **es wenig Zucker, aber dafür chemische Süßstoffe enthält.** • **(und) diese künstlichen Süßstoffe und Geschmacksverstärker gesundheitsschädlich sind.**
(2) Peter	Die Kennzeichnung von Lebensmitteln wäre sinnvoll für all diejenigen, die … • **keine Zeit haben, diese Dinge herauszufinden.** • **keine Lust haben, diese Dinge herauszufinden.** • **nicht das Wissen und die Erfahrung haben.** • **die Mehrheit der Verbraucher darstellen und dankbar für leicht verständliche Lebensmittelbeschriftungen wären.**

(3) Susan	Wenn Verbraucher weiterhin ungesunde Kaufentscheidungen treffen, geht uns das alle etwas an, weil ... • **dadurch Druck auf das Gesundheitssystem entsteht.** • **das Geld der Steuerzahler verschwendet wird, um sich um Personen zu kümmern, die schlechte und ungesunde Ernährung für sich wählen.**
(4) Don	Eine durchdachte Lebensmittel-App wäre die bessere Alternative zur Lebensmittelkennzeichnung, weil ... • **die Empfehlungen der Nahrungsmittelhersteller überflüssig wären.** • **Kunden nach Produkten für ihre persönlichen Bedürfnisse suchen könnten.** • **Kunden bei den Zutaten etwas, gegen das sie allergisch sind, ausschließen könnten.** • **es das Leben so viel leichter machen würde.**

zu (1) Tom: "*it is low in sugar but contains chemical sweeteners*" / "*these artificial sweeteners and flavor intensifiers are dangerous for our health.*"

zu (2) Peter: "*they either lack the time, the knowledge, and the experience or just don't care about working these things out. The majority of consumers would be grateful for easy-to-understand food labels.*"

zu (3) Susan: "*others are putting pressure on the health system*" / "*so much of our tax will have to be diverted to looking after people who make poor and hence unhealthy choices.*"

zu (4) Don: "*any recommendations by the food companies themselves would be irrelevant.*" / "*Plus, people could search for products that fit their particular needs.*" / "*or EXCLUDE something they are allergic to in the ingredients.*" / "*It would make life so much easier!*"

Aufgabe 1 b – Offene Fragen

Transkript:

PAM: Hello and welcome to Global Issues here on radio CNB. My name is Pam Templeton. I'm joined by Fred Pearce, English science writer. Fred, you have recently published the book "The Land Grabbers. The new fight over who owns the earth". So what inspired you to write about land grabbing?

FRED: Over the last few years, I've become aware of this hidden revolution taking place around the world: Land grabbing actually means the purchase of large pieces of land in developing countries by big companies, foreign governments, and individuals. Speculators and investors then started piling in on the back of that.

PAM: A hidden revolution … so it's a relatively new thing then? How did you research the book?

FRED: Right, it's a new trend, but I'm an old-fashioned reporter – I want to go and see. So I'd read about a big land deal in the papers and went to find out what was going on. In 2007 and 2008, soaring grain prices made countries such as Saudi Arabia and South Korea worry about their national food security and start buying up land overseas. I travelled to quite a few countries where the most shocking land grabbing is taking place, e. g. the savannah of Brazil, the forests of Indonesia and the inner Niger delta of Mali.

PAM: It seems to be happening all over the world. So let's talk details. How much land has been grabbed?

FRED: Mmh, difficult question. Some say more than two million square kilometres in the last decade have been grabbed, two-thirds of them in Africa. That's like Spain, France, Britain, Italy and Germany put together. The point is a lot of reported deals never happen, but on the other hand, a lot of the largest ones are done secretly.

PAM: I see and in your book you reveal the identities of the land grabbers: Gulf sheikdoms, Chinese state corporations, Russian oligarchs. So who's losing out?

FRED: I think the net result is that poor farmers and cattle herders across the world are being thrown off their land. They are forced to go to the nearest town and they lose absolutely everything. Land grabbing is having more of an impact on poor people's lives than climate change.

PAM: Ah, climate change, … I remember, you wrote the first popular book on climate change, "Turning up the Heat". How's that story going?

FRED: Oh well, we have started a number of projects …

Based on: Fred Pearce: Land grabbing has more of an impact on the world's poor than climate change. Interview by Tom Templeton. In: The Observer, 20 May 2012

✏ Bei dieser Aufgabe sollen Sie die unten stehenden Fragen in verständlichen Stichworten auf Deutsch beantworten. Sie hören das Interview zweimal.
✏ Während des Hörens dürfen Sie sich Notizen machen. Notieren Sie sich spontan alles, was Sie verstehen, da Sie vorher nicht wissen können, ob noch weitere Informationen zu diesem Punkt kommen werden.
✏ Nutzen Sie wiederum die Hörpausen zum Schreiben, um nichts zu versäumen.

1	Wie erklärt Fred Pearce „Land grabbing"?
	• **Der Kauf von großen Landstücken in Entwicklungsländern durch große Firmen, ausländische Regierungen und Einzelpersonen**
2	Aus welchem Grund begannen Saudi-Arabien und Südkorea in den Jahren 2007 und 2008 mit dem „Land grabbing"?
	• **Machten sich Sorgen um ihre nationale Lebensmittelversorgung / um die Sicherheit ihrer Lebensmittelversorgung**
3	Warum gibt es keine verlässlichen Angaben über das Ausmaß von „Land grabbing"?
	• **Viele gemeldete Abschlüsse / Geschäfte finden nicht statt** • **Viele der größten Geschäfte werden heimlich abgeschlossen**
4	Wer ist von „Land grabbing" betroffen und welche Folgen hat dies für die Betroffenen?
	• **Arme Bauern und Viehhirten auf der ganzen Welt sind betroffen** • **Werden von ihrem Land vertrieben / Werden gezwungen, in die nächste Stadt zu ziehen / Verlieren wirklich alles**

✏ **zu 1:** "Land grabbing actually means the purchase of large pieces of land in developing countries by big companies, foreign governments, and individuals."
✏ **zu 2:** "In 2007 and 2008, soaring grain prices made countries such as Saudi Arabia and South Korea worry about their national food security"
✏ **zu 3:** "a lot of reported deals never happen, but on the other hand, a lot of the largest ones are done secretly."
✏ **zu 4:** "poor farmers and cattle herders across the world are being thrown off their land. They are forced to go to the nearest town and they lose absolutely everything."

Teil B: Leseverstehen

Aufgabe 2 – Mediation

✏ Bei dieser Aufgabe sollen Sie das Konzept der „Smart City" erläutern und dabei in einem Handout für eine Präsentation auf umweltfreundliche, innovative Technologien eingehen. Das heißt im Klartext: Sie müssen einen eigenen Text in Form eines Handouts erstellen, mit einer Überschrift, einer Einführung (z. B. einer Definition

- von „Smart City") und zwei bis drei Unterpunkten mit entsprechenden Überschriften, die den Text strukturieren, z. B.: „Was Großstädte zu ‚Smart Cities' macht", „Fazit" oder „Appell". Hierbei soll eine Struktur auf den ersten Blick erkennbar sein. Sie sollen zudem, wie im Arbeitsauftrag gefordert, in ganzen Sätzen formulieren. Dies sollten Sie vor allem innerhalb der einzelnen Unterpunkte tun.
- Die notwendigen Informationen für Ihr Handout entnehmen Sie dem vorliegenden englischen Text. Achten Sie dabei darauf, nur diejenigen Informationen zu übernehmen, die zum Thema passen, und versuchen Sie nicht, Teile des Textes einfach zu übersetzen. Sie riskieren sonst, dass Ihre Arbeit mit 0 Punkten bewertet wird.
- Es gibt insgesamt 15 VP für diese Aufgabe, wobei Inhalt und Sprache gemeinsam gewertet werden, d. h., es gibt keine getrennte Wertung von Inhalts- und Sprachpunkten.
- 15 oder 14 VP gibt es beispielsweise, wenn Sie alle wesentlichen Inhaltspunkte in Ihrem Artikel haben und die Aufgabe angemessene und variantenreiche Formulierungen enthält, d. h. in gutem Deutsch geschrieben ist (Sprache, Stil, Rechtschreibung und Zeichensetzung). In der folgenden Musterlösung sind die wesentlichen Inhaltspunkte (VP) kenntlich gemacht.

Handout: Umweltfreundliche Technologien in der „Smart City"

Definition: Eine „Smart City" verbindet die üblichen städtischen Dienstleistungen mit neuen, umweltfreundlichen Technologien, um Ressourcen einzusparen und auf diese Weise Einkünfte zu erzielen.

Was Großstädte zu „Smart Cities" macht:
Großstädte verbessern ihre Infrastruktur zur Steigerung der Effizienz *(VP)* und überprüfen ihre bestehenden Dienstleistungen auf Einsparungsmöglichkeiten *(VP)*:
– Barcelona beispielsweise investiert in den Ausbau des Hochgeschwindigkeitsinternets in der gesamten Umgebung *(VP)* und in Ladestationen für Elektroautos und -motorräder *(VP)*. Sensoren, die an Müllcontainern angebracht sind, informieren zudem die Entsorger, wenn sie geleert werden müssen *(VP)*.
– Ein weiteres Beispiel ist die Installation von Sensoren in öffentlichen Parkanlagen, welche die Bodenfeuchtigkeit feststellen und Bewässerungsanlagen steuern *(VP)*, wodurch sich der Wasserverbrauch erheblich reduziert *(VP)*.
– Doch auch bestehende Strukturen werden genutzt, wie die Stromnetze, die mit internetfähigen Haushaltsgeräten verbunden werden, z. B. Kühlschränken, die automatisch Bestellungen an den nächsten Supermarkt schicken, wenn sie aufgefüllt werden müssen *(VP)*.

Neue Technologien machen Städte „noch smarter":
Zur Einsparung wichtiger Ressourcen und zur Steigerung des Einkommens arbeiten viele Städte zudem mit Firmen zusammen, die neue, innovative Projekte und Technologien entwickeln:
– Ein Projekt der Firma Nest Labs beschäftigt sich mit energiesparenden Geräten wie internetfähigen Rauchmeldern, die die typischen Verhaltensweisen von Verbrauchern beobachten und die Thermostate entsprechend steuern, wobei Kosten für Heizung und Klimatisierung eingespart werden *(VP)*.

– Ein anderes Projekt der Firmen Philips und Ericsson nutzt die Kombination energiesparender Straßenlaternen mit der Mobilfunkinfrastruktur: Straßenlampen werden von der Stadt an Provider vermietet, welche ihre Netzabdeckung erweitern wollen, was eine gute Einkommensquelle darstellt *(VP)*; außerdem ermöglichen Straßenlaternen, die mithilfe von Smartphones gesteuert werden, eine Energieeinsparung von bis zu 50 % gegenüber normaler Beleuchtung *(VP)*.
– Eine neue App von „Citymapper", die die Benutzung des öffentlichen Nahverkehrs erleichtert, indem sie Fahrgästen hilft, sich in komplizierten Bus- und U-Bahnplänen zurechtzufinden *(VP)*, fördert den öffentlichen Nahverkehr und verringert die Anzahl von Autos – und damit den CO_2-Ausstoß *(VP)*.
– Des Weiteren gibt es ein System, das die Parkplatzsuche erleichtert und den Parksuchverkehr reduziert *(VP)*. Sensoren zeigen verfügbare Parkplätze an und geben Informationen darüber an Kunden weiter. Diese können diese Parkplätze über eine App stundenweise buchen *(VP)*.

Fazit: Es gibt sehr viele neue Möglichkeiten für Städte und Bewohner, Zeit und Geld zu sparen und gleichzeitig etwas für die Umwelt zu tun, indem man den Energieverbrauch senkt und Ressourcen spart.
Appell: Es wäre schön, wenn alle Städte zu „Smart Cities" würden!

Teil C: Textproduktion

Aufgabe 3 – Materialgestützter Aufsatz

Bei Aufgabe 3 müssen Sie <u>zwischen zwei Themen</u> (Composition 1 oder Composition 2) <u>wählen</u>. Zu einem dieser Themen schreiben Sie einen Aufsatz, wobei Ihnen fünf verschiedene Materialien inhaltlich als Grundlage zur Verfügung stehen. Davon müssen Sie <u>mindestens drei</u> inhaltlich einfließen lassen. Geben Sie zu Beginn Ihres Aufsatzes an, welche Materialien Sie verwenden. Sie können natürlich auch Bezug auf vier oder alle fünf Materialien nehmen und eigene Kenntnisse einbringen. Achten Sie darauf, die Informationen in einem einzigen, zusammenhängenden Text unterzubringen und nicht fünf Einzeltexte zu schreiben. Es empfiehlt sich, zunächst alle fünf Materialien zu sichten im Hinblick auf die Argumente und Aspekte, die Sie daraus für Ihren Aufsatz entnehmen können.
Anschließend sollten Sie die für Sie ansprechendsten auswählen, sie in eine schlüssige Reihenfolge bringen und sie mit passenden Überleitungen miteinander verknüpfen. Sie müssen die Materialien nicht getrennt voneinander behandeln, denn manchmal können sie geschickt miteinander kombiniert werden (s. Composition 1).
Sie haben für die Aufgabe 90 Minuten Zeit und können bis zu 10 Inhalts- und 20 Sprachpunkte bekommen. Es wird erwartet, dass Sie sowohl eine Einleitung als auch einen Schluss schreiben und Ihren Aufsatz mit einem Fazit oder einer persönlichen Stellungnahme abschließen. Achten Sie besonders auf korrektes Englisch. Die Textmenge für eine gute Leistung umfasst in der Regel ca. 500 Wörter. Die folgenden Lösungsvorschläge sind ausführlicher gefasst, da sie alle Materialien berücksichtigen.

Composition 1

Unter Verwendung aller Materialien:

Immigration to Europe, which is one of the most highly discussed topics in public at the moment, is a rather complex issue and a highly emotional one, too. On the one hand, refugees flee their home country because they fear for their own lives, but on the other hand, Europeans also have fears due to the high numbers of refugees coming. In the following I will discuss this difficult matter in further detail.

First of all, let's have a look at why these refugees come to Europe. From statistics about migrant flow, we can see that most of them come because Europe is closer than other rich countries, so that they don't have to travel too far and pay much for transport. We also learn that more people come from continents with poorer living conditions like Africa and South America than from Australia and North America. *(Material 2)*

Now let's look at the motivation of refugees coming to Europe. We learn from a text about African refugees that immigrants are fleeing their homelands mostly because there is no hope for them to lead a decent life. They would face hunger, starvation and death if they stayed there and therefore risk their lives on overcrowded boats to reach Europe, in order to find work and better paid jobs. Another motivation to leave their home country is that they are persecuted because of their religion or heritage. In these cases they are oppressed and threatened to be killed as quite often there is no real government but mere anarchy in these countries. The third and most important motive is that people want to escape violence and war, as in Syria at the moment, in order to save their own lives or those of their families. If they stayed there, they would probably be tortured or killed. In a quote, actress Angelina Jolie says that according to her own experience, most refugees would like to go back home after peace is restored and a political solution has been found for their native country. We can gather from this statement that most migrants would have stayed in their home countries if the living conditions had been better. *(Material 3, 4)*

Now let's turn to the anxieties of the European people. From a German text we learn that many Europeans think that their welfare state is in danger because these immigrants receive money and accommodation, supplied by communities which are financed from taxes the native population have to pay; that's why they are afraid that their own standard of living will eventually decrease if this continues for a longer period of time. Since most of these immigrants are in Europe for economic reasons and are not granted political asylum in the end, they feel that their social system is being misused by these refugees. However, Europeans shouldn't forget that many people in our history had a similar fate and were glad that others offered help and support and gave them a second chance in their countries. Kofi Annan reminds us not to forget the positive contribution refugees have made to societies in the past and would make in the future. These contributions are one reason why Europeans should appreciate the bravery of migrants. *(Material 1, 4)*

In addition, we must keep in mind that these immigrants really don't have a choice: either they flee or they starve or are killed. They take practically nothing with them and set off on a very dangerous journey, which cost many their lives, in the hope of

finding peace and security in Europe. This situation is well depicted in a cartoon where you can see an African standing on the edge of Africa with a bundle over his shoulder looking over towards the edge of Europe, which is only connected to Africa by a very large spoon. Between these two cliffs there is a deep gap. If he wants to survive and get food, he must walk over the spoon with his bundle. If he fails and falls down from the handle, his death is certain. *(Material 5)*
Considering both sides of this dilemma, we must come to the conclusion that the motives of the immigrants and their need for help are more important and more urgent than the fears of Europeans for the safety of their own standard of living and the misuse of their welfare system. If we really want to prevent people from entering dangerous boats to come to Europe, we must help them in their home countries by improving their livelihood, so that they needn't starve, and by restoring peace and tolerance there, so that they may feel safe and secure. *(766 words)*

Composition 2

Unter Verwendung aller Materialien:

Do the producers of Fairtrade goods really profit from it, or is it another way of selling products more easily and getting more money out of consumers for things that they could have much cheaper if they bought non-Fairtrade goods? This is a very interesting but also very controversial topic, which is highly discussed in public, and I will examine it in the following.
First of all, let's have a look at some of the facts and figures about Fairtrade to understand how significant the trade with those products is and how much money is involved. In a German text we learn that Fairtrade is flourishing and on the rise. At the moment 30,000 products are offered in 125 countries, and the worldwide sales were 5.5 billion Euros in 2013 and increased by 15 % in comparison to 2012. Great Britain sells the most products, with a turnover of 2 billion Euros, followed by Germany. From these figures we can see that there is quite a lot of money involved in Fairtrade and the figures and numbers of products are going up constantly. *(Material 2)*
Now we should have a look at the differences between "normal" trade and Fairtrade. In a cartoon about two packs of coffee, these differences are depicted next to each other. The considerably higher price of the Fairtrade coffee is justified at the bottom of the pack by mentioning organic and sustainable farming practices by small farm cooperatives, environment-friendly production and transport, and the recycled packaging. In contrast to this, the coffee of the "unfair" trade contains pesticides, is produced with slave labor under brutal dictatorships, packed in toxic plastic bags and dumped in huge supermarkets by petrol wasting four-wheel drive cars – but only costs about one third of the price of Fairtrade coffee. *(Material 5)*
These differences are also emphasized by a marketing poster for Fairtrade shoes. Left of the shoes you can read that there is "no plastic", "no child labour", "no exploitation" and "no bad karma" in them. That means they are environment-friendly, support human rights and improve the living conditions of the workers, and that's why

buying Fairtrade shoes is good for the "Karma" of the consumers; they don't have to have a bad conscience when buying them. *(Material 3)*

In a quote by Mr Ohemeng-Tinyase, we read that buying Fairtrade products has many positive effects on the people living in areas where those products are produced. It improves their lives because they get better healthcare, a better education and their standard of living improves. In another quote by Martin Luther King, he says that we should be aware that we consume products from all over the world and that we contribute to peace on Earth if we consume responsibly. *(Material 4)*

However, are all these good aspects and promises really true? In an English text we read that a British study comparing the production of flowers, coffee and tea on Fairtrade farms with farms producing without Fairtrade certification in Ethiopia and Uganda revealed that Fairtrade employees received lower wages and that the working conditions on Fairtrade farms were worse than those on farms without the Fairtrade label. If this was really true in all countries which produce for Fairtrade, the consumers' money would simply be wasted on the organization of Fairtrade, and decent people who care about the farmers in Africa would be deceived. *(Material 1)*

All in all, we can say that the idea of Fairtrade is a concept of helping people who produce things for us, in order that they might have a decent life and one of supporting their development in their own country. However, we must be careful that this positive initiative is not misused as it was in Ethiopia and Uganda, so that the image of Fairtrade is not damaged irreparably. In my opinion, it could be worthwhile supporting and buying Fairtrade products, because positive changes can be achieved if we all help und contribute to a better world. *(654 words)*

Fachhochschulreife Englisch (Berufskolleg Baden-Württemberg)
Schriftliche Hauptprüfung 2016

Teil A: Hörverstehen

Aufgabe 1a – Satzergänzungen (8 VP)

Soziale Netzwerke am Arbeitsplatz

Radio CNB hat bei seinen Hörern eine Umfrage zum Thema Soziale Netzwerke am Arbeitsplatz gestartet. Einige der Beiträge werden im Radio vorgestellt.

▶ Hören Sie aufmerksam zu und vervollständigen Sie auf Deutsch die unten stehenden Sätze. Entnehmen Sie jeder Aussage mindestens **zwei** Aspekte.

(1) Tom	Während der Arbeit sollten Angestellte keine Zeit in sozialen Netzwerken verbringen, da …
(2) Peter	Die Nutzung sozialer Netzwerke am Arbeitsplatz bereitet den Arbeitgebern berechtigte Sorge, weil …
(3) Susan	Vernünftige Arbeitgeber sollten …
(4) Don	Es ist leider traurige Realität, dass …

2016-1

Aufgabe 1 b – Offene Fragen *(7 VP)*

Zucker

Francesco Branca stellt die neuen Empfehlungen der Weltgesundheitsorganisation (WHO) für den Konsum von Zucker auf einer Pressekonferenz vor.

▶ Hören Sie aufmerksam zu und bearbeiten Sie die Fragen auf Deutsch in Stichworten.

1	Beschreiben Sie die weltweite Entwicklung von Fettleibigkeit.
	(2 VP)
2	Wie definiert die WHO den Begriff „free sugars"?
	(2 VP)
3	Welche drei Empfehlungen gibt die WHO bezüglich des individuellen Zuckerkonsums?
	(3 VP)

Teil B: Leseverstehen

Aufgabe 2 – Mediation (15 VP)

Anlässlich des diesjährigen Internationalen Weltkindertags am 1. Juni erstellen Sie für den Ethikunterricht eine schriftliche Ausarbeitung zum Thema „Lebens- und Arbeitssituation der Kinder auf westafrikanischen Kakaoplantagen". Bei der Recherche sind Sie auf folgenden Text gestoßen.

▶ Entnehmen Sie dem vorliegenden Artikel die dafür notwendigen Informationen.
▶ Formulieren Sie ganze deutsche Sätze.

Child Labor and Slavery in the Chocolate Industry

Chocolate is a product of the cocoa bean, which grows primarily in the tropical climates of Western Africa, Asia, and Latin America. Western African countries, mostly Ghana and the Ivory Coast, supply more than 70 % of the world's cocoa.

In recent years, a handful of organizations and journalists have revealed the widespread use of child labor, and in some cases slavery, on cocoa farms in Western Africa. Since then, the industry has become increasingly secretive, making it difficult for reporters to access farms where human rights violations still occur. At least one journalist investigating this topic has been killed. The farms of Western Africa supply cocoa to international giants such as Hershey's, Mars, and Nestlé – revealing the industry's direct connection to the worst forms of child labor and slavery.

In Western Africa, cocoa is a crop grown primarily for export; 60 % of the Ivory Coast's export revenue comes from its cocoa. As the chocolate industry has grown over the years, so has the demand for cheap cocoa. On average, cocoa farmers earn less than $ 2 per day, an income below the poverty line. As a result, they often use child labor to keep their prices competitive.

The children of Western Africa are surrounded by intense poverty, and most begin working at a young age to help support their families. Some children end up on the cocoa farms because they need work and they are told that the job pays well. Other children are "sold" to farm owners by their own relatives, who are unaware of the dangerous work environment and the lack of any education. Once they have been taken to the cocoa farms, the children may not see their families for years, if ever.

Most of the children labouring on cocoa farms are between the ages of 12 and 16, but reporters have found children as young as 5. In addition, 40 % of these children are girls, and some stay for a few months, while others end up working on the cocoa farms through adulthood.

A child's workday typically begins at six in the morning and ends in the evening. Some of the children use chainsaws to clear the forests. Other children climb the cocoa trees to cut bean pods[1] using a machete. These large, heavy, dangerous knives are the standard tools for children on the cocoa farms, which violates international labor laws and a UN convention on eliminating the worst forms of child labor.

Once they have cut the bean pods from the trees, the children pack the pods into sacks that weigh more than 100 pounds when full and drag them through the forest.

Aly Diabate, a former cocoa slave, said, "Some of the bags were taller than me. It took two people to put the bag on my head. And if you didn't hurry, you were beaten."

Holding a single large pod in one hand, each child has to strike the pod with a machete and cut it open with the tip of the blade to expose the cocoa beans. Every strike of the machete has the potential to cut a child's flesh. The majority of children have scars on their hands, arms, legs or shoulders from the machetes.

In addition to the dangers of using machetes, children are also exposed to agricultural chemicals on cocoa farms in Western Africa. Tropical regions such as Ghana and the Ivory Coast consistently have plagues of insects and spray the pods with large amounts of industrial chemicals. In Ghana, children as young as 10 spray the pods with these toxins without wearing protective clothing.

The farm owners using child labor usually provide children with the cheapest food available, such as corn paste and bananas. In some cases, the children sleep on wooden planks in small windowless buildings with no access to clean water or bathrooms.

On cocoa farms, 10 % of child laborers in Ghana and 40 % in the Ivory Coast do not attend school, which violates the International Labour Organization's (ILO) Child Labour Standards. Depriving these children of an education has many short-term and also long-term effects. Without an education, the children of the cocoa farms have little hope of ever breaking the cycle of poverty.

To date, relatively little progress has been made to reduce or eliminate child labor and slavery in the cocoa industry of Western Africa. Approximately 1.8 million children in the Ivory Coast and Ghana may be exposed to the worst forms of child labor on cocoa farms. *(749 words)*

© *Food Empowerment Project, www.foodispower.org/slavery-chocolate*

Annotation
1 cocoa bean pod – Kakaofrucht

Teil C: Textproduktion

Aufgabe 3 – Materialgestützter Aufsatz   *(30 VP: 10 VP Inh./20 VP Spr.)*

Choose between Composition 1 or Composition 2.

Write a composition about the chosen topic.
- Use the information of at least three of the given materials.
- Name which ones you are using.
- Make use of your own ideas.
- Do not write three separate compositions but one covering all the materials chosen.

Composition 1

Partying and drinking in public is a common pastime for people of all ages. For some this is a great way of socializing, for others it is a real nuisance. More and more city councils are thinking about introducing alcohol-free zones in public places. Discuss the pros and cons of this idea.

Material 1

Alcohol-free zone plan considered

Parts of South London could become alcohol-free zones under proposals being considered by a local authority. Lambeth Council is considering introducing a controlled drinking zone (CDZ) to combat alcohol related anti-social behaviour. It would allow police to confiscate alcohol or stop people from drinking in any of the borough's streets. Public areas subject to the ban could include streets, parks and open spaces.

Critics have insisted the laws are oppressive but the council said it would only target problem drinkers.

"People have a right to walk along the street without being intimidated by problem drinkers," said Lambeth Council's Ann Corbett. "These extra powers will help the police, council, and partner agencies take action against street drinkers and get to the root cause of the problem."

But opponents said such laws are a sign of "hyper-regulation". Josie Appleton, from the anti-regulation campaign group the Manifesto Club, said: "Across the country people sitting with friends enjoying a beer in a picnic or walking through town are having that beer confiscated. This is outrageous, it's completely unreasonable. They're not doing anyone harm. This law is actually anti-social and we think the police shouldn't have these powers."

© *BBC News, June 30, 2009*

Material 2

© INKCINCT Cartoons, www.inkcinct.com.au

Material 3

© Fröse-Probst Claudia

Material 4

Quotes about partying and drinking

1. "That's the problem with drinking, I thought, as I poured myself a drink. If something bad happens you drink in an attempt to forget; if something good happens you drink in order to celebrate; and if nothing happens you drink to make something happen."
   Charles Bukowski, amerikanischer Autor
   aus: *Charles Bukowski: Women. Boston: Black Sparrow Press 1978.*

2. "I had years of partying, and I was kind of surprised and happy I survived it all. Now, being a parent, I look back on it thinking: Oh God, the things you did!"
   Jeff Bridges, amerikanischer Schauspieler
   aus: *John Patterson: The Dude will see you now. Interview with Jeff Bridges. In: The Guardian, 24 Oct, 2003.*

Material 5

Jugend mit Vorbildern

Sie grölen herum, sie sind rücksichtslos, sie verrichten ihr Geschäft in Vorgärten. Und sie sind schwer betrunken. Die Rede ist nicht von den frei laufenden Jugendlichen, die, glaubt man Sicherheitskräften, Bürgermeistern und einigen Mitgliedern der Regierungskoalition, sich zu Horden an Tank- und Haltestellen zusammenrotten, um anschließend als marodierende Masse die Innenstädte zu verwüsten. Die Rede ist vielmehr von animierten Besuchern durchschnittlicher Dorf-, Feuerwehr-, Volks- und Stadtteilfeste, von Angehörigen aller Altersklassen, die der verbreiteten Auffassung anhängen, sie könnten auch ohne Alkohol fröhlich sein, müssten aber nicht. [...]

Allenthalben erzählen Tourismuswerber und kommunale Eventmanager, Städte und Gemeinden seien umso lebenswerter, je mehr Stadtfeste, Weindörfer, Fischmärkte sie zu bieten hätten. Der Schultes sticht das Fass an, der Minister küsst weinselig die Weinkönigin, und kein Mitglied der Regierungsbank kann es sich leisten, nicht wenigstens einmal pro Saison auf dem Cannstatter Wasen den Humpen in die Kamera zu heben. Alkohol gilt als Kulturgut und fungiert als Schmiermittel unserer Gesellschaft; das Recht auf Rausch ist unbestritten. Und unsere Jugend wächst da hinein. [...]

Herumpöbeln, die Ruhe stören, Passanten beleidigen, öffentliches Ärgernis erregen – gegen all das kann die Polizei jetzt schon vorgehen. Bürger, denen alkoholbetäubte Jugendliche ein Dorn im Auge sind, Eltern, die sich um ihre heranwachsenden Kinder sorgen, kurz: wir alle sollten über das Vorbild nachdenken, das wir abgeben.

© *Ruf Reiner, www.stuttgarter-zeitung.de*

Composition 2

Women in "typically male" professions – a minority.
Explain reasons and describe possible changes.

Material 1

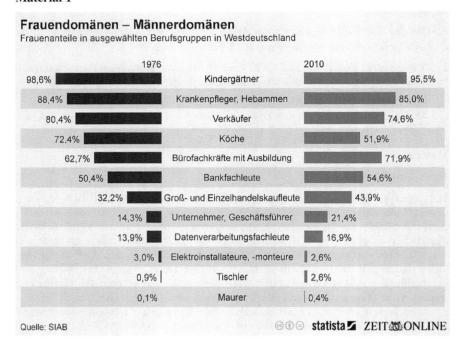

Frauendomänen – Männerdomänen
Frauenanteile in ausgewählten Berufsgruppen in Westdeutschland

1976	Beruf	2010
98,6%	Kindergärtner	95,5%
88,4%	Krankenpfleger, Hebammen	85,0%
80,4%	Verkäufer	74,6%
72,4%	Köche	51,9%
62,7%	Bürofachkräfte mit Ausbildung	71,9%
50,4%	Bankfachleute	54,6%
32,2%	Groß- und Einzelhandelskaufleute	43,9%
14,3%	Unternehmer, Geschäftsführer	21,4%
13,9%	Datenverarbeitungsfachleute	16,9%
3,0%	Elektroinstallateure, -monteure	2,6%
0,9%	Tischler	2,6%
0,1%	Maurer	0,4%

Quelle: SIAB   statista ZEIT ONLINE

Material 2

**Women and work: Do they opt out or are they pushed out? –
The US story in data**

1   Some call women leaving the workforce in order to balance work and family life "opting out". Social scientists who study workplace culture say it's more like they were "pushed out" because workplaces require long, demanding hours of face time and see flexible or part-time work as almost a sign of weakness. And, unlike in other
5   advanced economies, there are no policies or laws that give real support to working families.
    Economist Sylvia Ann Hewlett of the Center for Talent Innovation, who studies the phenomenon, calls it a "hidden brain drain" that not only hurts women, keeping them down or out of the workforce. It also hurts men by tying them to work even
10   though more, particularly younger men, say what they most want is to spend more

time with their children and be equal partners at home. The phenomenon, Hewlett argues, hurts businesses, families and the economy.

Brigid Schulte: Women and work: Opt out or pushed out? The story in data. In: Washington Post, June 9, 2014. © Brigid Schulte. URL: www.washingtonpost.com/blogs/she-the-people/wp/2014/06/09/women-and-work-opt-out-or-pushed-out-the-story-in-data/

Material 3

Girls' Day macht Schule

Mädchen haben im Schnitt die besseren Schulabschlüsse und Noten. Trotzdem wählt mehr als die Hälfte der Mädchen aus nur zehn verschiedenen Ausbildungsberufen im dualen System – kein einziger naturwissenschaftlich-technischer ist darunter. In Studiengängen, wie z. B. in Ingenieurswissenschaften oder Informatik, sind Frauen deutlich unterrepräsentiert.

Als Lehrkraft und als Eltern spielen sie eine besonders wichtige Rolle bei der Berufsorientierung der Mädchen. Sie kennen ihre Stärken und Begabungen und können sie auf ihrem Entscheidungsweg unterstützen.

Quelle: www.girls-day.de © Kompetenzzentrum Bielefeld

Material 4

Carroll Zahn / cartoonstock.com

Material 5

Quotes about women and work

1. "A strong woman understands that the gifts such as logic, decisiveness, and strength are just as feminine as intuition and emotional connection. She values and uses all of her gifts."
   Nancy Rathburn, amerikanische Psychotherapeutin
   aus: 30 Empowering Quotes from Women Who Dare. Harpers Bazaar, Mar 8, 2016

2. "The gender stereotypes introduced in childhood are reinforced throughout our lives and become self-fulfilling prophesies. Most leadership positions are held by men, so women don't expect to achieve them, and that becomes one of the reasons they don't."
   Sheryl Sandberg, Chief Operating Officer von Facebook
   aus: Sheryl Sandberg: Lean in. Women, work, and the will to lead. New York: Alfred A. Knopf 2013

3. "You can have unbelievable intelligence, you can have connections, you can have opportunities fall out of the sky. But in the end, hard work is the true, enduring characteristic of successful people."
   Marsha Evans, amerikanische Schriftstellerin
   aus: Barry J. Farber: Diamond Power. Gems of Wisdom from America's Greatest Marketer. Franklin Lakes: Career Press 2003

Lösungsvorschläge

Teil A: Hörverstehen

Aufgabe 1a – Satzergänzungen

Transkript:

Hello and welcome to Current Issues here on CNB. My name is Jane Clover and today our topic is social media at work and whether social network sites should be banned at the workplace. Let's see what our listeners have to say.

Let's listen to our first call from Tom. He is from Dayton, Ohio. Tom tell us your opinion.

(1) Tom	An employee attends work to earn his salary. His time at work should be spent dealing with the job requirements, which means giving complete effort and attention to the job at hand. Work is not a place where time can be wasted on meaningless social chitchat, since this has no benefit to the employer and costs businesses millions of euros in lost productivity. Social media should be reserved for one's free time, which is precisely what they were developed for.

Thank you, Tom. Rhode Island resident Peter adds a further interesting aspect to our discussion:

(2) Peter	Work is a major part of our lives and staff have always discussed aspects of their jobs in private. Now many of these private conversations are written on the Web and are potentially searchable by the public which is problematic for sure. Employers may have reasonable concerns about keeping confidential information secret or about reputation damage, but should still not overreact by attempting to stop staff from using such tools at all. WhatsApp and co. help us to organize our personal lives – that's all.

Our next call is from Susan in Melbourne.

(3) Susan	Even if employers have the right to stop staff from using social-networking sites at work, a total ban is an overreaction. I think sensible employers should do two things: First, they should make sure they have policies that cover their use, so that there are no unpleasant surprises for either employer or employee if things should go wrong. Second, all of us spend many of our waking hours at work and should be allowed to use social media during breaks e. g. for "poking" friends or making plans for after office hours.

Thank you, Susan, for your point of view. And finally we've got another call on this topic from Don:

(4) Don	This all sounds good to me, but the sad fact is that, with human nature being what it is, employees will always stretch to the limit any concessions made by employers, so that even limited access will soon be misused because of the very structure of these sites. Facebook, for example, has games on its site, which can take up huge amounts of time – time that is being paid for by the employer.

Thank you, Don. The response to this topic has been amazing. My name is Jane Clover. Thanks a lot for listening …

Adapted from: Peter Mooney: Should networking sites be banned from work?
In: Handelsblatt, 11 Aug, 2010; Employers need to face up to the age of Facebook.Trades Union Congress, Press Release, 30 Aug, 2007; Brendan Barber: Should networking sites be banned from work? In: Business Spotlight, 11 Aug, 2010

Bei dieser Aufgabe sollen Sie die vorgegebenen Satzanfänge auf Deutsch vervollständigen. Sie hören den Text zweimal. Lesen Sie sich die Aufgabenstellung, d. h. die vier Satzanfänge, genau durch, bevor Sie sich die Kommentare aus der Radiosendung anhören. Während des Hörens dürfen Sie sich Notizen machen. Notieren Sie alles, was Sie verstehen, da das Hörverstehen sehr schnell abläuft und wenig Zeit zum Nachdenken bleibt. Sie erhalten für diese Aufgabe insgesamt 8 Punkte. Das bedeutet, dass Sie pro Kommentar zwei Informationen erfassen müssen. Pro richtige Information erhalten Sie einen Verrechnungspunkt. Bei (1) Tom und (4) Don sind alternative Nennungen angegeben. Es werden aber nur jeweils zwei Nennungen gewertet. Nutzen Sie zum Schreiben vor allem die Pausen zwischen dem 1. und 2. Hördurchgang, sowie nach dem 2. Abspielen des Textes, weil Sie in dieser Zeit keine Informationen versäumen können. Schreiben Sie alles, was Ihnen aus dem Gedächtnis heraus einfällt, auf, da es manchmal nur die zwei geforderten Informationen gibt.

(1) Tom	Während der Arbeit sollten Angestellte keine Zeit in sozialen Netzwerken verbringen, da …
	• **ein Angestellter zur Arbeit geht, um sein Gehalt zu verdienen.** / **ihre Arbeitszeit mit den Anforderungen des Arbeitsplatzes zugebracht werden sollte.** / **sie ihre gesamte Mühe und Aufmerksamkeit der Arbeit widmen sollten.** / **die Arbeit kein Ort ist, an dem Zeit mit belanglosem Smalltalk vergeudet werden sollte.** • **dies keinen Nutzen für den Arbeitgeber hat.** • **es Firmen Millionen von Euro durch verlorene Produktivität kostet.** • **diese für die Freizeit reserviert sein sollen, wofür sie eigentlich entwickelt wurden.** *(2 Nennungen sind verlangt)*

(2) Peter	Die Nutzung sozialer Netzwerke am Arbeitsplatz bereitet den Arbeitgebern berechtigte Sorge, weil … <ul><li>sie befürchten, dass vertrauliche Informationen nicht mehr geheim bleiben.</li><li>sie Rufschädigung befürchten. / sie befürchten, dass der Ruf ihrer Firma Schaden nimmt.</li></ul>	
(3) Susan	Vernünftige Arbeitgeber sollten … <ul><li>sicherstellen, dass sie Regeln für die Nutzung sozialer Netzwerke haben, um negative Überraschungen zu vermeiden.</li><li>die Verwendung von sozialen Netzwerken in den Pausen erlauben.</li></ul>	
(4) Don	Es ist leider traurige Realität, dass … <ul><li>Arbeitnehmer Zugeständnisse ihres Arbeitgebers immer bis zum Limit ausnutzen.</li><li>sogar ein begrenzter Zugang sehr bald missbraucht werden wird.</li><li>Spiele in sozialen Netzwerken (wie Facebook) eine Menge Zeit verschwenden, die vom Arbeitgeber bezahlt wird.</li></ul> *(2 Nennungen sind verlangt)*	

zu (1) Tom: "An employee attends work to earn his salary. His time at work should be spent dealing with the job requirements, which means giving complete effort and attention to the job at hand. Work is not a place where time can be wasted on meaningless chitchat" / "since this has no benefit to the employer" / "costs businesses millions of euros in lost productivity" / "Social media should be reserved for one's free time, which is precisely what they were developed for."

zu (2) Peter: "Employers may have reasonable concerns about keeping confidential information secret" / "or about reputation damage"

zu (3) Susan: "they should make sure they have policies that cover their use, so that there are no unpleasant surprises" / "all of us […] should be allowed to use social media during breaks"

zu (4) Don: "employees will always stretch to the limit any concessions made by employers" / "even limited access will soon be misused" / "Facebook, for example, has games on its site, which can take up huge amounts of time – time that is being paid for by the employer."

Aufgabe 1 b – Offene Fragen

Transkript:

Francesco Branca: "Ladies and gentlemen, good morning. We're here today to present the World Health Organization (WHO) results regarding the impact of sugars on people's health and particularly the consequences the intake of free sugars has on two very common public health issues – obesity and tooth decay. Obesity now affects half a billion people worldwide and it is particularly on the rise in low and middle-income countries. Tooth decay is one of the most common non-infectious diseases. It creates discomfort, pain and eats up about 5 % of the global health budget.

Today, we're discussing the impact of free sugars, particularly the question of what free sugars are. Free sugars are sugars that are added to food artificially or are naturally present in honey, in fruit syrups and fruit concentrates. Sometimes we're not really able to see the free sugars so I've brought some examples of foods that have a high content of free sugars with me today. Here is a soda, an average soft drink. An average serving contains up to 35 g – this particular one contains 35 g of sugar.

You can also find free sugars in cereals – these here are breakfast cereals. In this average sized bowl, for example, we have approximately 14 g of sugar. We sometimes don't realize how much sugar content there is because it is only listed in the list of ingredients in small print. A standard, typical sauce that is added to meat can contain up to 7 g of sugar. So, free sugars are hidden in food, we don't see them.

The question is: How much sugar is appropriate? We have developed a new guideline that we're opening for consultation today.

The new draft recommendations make three points. The first point is that WHO recommends a reduced intake of free sugars throughout the course of your life. The second recommendation is that the intake of free sugars in both adults and children should not exceed 10 % of total energy intake. Now, this for an adult means approximately the equivalent of 50 g of sugar per day. For children it's even less – about no more than 3 teaspoons for an 8-year-old child.

But we also make a third recommendation and that is that the further reduction to less than 5 % of total energy intake gives additional health benefits.

We are opening the public consultation today. People who are interested are invited to submit a declaration of interest through the WHO website and give their comments, which will be thoroughly analyzed by the WHO Secretariat. Thank you."

Public consultation on WHO draft sugars guidelines. WHO virtual press conference, 5 Mar, 2014, pp. 2-3. Copyright 2014.
URL: www.who.int/mediacentre/multimedia/who_food_safety_sugar_consumption_05mar2014.pdf
[last accessed on 9 Jun, 2016]

Bei dieser Aufgabe sollen Sie in verständlichen Stichworten auf Deutsch antworten. Sie hören den Text zweimal. Lesen Sie zunächst die Aufgabe genau durch. Während des Hörens und in den Pausen dürfen Sie sich Notizen machen. Sie erhalten für diese Aufgabe insgesamt 7 Punkte. Pro Nennung, d. h. Satz bzw. Stichpunkt erhalten Sie einen Punkt. Achten Sie auf die Angabe der zu vergebenen Punkte; bei Aufgabe 3 sind drei Verrechnungspunkte zu erreichen.

1	Beschreiben Sie die weltweite Entwicklung von Fettleibigkeit. (2 VP) <ul><li>**Es sind bis jetzt eine halbe Milliarde Menschen weltweit davon betroffen.**</li><li>**Sie nimmt besonders in Ländern mit niedrigen und mittleren Einkommen zu.**</li></ul>
2	Wie definiert die WHO den Begriff „free sugars"? (2 VP) <ul><li>**Es sind Zuckerarten, die Nahrung(smitteln) künstlich zugefügt werden**</li><li>**oder natürlich in Honig, Sirup oder Fruchtkonzentraten enthalten sind.**</li></ul>
3	Welche drei Empfehlungen gibt die WHO bezüglich des individuellen Zuckerkonsums? (3 VP) <ul><li>**Sie empfiehlt, den Konsum von (freien) Zucker(arten) das ganze Leben lang zu reduzieren.**</li><li>**Der Konsum von Zucker sollte sowohl bei Erwachsenen als auch bei Kindern 10 % des täglichen Energiebedarfs nicht übersteigen. / Erwachsene sollten nicht mehr als ca. 50 Gramm Zucker pro Tag zu sich nehmen, ein achtjähriges Kind beispielsweise nicht mehr als drei Teelöffel.**</li><li>**Eine weitere Reduzierung des Zuckers auf weniger als 5 % des täglichen Energiebedarfs wirkt sich zusätzlich positiv auf die Gesundheit aus.**</li></ul>

zu 1: "Obesity now affects half a billion people worldwide" / "it is particularly on the rise in low and middle-income countries."

zu 2: "Free sugars are sugars that are added to food artificially" / "are naturally present in honey, in fruit syrups and fruit concentrates."

zu 3: "WHO recommends a reduced intake of free sugars throughout the course of your life." / "the intake of free sugars in both adults and children should not exceed 10 % of total energy intake." / "this for an adult means approximately the equivalent of 50 g of sugar per day. For children it's even less – about no more than 3 teaspoons for an 8-year-old child." / "the further reduction to less than 5 % of total energy intake gives additional health benefits."

Teil B: Leseverstehen

Aufgabe 2 – Mediation

Bei dieser Aufgabe sollen Sie an dem diesjährigen Weltkindertag am 1. Juni für den Ethikunterricht eine Ausarbeitung zum Thema „Lebens- und Arbeitssituation der Kinder auf westafrikanischen Kakaoplantagen" anfertigen.

Sie müssen also einen eigenen Text in ganzen Sätzen erstellen, mit dem Thema als Überschrift, einem Einführungssatz und zwei bis drei Unterüberschriften, die den Text strukturieren sollen. Unter diesen Überschriften sollen Sie die Beschreibung der Situation der Kinder in den beiden vorgegebenen Bereichen gliedern. Am Ende folgt ein Fazit, das in dieser Beispiellösung einen Appell beinhaltet, etwas gegen das Problem zu unternehmen.

Alle notwendigen Informationen entnehmen Sie dem englischen Text zu diesem Thema, der Ihnen quasi als Steinbruch dient, aus dem Sie die Fakten und Ideen für Ihren eigenen Text herausholen können. Suchen Sie aber nur diejenigen Informationen heraus, die zu Ihrem Thema passen.

Versuchen Sie nicht, Teile des Textes zu übersetzen, weil dies dazu führt, dass Sie die gestellte Aufgabe nicht erfüllen. Deshalb müsste eine reine Übersetzung des Textes in jedem Fall mit 0 Punkten bewertet werden.

Es gibt insgesamt 15 VP für diese Aufgabe, wobei Inhalt- und Sprachpunkte gemeinsam gewertet werden, d. h., es gibt keine getrennte Wertung von Inhalts- und Sprachpunkten. Zur Orientierung: 15 oder 14 VP gibt es, wenn die kontextbezogene Aufgabe vollständig und umfassend gelöst ist, d. h., wenn sie alle wesentlichen Inhaltspunkte in ihrem Artikel haben, <u>und</u> die Aufgabe in angemessenem, variantenreichem und korrektem Deutsch geschrieben ist, was Sprache, Stil, Rechtschreibung und Zeichensetzung angeht. In der folgenden Musterlösung sind die wesentlichen Inhaltspunkte (VP) kenntlich gemacht.

Die Lebens- und Arbeitssituationen der Kinder auf Kakaoplantagen

Auf den Kakaoplantagen in Westafrika, auf denen mehr als 70 % des Kakaos der Welt hergestellt wird, ist Kinderarbeit und in manchen Fällen sogar Sklaverei weit verbreitet. *(VP)* Da die Nachfrage nach billigem Kakao sehr groß ist und die Bauern dort weniger als zwei Dollar am Tag verdienen, nutzt man oft Kinderarbeit, um den Preis niedrig zu halten. *(VP)*

Die Lebenssituation der Kinder in Westafrika
Die Kinder in Westafrika kommen aus sehr armen Verhältnissen und beginnen im frühen Alter zu arbeiten, um ihre Familien zu unterstützen. *(VP)* Sie landen auf den Kakaoplantagen weil sie Arbeit brauchen und ihnen gesagt wird, dass die Arbeit gut bezahlt ist. *(VP)* Manche Kinder werden von ihren eigenen Verwandten, denen nicht bewusst ist, dass die Arbeitsbedingungen auf den Plantagen sehr schlecht sind, als Sklaven verkauft. *(VP)*

Viele Kinder sehen ihre Familie oft jahrelang nicht mehr, manche auch nie wieder. Manche bleiben nur ein paar Monate und andere arbeiten dort ihr gesamtes Erwachsenenleben hindurch. *(VP)* Die meisten Kinder, von denen 40 % Mädchen sind, sind zwischen 12 und 16 Jahre alt. Es gibt aber auch Kinder im Alter von 5 Jahren. *(VP)*

Arbeitsbedingungen der Kinder auf Kakaoplantagen
Die Kinder müssen von früh morgens um 6 Uhr bis spät abends arbeiten und sie verwenden oft gefährliche Werkzeuge, wie zum Beispiel Kettensägen. *(VP)* Sie müssen oft sehr schwere Säcke durch den Wald transportieren und wenn sie die Arbeiten nicht schnell genug machen, werden sie geschlagen. *(VP)*
Die Mehrzahl der Kinder hat Narben von Schnittwunden am ganzen Körper, verursacht durch die Macheten, mit denen sie arbeiten müssen. *(VP)* Außerdem werden Sie giftigen Chemikalien ausgesetzt, ohne dass sie Schutzkleidung tragen. *(VP)* Sie werden nur mit den billigsten Nahrungsmitteln versorgt, wie z. B. mit Bananen und Maispaste *(VP)*, und manche schlafen auf Holzböden in kleinen Gebäuden ohne Fenster und ohne Zugang zu sauberem Wasser oder einem Waschraum. *(VP)*
Einige Kinder, die auf Kakaoplantagen arbeiten, besuchen keine Schule, ohne die sie keine Chance haben, den Teufelskreis der Armut zu durchbrechen. *(VP)*

Fazit
Bis heute ist es nicht gelungen, die Kinderarbeit auf Kakaoplantagen, von der etwa 1,8 Millionen Kinder betroffen sind, zu reduzieren. *(VP)*
Es ist notwendig, Druck auf die großen Schokoladegiganten wie Mars und Nestlé auszuüben, um die Kinder- und Sklavenarbeit in Westafrika in den Griff zu bekommen, da auch diese von dort die größte Menge ihres Kakaos beziehen.

Teil C: Textproduktion

Aufgabe 3 – Materialgestützter Aufsatz

Bei dieser Aufgabe müssen Sie einen Aufsatz über eines der vorgegebenen Themen (Composition 1 oder Composition 2) schreiben, wobei Ihnen jeweils fünf verschiedene Materialien inhaltlich als Grundlage zur Verfügung stehen. Davon müssen Sie mindestens drei Aspekte inhaltlich in Ihren Aufsatz mit einfließen lassen. Geben Sie zu Beginn Ihres Aufsatzes an, welche Materialien Sie für Ihren Aufsatz verwendet haben. Sie können natürlich auch vier oder alle fünf Materialien einbringen und auch noch eigene Kenntnisse ergänzen. Achten Sie aber darauf, die Informationen in einem einzigen zusammenhängenden Text unterzubringen.
Es empfiehlt sich, zunächst alle fünf Materialien gründlich zu sichten im Hinblick auf die Argumente und relevanten Aspekte, die Sie daraus für Ihren Aufsatz entnehmen können.
Sie haben insgesamt 90 Minuten Zeit und können insgesamt maximal 10 Inhalts- und 20 Sprachpunkte bekommen. Es wird erwartet, dass Sie sowohl eine Einleitung als auch einen Schluss schreiben und mindestens drei Aspekte ausführlich diskutieren, um die Aufgabe vollständig zu bearbeiten. Die Textmenge für eine gute Leistung umfasst in der Regel ca. 500 Wörter. Die folgenden Lösungsvorschläge berücksichtigen jeweils vier Materialien.

- *Beim ersten Thema sollen Sie einen Aufsatz schreiben, in dem Sie die Vor- und Nachteile des Alkoholverbots auf öffentlichen Plätzen diskutieren. Es handelt sich hierbei also um einen dialektischen Aufsatz, bei dem es die Vor- und Nachteile zu beschreiben und gegeneinander abzuwägen gilt.*
- *Beim zweiten Thema sollen Sie einen Aufsatz verfassen, in dem Sie über Frauen in typischen Männerberufen schreiben. Es handelt sich also um keinen dialektischen (Pro/Kontra) Aufsatz, sondern um einen linearen Aufsatz mit zwei verschiedenen Blickpunkten, die es zu betrachten gilt, nämlich einerseits die Gründe für diese Besonderheit und die möglichen Veränderungen, die es zu beobachten gibt.*

Composition 1

Verwendete Materialien: 1, 3, 4 und 5

"Partying and drinking in public places" is a very controversial issue which is often discussed in the media. That is why it is worthwhile discussing whether it would be a good or bad idea to introduce alcohol-free zones in public places in city centres. This is what I am going to do in the following in further detail. *(Introduction)*

First of all, let's have a look at some statistics concerning alcohol consumption. From these statistics we can clearly see that drinking alcohol can be fun, can make you feel better and can also help you to relax. It is a way to escape from your problems, and it makes it easier for you to get into social contact with other people. But on the other hand, drinking can also have negative effects on people such as feelings of dizziness or sickness, and it may also contribute to addiction and boost bad behaviour towards other people. In addition, due to the lack of concentration, there is a much greater risk of accidents happening, and the dangers of hurting oneself or others are increased when you drink and drive. *(Material 3)*

Another aspect of this matter is described in a quote by Charles Bukowski, in which he explains that there is always a good reason to drink. If you are happy, you drink in order to celebrate; and if you are sad, you drink in order to forget; and if there is no special reason, you drink anyway. We can learn from this statement that we do not have a problem with drinking, but that drinking is the problem. *(Material 4)*

From another text about role models we learn that not only youngsters are responsible for causing trouble in inner cities, but rather society itself is responsible by showing that alcohol is socially acceptable by organizing events such as wine and beer festivals. Even the town's mayor and other celebrities drink alcohol in public at such events. This way they are bad role models for youngsters who imitate the bad behaviour of the adults. *(Material 5)*

Let's turn to a text explaining why cities want to establish alcohol-free zones. Londoners want to introduce such a thing because then the police could act and take measures against people who behave badly when they are drunk. They can take away their alcohol and stop them from going on drinking in the city centre. The goal of this measure is to stop binge drinkers from harassing tourists and passers-by. *(Material 1)*

All in all, we can say that it is quite hard to decide which is right or wrong because many towns and cities use these wine and beer festivals to attract people to their communities and thus lure guests and tourists.

My suggestion would be to introduce alcohol-free zones in public places so that children do not get bad ideas about what they can do in their free-time. And I would also allow cities to make an exception from the rule for their public festivals once a year. *(Conclusion, own opinion)* *(495 words)*

Composition 2

Verwendete Materialien: 1, 2, 3 und 5

Everybody knows that women who work in so-called male jobs are a minority. In this context the question comes up why this is and what the possible consequences could be. In the following I am going to discuss this difficult matter in further detail. *(Introduction)*

To begin with, let's have a look at some statistics to find out in which kinds of jobs you hardly see any women at all. We can see from the statistics that in most fields of manual labour such as electricians, joiners, bricklayers there are hardly any women because this is hard physical work. The other kinds of jobs are time-consuming ones like computer experts and programmers or managers and bosses who have to put in many hours of work. Obviously, these jobs are incompatible with organizing a family with children. *(Material 1)*

This aspect is especially emphasized by an American text in which we can read that it is becoming increasingly difficult to combine a job with household and family life. Because of these circumstances, women do not choose to give up their jobs or careers but rather are driven out of their jobs by requirements of the labour market like long working hours. And there are no laws helping or supporting working mothers to stay in their jobs. This trend has negative effects not only on families but also on businesses and the economy of a country as a whole. *(Material 2)*

The reasons for this are explained in a text in which we can read that girls usually do better at school than boys but, in spite of that, they only choose from a small range of jobs for their apprenticeships or trainings. They are underrepresented in certain university courses such as science and technology. That is why women should play a role to change this trend by being mothers or teachers who show girls that they can do these jobs. *(Material 3)*

In quotes about women and work it is explained how this could be done. We can read that women should be aware of all their abilities and should not restrict themselves to the traditional "female skills" like cooking or caring for other people. The traditional roles in which girls are brought up hinder them from trying to get into higher positions in their later lives. Most of one's success is really hard work, which is always difficult and takes up a lot of time and energy. *(Material 5)*

To sum up, we can say that the reasons why women are a minority in "male jobs" range from insufficient physical strength and time-consuming working hours in business jobs to lack of support for girls to get into jobs which are dominated by men. Possible changes of this old-fashioned job pattern would have positive aspects on families, companies and for the economy – as we can see in France and Germany where working mothers are supported by the state. There is a lot to be gained for society as a whole by breaking up the traditional stereotypes of job roles.

Interestingly enough, in the statistics mentioned above we can see that some changes have already started because the percentage of women in typically "male jobs" has risen, and some men are equally entering "female domains", too. *(Own opinion, conclusion)* *(538 words)*

Notizen

Notizen

Notizen

Notizen

Liebe Kundin, lieber Kunde,

der STARK Verlag hat das Ziel, Sie effektiv beim Lernen zu unterstützen. In welchem Maße uns dies gelingt, wissen Sie am besten. Deshalb bitten wir Sie, uns Ihre Meinung zu den STARK-Produkten in dieser Umfrage mitzuteilen:

www.stark-verlag.de/feedback

Als Dankeschön verlosen wir einmal jährlich, zum 31. Juli, unter allen Teilnehmern ein aktuelles Samsung-Tablet. Für nähere Informationen und die Teilnahmebedingungen folgen Sie dem Internetlink.

Herzlichen Dank!

Haben Sie weitere Fragen an uns?
Sie erreichen uns telefonisch **0180 3 179000***
per E-Mail **info@stark-verlag.de**
oder im Internet unter **www.stark-verlag.de**

Lernen • Wissen • Zukunft
STARK

*9 Cent pro Min. aus dem deutschen Festnetz, Mobilfunk bis 42 Cent pro Min. Aus dem Mobilfunknetz wählen Sie die Festnetznummer: **08167 9573-0**

Erfolgreich durchs Abitur mit den **STARK** Reihen

Abiturprüfung

Anhand von Original-Aufgaben die Prüfungssituation trainieren. Schülergerechte Lösungen helfen bei der Leistungskontrolle.

Abitur-Training

Prüfungsrelevantes Wissen schülergerecht präsentiert. Übungsaufgaben mit Lösungen sichern den Lernerfolg.

Klausuren

Durch gezieltes Klausurentraining die Grundlagen schaffen für eine gute Abinote.

Kompakt-Wissen

Kompakte Darstellung des prüfungsrelevanten Wissens zum schnellen Nachschlagen und Wiederholen.

Interpretationen

Perfekte Hilfe beim Verständnis literarischer Werke.

Und vieles mehr auf www.stark-verlag.de

Abi in der Tasche – und dann?

In den **STARK** Ratgebern findest du alle Informationen für einen erfolgreichen Start in die berufliche Zukunft.

Alle Titel zu Beruf & Karriere
www.berufundkarriere.de

Lernen • Wissen • Zukunft
STARK

Bestellungen bitte direkt an
STARK Verlagsgesellschaft mbH & Co. KG · Postfach 1852 · 85318 Freising
Tel. 0180 3 179001* · Fax 0180 3 179001* · www.stark-verlag.de · info@stark-verlag.de

*9 Cent pro Min. aus dem deutschen Festnetz, Mobilfunk bis 42 Cent pro Min. Aus dem Mobilfunknetz wählen Sie die Festnetznummer: 08167 9573-0